BEHEADED BY
HITLER

Freedom is the sure possession
of those alone who have the courage to defend it—Pericles

The former German Chancellor Willy Brandt won the Nobel Prize for Peace in 1971.
Forced to flee from Nazism in 1933, he later defined a 'resister' as a person who 'takes
serious risks to act illegally in a world where right has become wrong'.

BEHEADED BY HITLER

CRUELTY OF THE NAZIS, CIVILIAN EXECUTIONS
AND JUDICIAL TERROR 1933–1945

COLIN PATEMAN

FONTHILL

Fonthill Media Language Policy
Fonthill Media publishes in the international English language market. One
language edition is published worldwide. As there are minor differences in spelling
and presentation, especially with regard to American English and British English,
a policy is necessary to define which form of English to use. The policy is to use
the form of English native to the author. Colin Pateman was born and eduated in
England therefore British English has been adopted in this publication.

Fonthill Media Limited
Fonthill Media LLC
www.fonthillmedia.com
office@fonthillmedia.com

First published in the United Kingdom
And the United State of America 2014

British Library Cataloguing in Publication Data:
A catalogue record for this book is available from the British Library

Typeset in 10.5 pt on 13 pt Minion Pro
Printed and bound in England

Contents

Acknowledgements

In this book the author has been respectful to the many thousands of men and women executed within the Nazi judiciary period. The images reproduced within this publication, in the vast majority of instances, were originally taken by Allied military sources, the photographers being unidentifiable and direct attribution impossible. In several instances, photographs have been included from the author's collection. The terms of the Open Government Licence facilitate the use of historic material from the National Archives, whilst other material, particularly photographic work, sits within the public domain created by the government prior to 1957. The author would like to acknowledge the original recipients of such documentary evidence, and where possible this has been done.

The *Bundesarchiv* images where identified have been duly acknowledged within their respective captions as required by the German Federal Archives directives in compliance with the Creative Commons Attribution-ShareAlike 3.0 Germany Licence.

It has been my intention to show the images of Fallbeil devices reverently and to acknowledge that subject matter appropriately. In many instances conjecture exists in relation to the types of machine and other technical aspects which have not been explored.

Wherever possible I have sought to credit all material with due diligence and integrity. Every care has been taken to trace copyright holders. However, I apologise if I have omitted anyone and will, if advised, make corrections to any future edition.

Preface

This book serves to inform those who, like the author, were unaware of the extent of the calculated legal terror that took place in Nazi Germany during the Third Reich against its own citizens and those from countries it occupied. Many people, the courageous minority when compared to the 'Final Solution', were executed because they did not conform to or fit German ideologies, or were believed to be resisters of Fascism. They paid the ultimate price of a dictatorship built on oppression; their life was terminated on the orders of a judge and prosecutor.

> We used to have a canary. When we learned of the law prohibiting Jews from keeping pets, my husband simply could not part with the bird … Maybe someone informed on him, because one day my husband was called in for questioning by the Gestapo … After many weeks of agony I received a note from the police that, for the fee of three Reichsmarks, I should pick up my husband's urn. (Anonymous, 1943)

Whether you were Jewish, a Jehovah's Witness, a Communist, a Social Democrat or someone who disagreed with the Third Reich and its brutal regime, there was a bloodstained judge ready to take away your very existence on the back of Hitler's dictatorship and his thirst for supreme power.

Colin Pateman

Introduction

This book draws upon conclusive evidence from events that took place within the judicial courts of the Third Reich period and demonstrates that the core principle of judicial independence from politics was suppressed. By failing to ensure that judicial proceedings were conducted fairly and that the rights of parties were respected, the judicial system in Germany became an instrument of terror. The public prosecutors and judges of the Nazi judicial system were responsible for the execution of at least 26,000 Germans and foreigners during the Second World War, a statistic established by Dr Thomas Dehler, the former West German Minister of Justice from 1949 to 1953.

The accounts of persecuted individuals and groups who dared to resist the Nazi movement or those who were simply deemed by the Reich to be unworthy to exist are at times difficult to comprehend. The manipulation of the judicial system allowed the Third Reich to remove any guarantee that the constitution or the laws of Germany would protect an individual. That manipulation by the Nazi movement prevented the judiciary from impartially deciding matters of fact whilst being free from inducement, interference or improper influences and, indeed, additional manipulation by directing rulings to other courts to suit preconceived objectives. Examples exist evidencing that one court ruling that may have been deemed unacceptable was simply removed to a higher court in order to seek the death sentence desired.

Death by beheading became a common occurrence throughout the People's Courts. On 18 March 1943, Judge Claassen sentenced Polish farm worker Kasimir Boszko for alleged possession of a sporting gun. The accused denied having the gun, and in fact no firearm had been discovered upon his arrest; only an old cleaning stick had been located. Boszko was executed upon the direction of the judge. A similar case involving Judge Moehl occurred on 11 December 1941, when Moehl was acting as the president in a special court in Leslau, Poland. Farmer Tadeusz Kowalski, a father of six children, was accused of allegedly possessing a firearm. A search revealed no weapon, but Moehl convicted the farmer and condemned him to death, satisfied by the evidence of a witness, Josef Pajewski, a person known to have owed money to the accused farmer for some time. A plethora of other cases can be found where common principles of evidence were not present to justify a conviction let alone a sentence of death.

This book is testimony to those mentioned within it and to the many thousands who walked the same path to the German guillotine described henceforth as the 'Fallbeil'. It is my hope that the subject of civilian executions inflicted by beheadings across Germany and the occupied territories during Nazi rule will become more recognised than they currently appear to be, an understandable situation in view of the horrific genocide committed in the Third Reich extermination camps that consumed so many lives.

CHAPTER 1

Hitler's Rise to Power

Born on 20 April 1889 in the Austrian town of Braunau, Adolf Hitler was the fourth child of Alois Schicklgruber and Klara Hitler. When Adolf was three years old, the family moved to Passau, on the German side of the border. A further family move followed, which saw them living for six months across from a large Benedictine monastery whose coat of arms had a most salient feature: a swastika. Poor health enveloped the family, with Adolf's father dying in 1903 after suffering a pleural haemorrhage and Adolf himself suffering from lung infections. This was eventually to result in him leaving school at the age of sixteen, partially because of ill health and partially the result of poor schoolwork.

In 1906, Adolf was permitted to visit Vienna but failed the entrance exam to gain admission to a prestigious art school. It was at this time that his mother developed terminal breast cancer and was treated by Dr Edward Bloch, a Jewish doctor who served the poor. She died on 21 December 1907, despite undergoing an operation and excruciatingly painful and expensive treatments with a dangerous drug. Adolf spent the next six years in Vienna, alone and without purpose, living on a small legacy from his father and an orphan's allowance. By 1909, he was almost destitute and slept in bars and shelters for the homeless around Vienna, some of which were ironically financed by Jewish philanthropists. It was during this time that Adolf began to develop his anti-Semitic beliefs, views that were commonly held by Catholic culture in Vienna. As his interest in politics developed he became influenced by politicians such as Karl Lueger and Georg Ritter von Schonerer, who vehemently believed in the superiority of the 'Aryan race'.

In May 1913, Hitler, financed by a small inheritance, left Vienna for Munich, the likely reason being to avoid military service in Austria. However, in the January of the following year the police came to his door bearing a draft notice from the Austrian government. The document threatened a year in prison and a fine if he was found guilty of leaving his native land with the intent of evading conscription. Hitler was taken to Salzburg to report for duty, but failed the physical exam for entry into the Austrian army, having been found to be 'unfit … too weak … and unable to bear arms' and so he returned to Munich, a place where his beliefs were encouraged by a more racially homogeneous area.

At the age of 25 in August 1914, when the German Empire entered the First World War, Hitler swiftly enlisted into the Bavarian army, eager to fight for the fatherland. His first engagement with the Bavarian regiment was against Belgian and British troops near Ypres and ended with 2,500 out of 3,000 men being either wounded, killed or missing in action. Hitler came through the battle without injury. Records indicate that Hitler was a keen soldier, and as a dispatch runner he would take messages to and from the command staff at the back of the fighting units. He was twice cited for bravery in action, receiving the Iron Cross Second Class in December 1915, and the Iron Cross First Class in August 1918. It is likely that he did not achieve a rank higher than a corporal due to not being a German citizen, something he did not become until 1932. Hitler was wounded in the leg by a shell fragment in October 1916 and, following hospitalisation in Germany, was assigned to light duties in Munich to aid his recovery. During this time he became dismayed at the apathy of German citizens coupled with anti-war sentiment, and blamed the Jews and Marxists for spreading unrest in an effort to undermine the war effort. Hitler requested to go back to the front, which he did in March 1917, finding that the morale of the front-line soldiers had declined as the reality of defeat was becoming a certainty. In October 1918, Hitler was partially blinded in a mustard gas attack near Ypres which resulted in him being sent to a military hospital. The inevitable news of the Armistice on 11 November 1918 reached him as he was convalescing; confirming that his beloved fatherland was now a republic and the war was over. Two days prior to the Armistice, Kaiser Wilhelm II abdicated and the Socialists gained control of the government. By this time, Hitler had become an impassioned German patriot carried along by an increasingly vicious political anti-Semitism that had seeped into the military hierarchy and been disseminated by right-wing extremists during the last two years of the war. The end of the war was an emotional disaster for Hitler. He later described his reaction in his book *Mein Kampf*: 'There followed terrible days and even worse nights—I knew that all was lost … in these nights hatred grew in me, hatred for those responsible for this deed.'

Under the terms of the Armistice it was agreed that the German Army could remain but with reduced numbers and surprisingly the German General Staff were not forced to admit defeat. Many German citizens, including Hitler, felt betrayed, and a 'stab in the back' theory existed to suggest that the army had not been defeated and that had it not been for the politicians, they could have fought on and won. The German politicians who signed the Armistice would become known as the 'November Criminals'.

Political turmoil had started to unfold within Germany. On 19 January 1919, Federal elections were held in Germany to elect 423 deputies to the National Assembly. The centrist parties swept to victory and the Weimar Republic took shape to replace the imperial form of government in Germany. Although it appeared that the new German Republic would put in place a constitution with power in the hands of the people to elect a president, a cabinet and a chancellor by majority vote in the

Reichstag, political and social chaos ensued. Left-wing Marxist groups in Munich and Berlin carried out Russian-style revolutions that were met with violence and opposition from the *Freikorps*, a volunteer organisation composed of vigilante war veterans who banded together to fight the growing Communist insurgency that was taking over Germany. With Communist-inspired insurrections shaking Germany, some Jews were cited as being leaders of these abortive revolutions, which further inspired the hatred of Jews as well as Communists. The *Freikorps* attempted to crush this insurgency, and its members were to form the nucleus of the paramilitary wing of the Nazi Party, known as the *Sturmabteilung* (SA) and nicknamed the Brownshirts.

On 28 June 1919, the Treaty of Versailles was signed by the German government and the Allies. The Germans had to accept responsibility for the war and therefore had to pay vast sums of money in war reparations to cover the civilian damage caused, as well as giving up land to Poland and France and limiting their army to 100,000 men without access to submarines or military aircraft. This had a humiliating effect on the German nation, and many, including Hitler, had a great desire to discard the treaty and its restrictions, and for Germany to become a dominant nation in the hands of a nationalist government. At this time, Hitler remained in the army where his anti-Semitic beliefs were being reinforced. He was stationed in Munich and carried out the role of an informer, naming soldiers in his own barracks and across the ranks that supported the Marxist uprisings, which led to their arrest and executions. Within the military intelligence unit in which Hitler served, he was assigned to investigate the German Workers' Party (*Deutsche Arbeiterpartei* or DAP), a small group in Munich. At the time it comprised only a handful of members, disorganised and with little forward vision. However, its members expressed right-wing principles in accord with Hitler's, as he found out when he attended a meeting in a beer hall, dressed as a civilian, on 12 September 1919. It was at one of the party's meetings the following month that Hitler captivated the audience with an emotional speech. He described the speech in *Mein Kampf*:

> I spoke for thirty minutes and what before I had simply felt within me, without in any way knowing it, was now proved by reality. I could speak! After thirty minutes the people in the small room were electrified and the enthusiasm was first expressed by the fact that my appeal to the self-sacrifice of those present led to the donation of three hundred marks.

News of this hypnotic and impassioned young man and his speeches on building a strong pro-military, nationalist and anti-Semitic party of working class people spread, resulting in a large number of Germans being eager to attend the meetings to listen to him and in turn providing much needed donations to the party funds. By this time, Hitler had officially entered the world of politics, having joined the German Workers' Party as a committee member. The money went towards the production of leaflets and advertising.

With the assistance of party staff, Hitler drafted a programme that was presented at a public meeting on 24 February 1920, with over 2,000 participants eager to hear him speak. After Marxist hecklers were removed by Hitler supporters armed with whips and rubber truncheons, Hitler gave an impassioned speech which electrified the audience. He outlined a twenty-five-point programme that included his condemnation and rejection of the Versailles Treaty, citizenship to be determined by race, with no Jew being recognised as a German, religious freedom except for those religions that endangered the German race, and a robust central government to execute effective legislation. Hitler sought and received approval from the boisterous crowd for each point as he raised it, and the meeting proved to be an enormous success.

By the end of 1920, the party membership had swelled to over 3,000. In order to improve the identity of the party, the name was changed by Hitler to include the term National Socialist, thus becoming the National Socialist German Workers' Party (NSDAP) or more commonly known as the Nazi Party. Realising that the party needed a recognisable symbol, Hitler chose the swastika, an image he had grown up with when he had lived close to the Benedictine Monastery in Austria. Hitler described the representation involved after the swastika had been placed inside a white circle on a red background:

> In the red we see the social idea of the movement, in the white the national idea, in the swastika the mission to struggle for the victory of Aryan man and at the same time the victory of the idea of creative work which is eternally anti-Semitic and will always be anti-Semitic.

At this time he was also recruiting into the party young men he had known in the army, aided by a new party member, Ernst Röhm, who would later play a major part in Hitler's rise to power. Through his relentless efforts to make the party succeed, Hitler had converted it from a passive discussion group to an actual political party and, in July 1921, he succeeded in becoming the leader (Führer) of the Nazi Party.

Earlier in the same year, the victorious European Allies demanded that Germany pay for damages caused in a war it had started, and so they presented a bill for $33 billion. The immediate effect of this was out-of-control inflation that reduced workers' earnings to next to nothing. Prior to the First World War, one US dollar was equivalent to approximately four German Reichsmarks. By the beginning of 1923, this had risen to 18,000 marks per dollar, followed by an astronomical increase to 350,000 by July and rising further to an unbelievable one hundred million marks in September of the same year.

Germany's Weimar Republic was now at crisis point and Hitler's party benefited by the people's reaction to the state of the country, exploiting it by holding mass protest rallies despite a ban on such events by the local police. Violence erupted with regular street fights between political opponents—Communists, Nazis, Socialists and others who felt violence was the way forward in order to silence their opponents. The Nazi Party began drawing in thousands of new members, many of whom were victims of hyperinflation and, like Hitler, found comfort in blaming the Jews for this trouble. Economic uncertainty meant political upheaval and Germany in the 1920s was no exception.

With the country in turmoil, Hitler carried out an attempt to seize power in Munich with his Nazi followers. The Bavarian government defied the Weimar Republic, accusing it of being too far left. Hitler endorsed the fall of the Weimar Republic, and declared at a public rally on 30 October 1923 that he was prepared to march on Berlin to rid the government of Communists and Jews. On 8 November 1923, inspired by the success the previous year of Mussolini's March on Rome, which had seen a Fascist government installed in Italy, Hitler and his armed henchmen stormed a rally of 3,000 people which was being held by the Bavarian government and attempted to hold the officials hostage until they expressed their support for his revolution. The incident became known as the 'Beer Hall Putsch'. The coup was not met with the enthusiasm that Hitler expected, so with a reduced chance of success, he led 2,000 supporters through the streets of Munich where they were confronted by the police. Fourteen Nazis were killed that day but Hitler escaped, only to be captured two days later, following which he was tried for high treason. The trial received significant press coverage both nationally and internationally. With the judges for his trial having been chosen by a Nazi sympathiser in the Bavarian government, Hitler was able to use the courtroom for propaganda purposes and admitted to wanting to overthrow the government, portraying himself as a German patriot whilst citing the government as the criminals, the politicians having prematurely ended the Great War and thus caused political turmoil in the country through a weak and failing democratic republic. Press reports on his speeches in the courtroom served to increase the following of the Nazi Party. At the conclusion of the trial Hitler was found guilty of high treason, but despite a life sentence being the likely outcome for high treason, incredibly, Hitler was given only a five-year sentence, eligible for parole in six months.

Hitler was incarcerated in Landsberg Prison and during his confinement, which he served in a spacious cell, he wrote *Mein Kampf*, a book that set out his political philosophy and planned conquest of Europe. He was given his own secretary to assist him, Rudolph Hess, who had also been arrested alongside Hitler and later became Deputy Führer in 1933. A report written in September 1924 by the then governor of Landsberg Prison following a request by the State Attorney's office in Munich provides an insight into what life was like for Hitler during his period of confinement:

> The political offender Adolf Hitler was consigned to the Fortress of Landsberg on 1 April 1924. Up to the present date he has served five and a half months. By October 1st he will have expiated his offences by ten and a half months' detention. Hitler has shown himself to be an orderly, disciplined prisoner, not only in his

own person but also with reference to his fellow prisoners, among whom he has preserved good discipline. He is amenable, unassuming and modest. He has never made exceptional demands, conducts himself in a uniformly quiet and reasonable manner, and has put up with the deprivations and restrictions of imprisonment very well. He has no personal vanity, is content with the prison diet, neither smokes nor drinks, and has exercised a helpful authority over other prisoners.

As a man unused at any time to personal indulgences, he has borne the loss of his freedom better than the married prisoners. He has no interest in women, and received the visits of women friends and followers without any particular enthusiasm but with the utmost politeness, and never allowed himself to be drawn into serious political discussions with them. He is invariably polite and has never insulted the prison officials.

At the beginning of his imprisonment he received a large number of visitors, but in the last few months he has discouraged them and withdrawn himself from political discussion. He writes very few letters, and for the most part, they are letters of thanks. He is entirely taken up with the writing of his book, which is due to appear in the next few weeks. It consists of his autobiography together with his thoughts about the bourgeoisie, Jewry and Marxism, the German revolution and Bolshevism, and the National Socialist movement with the events leading up to 8 November 1923. He hopes the book will run into many editions, thus enabling him to fulfil his financial obligations and to defray the expenses incurred at the time of his trial.

Hitler will undoubtedly return to political life. He proposes to re-form and reanimate his movement, but in the future he proposes not to run counter to the authorities, but to make use of all possible permissible means, short of a second bid for power, to attain his ends.

During his ten months under detention while awaiting trial and while under sentence, he has undoubtedly become more mature and calm. When he returns to freedom, he will do so without entertaining revengeful purposes against those in official positions who opposed him and frustrated him in November 1923. He will not agitate against the government, nor will he wage war against other nationalist parties. He is completely convinced that a state cannot exist without internal order and firm government.

Adolf Hitler is undoubtedly a man of many-sided intelligences, particularly political intelligence, and possesses extraordinary will-power and directness in his thinking. In view of the above facts, I venture to say that his behaviour while under detention merits the grant of an early release. He is counting on the decision of the Court to suspend his sentence as from October 1st of this year, when he will have earned a probationary period after completing six months of his sentence from 1 April 1924. In many of his letters Hitler anticipates that he will be released on 1 October.

Signed, Leybold

No doubt the experience of Hitler's failed attempt at seizing power through violence, and his subsequent imprisonment, had taught him that alongside violence, other factors needed to be brought into play, one of these being the manipulation of the deteriorating political system in Germany. Once released from prison, Hitler decided to seize power constitutionally through being elected and gaining a majority in the German parliament rather than by force of arms. Even though there were some members within the Nazi Party who feared the increasing dictatorial control that Hitler had over them, there was no doubt that through impassioned public speaking, Hitler reached out to mass audiences, calling for the German people to resist the burden of Jews and Communists, and to create a new empire which would rule the world. In 1927, a second volume of *Mein Kampf* was printed, which included Hitler's directives on how to obtain and retain political power. The book was received favourably by disillusioned German citizens and over five million copies were sold.

Hitler began to reorganise his Nazi storm troopers, the SA (*Sturmabteilung*), and they were initially used to prevent Nazi meetings being disrupted by Marxists. The SA men were often called Brownshirts due to the colour of their uniform, clothing that had been cheaply available after the First World War, having originally been ordered for the troops posted to Germany's former African colonies. They wore a swastika armband, badges and a cap to improve their visibility and recognition with members of the public. In addition to the SA, a unit was formed by Hitler to serve as his personal bodyguard: the staff guard, *Schutzstaffel* or SS for short. Rather than adopt the brown uniform, the SS wore black, an identity similar to the Italian Fascists.

The popularity of the Nazi Party continued to rise, the party capturing 18 per cent of the popular vote in the 1930 election. Building on this success, Hitler ran for President in 1932 and won 30 per cent of the vote, which forced his opponent, Great War veteran Field Marshal Paul von Hindenburg, into a run-off election. In order to try and curtail Hitler's bid for future supremacy, Hindenburg appointed Hitler as Chancellor in exchange for his political support, and he assumed this office in January 1933. Within a month Hitler had defined the foreign policy of the Nazis, with the prime objective being to secure *lebensraum*, 'living space' for the German master race. Hitler's rise to power had not only been cemented by the German people's resentment towards the government due to the political and economic crisis within their country but also through Nazi propaganda and the terror of his storm troopers to increase support for the Nazi Party and Fascism.

It must be remembered that there is a clear distinction between a Socialist and a Fascist. The full name of the German Nazi Party was the National Socialist German Workers' Party. On the face of it, the party represented a positive change towards a socialist economic system, one of productivity and distribution organised to directly satisfy economic demands of the German population. In reality however, Nazi Party members were Fascists controlled by a charismatic leader, Hitler, who sought unconditional authority with a focus on glorifying and strengthening the state through constant military conquests.

President Hindenburg underestimated Hitler's political resolve to gain power through a campaign to destabilise public support for the democratic government. On 27 February 1933, a fire swept through the Reichstag building, the seat of the German Parliament in Berlin. Capitalising on fear, Hitler was able to accelerate the banning of the Communist Party.

A witness to the fire, D. Sefton Delmer, reported in the *Daily Express* on Hitler's verbal reaction to the event:

> This is a God-given signal! If this fire, as I believe, turns out to be the handiwork of Communists, then there is nothing that shall stop us now crushing out this murder pest with an iron fist.

There are many theories surrounding who started the fire and for what purpose, and whether it had in fact been the Nazis. Regardless of speculation, the Nazis took advantage of the situation and blamed the Communists in order to seize power when a Dutch Communist, Marinus van der Lubbe, was arrested at the scene along with Ernst Torgler, a German Communist, and three Bulgarian Communists, Georgi Dimitrov, Simon Popov and Vassili Tanev.

The very next day, Chancellor Hitler along with President Hindenburg invoked Article 48 of the Weimar Constitution, which enabled civil liberties to be effectively suspended in times of a national emergency. The political landscape was starting to turn towards Hitler, his dictatorship and Fascism. The Decree of the Reich President for the Protection of the People and State annulled the following constitutional protections:

- Restrictions on personal liberty
- Free expression of opinion, including freedom of the press
- Right to privacy of postal and electronic communications
- Individual property rights
- Protection against unlawful searches and seizures
- Right of assembly and association
- States' right of self-government

Following the emergency decree, the SA and SS took to the streets and rounded up thousands of Communists, Social Democrats and Liberals who were taken away to SA barracks where they were beaten and tortured. The Nazis began a systematic takeover of the state government throughout Germany, using the emergency decree to displace legitimate office holders and replace them with Nazi Reich commissioners.

German trials at that time were based upon continental civil law procedures that permitted hearsay testimony: a witness was able to recount what somebody else told him or her, or what he or she overheard being said. Hermann Goering was later summoned to appear as a witness for the prosecution. On 4 November 1933, the bombastic Goering took centre stage at 10.30 hours, having kept the court waiting for an hour.

Several government officials were in attendance. Goering wore his storm trooper uniform and initiated the Hitler salute which was echoed by the party members present. He then spoke for approximately three hours, using the opportunity to make speculations upon the Communist movement, rhetoric which received noisy support from many of the audience. Joseph Goebbels, Hitler's newly appointed Minister of Public Enlightenment and Propaganda, appeared as another witness four days later. He, like Goering, was robustly cross-examined by the defence, particularly about the claims that Communists had started the fire and Goebbels' accusations that the Social Democrats had also been involved. Judge Buenger appeared to shield these high-profile witnesses as the trial progressed, which enabled the Nazi political and propaganda machine to be in full flow, utilising the Reichstag trial for the party's own purposes. At the end of the trial, the judges gave a lengthy summary of the evidence. Van der Lubbe was pronounced guilty of high treason, insurrectionary arson and attempted common arson, whilst the other defendants were acquitted. The judge's summary concluded:

> Even though ... the defendant Torgler and the Bulgarians Dimitrov, Tanev and Popov could not be convicted as accessories, nonetheless no doubt exists as to the camp in which these accessories were to be found ... The burning of the Reichstag was undoubtedly a political act. The enormity of the crime, that is to say, of the means points to the importance and violence of the goal. This can only have been the seizure of power ... The crime can only be the work of radical left-wing elements, who hoped to exploit it for the purpose of overthrowing the government and the constitution, and seizing power ... The Communist Party has proclaimed such treasonable goals as its programme. It was the party of treason.

Although van der Lubbe suffered from a mental impairment, following his conviction he was sentenced to death. His execution by beheading took place in a Leipzig prison yard and was widely reported in newspapers. *The New York Times* published the following account on 11 January 1934:

> At dawn van der Lubbe was shaved and led into the yard where Dr Wilhelm Buenger, the presiding judge at the Reichstag fire trial, Chief Prosecutor Werner, several physicians and twelve citizens of good repute in accordance with the law were assembled. Without showing the least emotion van der Lubbe listened with bowed head as the death sentence was read by Dr Buenger and silently shook his head when asked whether he wanted to make a statement. Dr Werner then said, 'I surrender you to the executioner.' The latter, Herr Goebler of Magdeburg dressed in evening clothes and wearing white gloves, laid his hand on van der Lubbe's shoulder.

Meekly the young man ascended the scaffold, where he was tied down, and in thirty seconds it was all over …

Hermann Goering had previously declared, on 3 March 1933, 'I don't have to worry about justice; my mission is only to destroy and exterminate, nothing more.' In order to incite further distrust against the Communists, Nazi publications were printed and issued to the German people claiming that the Nazis were the only party who could prevent a Communist takeover. The state-run radio was used to broadcast Hitler's speeches and Nazi propaganda.

Following the fire, Hitler called for a general election which took place on 5 March 1933. Even though the police were under Nazi influence, Goering suppressed the majority of the opposition before the election. Hitler failed to gain an absolute majority, but with the Nazis being the largest party with 44 per cent of the seats, he persuaded the Centre Party to support him by promising to protect the Catholic Church as well as winning Nationalist Party support. Hitler had got what he wanted. He was now able to seal the demise of the German democratic government and realise his objective to become the dictator of Germany, but not before he put on a staged public display of unity with Hindenburg at the official opening of the newly elected Reichstag on 21 March 1933. Hitler used the occasion to show false alliance with Hindenburg through the union of established Prussian military traditions and the Nazi Reich, and this was played out to the world media reporting on the event.

The very same day, Hindenburg signed two decrees at Hitler's insistence: one offering full pardons to all Nazis held in prisons; and the second allowing for the arrest of anyone suspected of maliciously criticising the Nazi Party or the government. A further decree signed by Hitler and Vice-Chancellor Franz von Papen enabled the establishment of special courts to try political offenders. These courts were to be conducted in a similar style to a military court martial, with the defence having little or no access to counsel. Later that month, Hitler and his Nazi compatriots persuaded and bullied members of the newly appointed Reichstag to pass an Enabling Act that effectively gave Hitler absolute power to make laws without consulting the Reichstag and the authority to rule alone and unchallenged. The Communist Party had already been banned by the government after the Reichstag fire, but by using the powers of the Enabling Act, Hitler passed a law banning the formation of all political parties. This was just the start of his oppressive dictatorship.

During the twelve years of National Socialist rule, the damaged Reichstag building was unable to be used for parliamentary sessions. As a result, the Reichstag parliament subsequently convened in the former Kroll opera house in close proximity to the original Reichstag building, which was used for propaganda purposes—a factor which did nothing to dispel later thoughts that cast doubt on the conviction and decapitation of Marinus van der Lubbe.

In May 1933, trade unions were closed down and funds confiscated. In July that year, Hitler signed the Concordat with the Pope to retain Catholic support by promising not to interfere with the Catholic Church in Germany.

As Hitler gained in power, with the Enabling Act in place and with the establishment of the SS under the direction of Heinrich Himmler, there was concern over the swelling numbers of the SA under the direction of Ernst Röhm and the potential for a coup against Hitler due to their socialist beliefs which could threaten the dominance that Hitler sought to achieve over the German people. Although there was no evidence to support this perceived threat, and despite Röhm having been a loyal follower of Hitler since the early days of the Nazi Party, Himmler, Goering and Goebbels convinced Hitler that Röhm and the SA were a threat to his quest for dominance. The regular army of Germany also saw the SA as a threat to their authority, as Röhm had openly discussed his plans to take over the regular army and consolidate it into the SA. The army leaders were alarmed at this, and Hitler saw the opportunity at last to secure the allegiance of the army leaders by making a pact. It was agreed that if Röhm and the other SA key personnel were removed, the remaining SA men would come under the control of the regular army, but in doing so the army leaders would have to swear an oath of loyalty to Hitler.

What took place on the night of 29–30 June 1934 became known as the Night of the Long Knives and started the killing spree and executions on Hitler's orders that would terrorise German civilians for the next eleven years. On this night, the SS arrested the leaders of the SA and other political opponents. In excess of seventy men were shot and executed on charges of treason, with little regard to any substantiated evidence against them. A number of politicians, including former chancellors von Papen and von Schleicher, were also arrested. Röhm was arrested and given the option of taking his own life, but he refused and was shot without trial. Others were battered to death.

The German people found out about the killing spree when Hitler declared in front of the Reichstag that he and he alone was the judge, jury and executioner in Germany and that the SS carried out his orders within the remit of the 'law regarding measures for state self-defence' which had been passed on 3 July. Hitler justified his decision by telling the world that he had prevented a rebellion. The SS became a feared force in Nazi Germany, led by Himmler who had impressed Hitler greatly by carrying out his orders and eliminating the power of the SA through the atrocities that had taken place in June.

Some overseas reporting of the incident glamorised the actions of Hitler in the face of his patriotism for Germany. For example, on 2 July, the *Daily Mail*, under the influence of its co-founder Lord Rothermere, who for a short period was an admirer of both Hitler and Mussolini and was seen as initially sympathetic to German and Italian Fascism along with a number of other newspapers of the time, reported the following:

Herr Adolf Hitler, the German Chancellor, has saved his country. Swiftly and with exorable severity, he has delivered Germany from men who had become a danger to the unity of the German people and to the order of the state. With lightning rapidity he has caused them to be removed from high office, to be arrested and put to death. The names of the men who have been shot by his orders are already known. Hitler's love of Germany has triumphed over private friendships and fidelity to comrades who had stood shoulder to shoulder with him in the fight for Germany's future.

President Hindenburg died on 2 August 1934, along with the last remnants of Germany's democratic government. Hitler combined the role of President and Chancellor into one and the army swore an oath of loyalty to him only. He had now fulfilled his ambition in achieving total power over the German states and was acclaimed as 'der Führer'.

CHAPTER 2

The Nazi Judicial System—Background and Changes during the Third Reich

One of the most tyrannical aspects of the Third Reich was the manipulation of the legal structure in Germany. It did so in order to create a judicial system that did not have the constraints of conventional procedures and legal doctrines, and served to eliminate all political opponents of Hitler. Nazi judicial ideals were predicated on the basis that individuals were subordinate to the state and should conduct themselves as law-abiding and obedient citizens within a Fascist society. Well aware that most Germans had not supported him or the NSDAP before 1933, Hitler wanted to ensure that any opposition to him and his party was eradicated through law enforcement. Like most areas of public life after the rise to power of the Nazis, the German system of justice underwent 'coordination' to ensure it was realigned with Nazi goals. With Nazi Germany becoming a police state, the reinterpretation of *Schutzhaft* (protective custody) took place in 1933, resulting in police powers becoming independent of judicial control. In Nazi terminology this meant the arrest without a judicial review of real and potential opponents of the regime. 'Protective custody' prisoners were under the exclusive authority of the SS. The Third Reich was seen as a dual state, with the normal judicial system coexisting with the peremptory power of Hitler and the police. The main Nazi police agencies were:

- SS—(*Schutzstaffel* meaning 'Protective Echelon') Founded by Hitler as a small bodyguard unit in 1925, the SS took on immense police powers for civil and military matters and was headed up by Heinrich Himmler. Initially the SS was subordinate to the brown-shirted storm troopers of the SA, but following the purge of the SA members in 1934, Himmler consolidated the SS strength by gaining control of all Germany's police forces and expanding their responsibilities and activities. Special military SS units were also trained, resulting in the SS being divided into two groups: the *Allgemeine-SS* (general SS) and the *Waffen-SS* (armed SS). The SS personnel swore absolute obedience and loyalty to the Führer, and during the Second World War carried out executions of political opponents on an immense scale—Communist authorities, Jews, Gypsies, Partisan resisters and Russian prisoners of war.
- Gestapo—Formed in 1933 by Hermann Goering, the men were initially recruited

from the Prussian police service. In 1934, the Gestapo was amalgamated into the SS under the command of Himmler. The Gestapo was given wide ranging powers when it became a national agency in 1936 following Himmler becoming chief of all German police. The Gestapo's main activities were to remove threats to the state, including espionage, treason and any assassination attempts against Nazi leaders. Gestapo agents were able to search without a warrant, detain without trial, and interrogate without restraint. They were renowned for the use of brutal torture, intimidation and killings. The number of agents grew from approximately 5,000 before 1939 to more than 45,000 in the inter-war period.

- Kripo—(*Kriminalpolizei* meaning 'criminal police') The Kripo had existed under the Weimar government and before the Nazi Party took power. Its main purpose was to deal with serious criminal offences such as murder, arson and fraud, and not to get involved in investigating 'political crimes'. In an attempt to maximise a Fascist police state, in 1933 the Nazis absorbed the Kripo into the SS. Kripo detectives who were against Nazism were 'encouraged' to resign or take retirement, and this enabled loyal Nazi personnel to be drafted in. More conventional policing methods were used by the Kripo, as their actions could be reviewed by the courts.
- Sipo—(*Sicherhietspolizei* meaning 'security police') Sipo was an overarching term used to describe the state's two investigative police services: the Gestapo and the Kripo. Although both police services were merged in 1936, they continued to operate independently. Predictably, Himmler was appointed as commander-in-chief of the Sipo, which ensured he was in full control of both the political and criminal police forces.
- Orpo—(*Ordnungspolizei* meaning 'ordinary police') This was the uniformed police force of Germany which had been managed by the state and local governments until 1936 when it came under the SS and Himmler. Himmler reorganised the Orpo so that its responsibilities included the management of traffic and public transport, and the organising of air-raid precautions, fire safety and response. A number of the Orpo divisions were trained to act as a reservist military force and home guard.
- SD—(*Sicherheitsdienst* meaning 'Security Service') The SD was formed in 1931 and was a uniformed division of the SS responsible for gathering intelligence for the NSDAP and SS. Its key objective was to identify and eliminate opponents of the Nazi regime, thus working closely with the Gestapo. The status of the SD increased from 1940 when its influence in Germany and the occupied territories meant that its agents were infiltrating Jewish populations, investigating black-market rings and locating hidden persons. The SD in Amsterdam was responsible for raiding the home and hiding place of Anne Frank, one of many Jewish victims of the Holocaust.

The Nazi state enforced its political and ideological aims with the direct support of the police, many of whom shared the Nazi vision of a *Volksgemeinschaft*, a 'national community', based on racial exclusion. The police were a fundamental instrument of rule. Not only the Gestapo but also all other branches of the German police took part in the terror against the political and ideological opponents of the Nazi state.

The Nazis considered the civil and criminal courts to be too lenient on those who committed crimes or demonstrated opposition against Germany's laws and so they brought about change by voicing their discontent and ensuring that judges, legal experts and lawyers were accepting of their policies. Many senior jurists in Nazi Germany had served on the bench during the Weimar Republic (1918-1933) and before. Although most jurists of this time believed in legal principles such as the equality of all citizens and the concept of there being no crime without a sound basis in law, many during the Weimar Republic era were also cynical since it had come about by a revolution. This attitude meant severe sentences for left-wing defendants, who were considered with suspicion as agents of foreign powers, whilst more mercy was shown towards right-wing defendants, whose nationalist sentiments echoed their own.

During the mid-1920s, the supporters of the Weimar Republic demanded a temporary suspension of judicial independence and the removal of reactionary anti-democratic judges. Judges reacted with fury, and many considered that the criticisms had come from the political left and from parliament in order to undermine their authority. When Hitler came to power, he promised to re-establish their reputation and power even though he was actually curtailing their judicial independence through decrees designed to strip away civil rights and political freedoms.

The *Sondergerichte* (Special Court) and *Volksgerichtshof* (People's Court) were emergency courts set up by the Nazis for one purpose: to enforce Fascist laws in Germany and in the areas of other countries occupied by German troops in order to wipe out opponents of the Nazi regime. Judges and public prosecutors were selected to preside at the courts, a chairman and two assessors, from whom exceptional reliability and notable experience in dealing with political crimes were prerequisites. They were also some of the most loyal and merciless Fascists. Initially, Special Courts were established on 21 March 1933, following a decree of the Reich President 'for the protection of folk and state', which was put into effect from 28 February 1933. The courts enabled the Nazis to expedite cases, dismiss any appeals and exclude evidence that was not considered necessary for determining the outcome of a trial. The courts worked in collaboration with the Gestapo and denied defendants a fair judicial process. They held jurisdiction over a number of perceived wartime crimes that were considered insubordinate to Germany and its cause, which included listening to and distributing information from international radio broadcasts, making false or distorted statements that undermined the Third Reich's integrity, high treason, riotous conduct, breaches of the peace, and other political crimes.

In addition, civil demographic rights and freedoms were withdrawn from the German people and occupied territories. A notorious rancorous afterthought decree, which came into effect on 21 March 1933 and was replaced by a similar law of

20 December 1934, made the Special Courts competent for another criminal action in actual connection with a trial which was already opened in a local court or from the criminal division of a district court. The regulations and scope of the Special Courts provided them with the ability to get rid of all political opponents more quickly and radically than could be achieved by the regular upper provincial and district courts. Judges in the regular courts were also not yet sufficiently conscious of the law relating to the condemnation of individuals who offended the 'healthy folk instinct'.

Procedures in the Special Courts were subject to special regulations to provide the judges and prosecutors with the opportunity to deal swiftly with any opponent of Nazism, which included:

S.21 A legal preliminary inquiry does not take place.

S.22 The decision on opening the main proceedings is omitted … On receipt of the bill of indictment the chairman fixes the date for the opening of the main proceedings.

S.23 In all trials before the Special Court the sentence must follow immediately without delays, if the accused was caught in the act or if his crime is otherwise self-evident … In other cases there can be a delay of twenty-four hours.

S.26 Appeals against decisions of the Special Court are not permissible.

S.27 The results of the examination need not be included in the protocol of the main trial.

These were regulations that were deemed appropriate for the organisation of trials for opponents of the Third Reich.

All professional associations involved with the administration of justice were merged into the National Socialist League of German Jurists. In April 1933, Hitler passed one of the earliest anti-Semitic laws, the Law for the Restoration of the Professional Civil Service, which effectively purged Jewish, non-Aryan personnel, Socialist judges, lawyers and other court officers from their professions. This was followed by the Civil Service Law of 1937, which required all judicial officers to swear a personal oath of loyalty to Hitler.

The Special Court was able to impose punishment immediately where guilt was deemed apparent and in a court that never allowed an appeal, anyone convicted of a criminal case was likely to have the death penalty served upon them, as encouraged by the Reich Minister of Justice. The Minister held an influential position and one that harnessed the interference of Hitler and his political officials with the courts and the sentences handed out to defendants. Franz Schlegelberger, Reich Minister of Justice for 1941 and 1942, was a Nazi official who had been responsible for the authoring of bills such as the *Polenstrafrechtsverordnung* (Poland Penal Law Provision) under which Poles were executed for such actions as tearing down German posters. He played a pivotal role in the case of Markus Luftglass, an elderly Jew who had been convicted of stealing eggs. A brief report on the case appeared in a Berlin daily newspaper following his being given a prison term of two and a half years, and when it was brought to Hitler's attention, he dictated that the sentence had been too lenient and immediately ordered that Markus be sentenced to death. Schlegelberger disregarded due legal process and fulfilled the wish of Hitler by issuing the instruction that effectively sealed Markus's fate. He reported back to the then Reich Minister and Chief of the Reich Chancellery, Hans Lammers:

Most honoured Mr. Reich Minister Dr. Lammers

Upon the Führer-order of 24 October 1941 forwarded to me through Mr. State Minister and Chief of the Führer's and Reich Chancellor's Presidial Chancellery, I have handed the Jew Markus Luftglass, sentenced to two and a half years in prison by the Special Court in Kattowitz, over to the Gestapo for execution.

Heil Hitler!
Your most obedient …

The Auschwitz death registers confirm that Markus Luftglass was murdered on 4 November 1941. This case was highlighted in the Nuremberg Trials against Schlegelberger to demonstrate the personal reach that Hitler had over daily workings of the legal system and the dismissive bureaucratic response by Schlegelberger in confirming Hitler's callous orders had been carried out against a human being in his seventies. The trial transcripts recorded that Schlegelberger was involved in this type of order from Hitler many times.

The Reich Ministry of Justice had been influential in the setting up of the Special Court, and in 1934 all courts became Federal courts and subject to control from Berlin. The Reich Ministry of Justice effectively took control of all the administration of justice for all German states, including the preparation of legislation concerning all branches of law, and control of the courts and prisons. Letter were sent out by the Reich Ministry of Justice to public prosecutors and judges informing them of the results they must accomplish, and the Gestapo and SD regularly influenced cases by directing them in line with Nazi political ideals. In effect, the court system became an administrative terror arm of the Nazi Party.

The courts were also established in occupied territories. Jews and Poles were considered to be less sensitive due to their perceived inferiority, and were generally given more severe punishments, the death penalty being widely used. With the growth of the Hitlerite terror against demographic forces and with the growing threat of war, the scope of the Special Courts increased and they became extremely important as Hitler's instrument of perceived justice against political crimes. On 9 November 1938, a Supreme Court document, 5 T. 557/38, confirmed that Special Courts were 'tribunals outside the ordinary judiciary not only by name but also by nature'.

The higher courts had initially attempted to resist the Fascist oppression of the judicial system, as evidenced by the famous Reichstag fire trial in 1933. The Supreme Court in Leipzig, Germany's highest court, refused to convict four of the five defendants who had been indicted on charges of setting the Reichstag on fire, due to a lack of evidence. Dissatisfied with the 'not guilty' verdicts, Hitler removed all political cases from the jurisdiction of the Supreme Court and regular courts, and through the Reich Ministry of Justice ordered the creation of the People's Court to try major 'political' cases and those who were accused of treason. Established in Berlin during April 1934, it was headed up by the notorious Nazi lawyer and judge, Roland Freisler.

The People's Court became part of the Nazi system of terror, condemning tens of thousands of people as 'Volk Vermin' and thousands more to death for 'Volk Treason'. For each hearing five members sat, each appointed by Hitler for a five-year period alongside other personnel selected by the Reich Ministry of Justice.

Politics rather than natural justice was at the forefront of the Nazi judicial system. Shockingly, the People's Court handed down death sentences to 10 per cent of defendants in 1941, rising to 40 per cent between 1942 and 1944, which totalled approximately 12,891 death sentences. In addition to the professional judges that sat for each case, loyal representatives of the Nazi Party and of the Fascist Wehrmacht were also present as 'experts'. The procedures in the People's Court corresponded to those of the Special Court and placed defendants coming before it at a disadvantage as there was no appeal against the decisions reached. If a defendant wanted a defence counsel then this required the consent of the chairman of the court. Defendants were at the mercy of the Fascist system, and very few of them got away with their lives.

Political authorities increased their control over matters of the judiciary, and the Gestapo were permitted to interfere in political trials. An example of such manipulation of the judicial system by a German official in order to eradicate an individual concerns Carl Wentzel, an influential German farmer and agricultural contractor who had been involved with Hitler's four-year plan to improve agricultural production in order to reduce Germany's dependence on imports for raw materials. Wentzel was part of a discussion group of industrialists as well as other influential people in politics and science who met several times at his estate to discuss issues concerning economic and political developments under Nazi control. At one of these meetings in 1943, Carl Goerdeler, a German jurist, National Conservative politician and resistance fighter against National Socialism, voiced his opinion about likely consequences for economic policy should a regime change take place, and when the assassination attempt on Hitler took place on 20 July 1944, this conversation was recounted to Gestapo officials, Wentzel being arrested ten days later and accused of being involved in the coup plans. It is rumoured that the heavily indebted SS group leader and major-general of the police Ludolf-Hermann von Alvensleben, whose family estate of Schochwitz was leased long-term to Wentzel, accused him of being involved with the assassination in order to dissolve the tenancy and take back his property in order to resolve his financial problems. Despite a lack of evidence, the

People's Court, chaired by Freisler, sentenced Wentzel to death on 13 November, a sentence that was carried out at Plötzensee Prison in Berlin on 20 December 1944.

Goerdeler was also implicated in the July plot against Hitler and arrested in August 1944. In contrast to Wentzel, Goerdeler had been a known active resister of Nazi rule and had unsuccessfully tried to negotiate a peace deal with the Allies. He felt strongly that Hitler would never surrender unconditionally and therefore only the armed forces of Germany could defeat the Führer. Goerdeler did take part in the planning of the July plot, but it was due to his anti-Nazi activities that an arrest warrant was issued against him on 14 July. He fled to his West Prussian homeland but was betrayed, and following his arrest was sentenced to death on 8 September by the People's Court for 'treason against the nation'. The sentence was deferred for five months during which he was interrogated and tortured in an attempt to discover the names of other conspirators. He was finally executed on 2 February 1945 at Plötzensee Prison.

The People's Court was an instrument of death for influential political opponents of Hitler. Denied legal representation, their fate was inevitably sealed before they entered the courtroom and even where evidence existed to confirm an individual's involvement in matters against the state, they were denied the opportunity to mitigate their actions through a fair judicial process. Ulrich von Hassell had been the German Ambassador to Rome and was initially a supporter of Hitler. However, he became critical of the aggressive approach of the Nazi Party, particularly with regard to foreign policies. In 1938, he was sacked from his position and so became an active opponent of Nazism, joining forces with Goerdeler and other influential Germans in attempts to recruit leading German generals in order to negotiate a peace deal with the Allies. Although he was warned that he was under investigation by the Gestapo, he continued to conspire against Hitler and was arrested the day after the 20 July plot. He was convicted of high treason, having been denied a defence, and was executed on 8 September 1944.

The structure and procedures of the People's Court were in place in order to maintain Nazi rule. Roland Freisler in a speech at Berlin University on 16 January 1934 ('Deutsche Justiz', No. 1/1934) declared, 'In the interests of self-protection' the judge must not 'be bound by the barriers of rigid facts'. The phrase 'no punishment without law' was a product of 'liberalistic mental attitudes ... The punishment of a crime not expressly declared as punishable must be possible' if it accords with 'healthy folk conception'.

In 1933, Military Courts and Party Tribunals were also established to absorb a proportion of cases and these developments signalled the end of any independent powers for the old judiciary who were now controlled by government agents and utilised as an instrument of repression. Military Courts operated on the same judicial basis as Special Courts and the People's Courts. On 12 May 1933, Hitler's government passed a law reintroducing a military judicial system, as the previous system had been suspended by the Weimar Republic in times of peace. The Reich Military Courts became the highest court of the Wehrmacht and indicated that Hitler wanted such courts operational in readiness for a war. This indication is further supported by the 'Decree on the Use of Military Justice in War and on Special Operations' and the notorious 'Decree on Special Penal Law in War and on Special Operations' issued on 17 August 1938. The opening sentence of the first paragraph of the Military Justice Decree stated, 'Modified procedure (war procedure) is introduced for the protection of the Wehrmacht and for war purposes.' This 'modified procedure for war purposes' stated in paragraph 33 that no record of the proceedings of the court should be kept. Paragraph 48 stated that the accused need not be informed in advance of the charges, since it was sufficient to 'publish the charges by reading them in the main hearing'. Basic rights were denied; for example, there was no provision for an interpreter to support a defendant who could not speak German. According to figures made public by Dr Thomas Dehler, the former West German Minister of Justice, and confirmed on 19 October 1958 by Dr Max Güde, the Federal Prosecutor-General, the military judges of the Nazi Wehrmacht used these modified procedures to pass death sentences on 10,000 soldiers and officers of the German forces during the Second World War, often simply for making a remark that opposed the war or a comment that favoured peace or democracy.

In addition to the death sentences carried out against soldiers and officers of the German forces, many death sentences were also handed down against foreign citizens by the Nazi military judges. In a large number of cases, there was no clear line between the Military Courts and the Special Courts. Many non-German citizens were tried, with the judges pronouncing innumerable death sentences as well as many years of hard labour, particularly against the civilian population and anti-Fascist resistance movements in Poland, France, Denmark, Norway, the Netherlands, Belgium, Czechoslovakia, the Soviet Union and other countries occupied by German troops.

The notorious Special Penal Law in War was used as a basis for death sentences against thousands of soldiers and civilians who opposed Hitler and Nazism. Other decrees were issued to support the Military Courts across occupied territories. For example, in Czechoslovakia on 26 August 1939, the 'Decree of the Reich Protector in Bohemia and Moravia on Acts of Sabotage' was published. This decree defined sabotage as 'every interference with public life or the economy'. A supplement issued to the decree stated, 'Interference with public life can for instance be produced by … spreading hostile rumours which cause unrest amongst the population, or which disturb the peaceful life side by side of the Germans and the Czechs.'

CHAPTER 3

Key Personnel within the Judicial System

Paul Jorns

Born in Heinade on 14 December 1897, Paul Jorns was to become a German jurist and senior prosecutor in the People's Court. He was involved in a number of high-profile cases, including one which led to the eventual use of the 'Fallbeil' within Nazi Germany and throughout the Second World War. On 15 January 1919, Rosa Luxemburg and Karl Liebknecht, both co-founders of the anti-war Spartacus League which would become the Communist Party of Germany, were brutally murdered. The official version was that after the pair had been arrested and while Karl was being transferred under military escort to a Berlin prison by motor car he suffered a heavy blow to his head. Reportedly the car then developed engine trouble and Karl, who was bleeding profusely, was ordered to continue by foot. Whilst doing so he tried to escape and was shot. Rosa Luxemburg was reportedly attacked by a mob when she was first detained, until her military escort rescued her unconscious and put her into a car. Whilst in the car an unknown assailant jumped on the running board and fired a pistol at her, the car driving away until a crowd near the Landwehr Canal in central Berlin stopped it, upon which she was dragged away and thrown into the canal.

Rosa and Karl were well-known individuals who had opposed the First World War and had been imprisoned for leading a revolt in Germany and openly preparing to establish a soviet republic under the newly proclaimed Communist Party of Germany. This movement was violently opposed by Friedrich Ebert, the Social Democratic leader of the provisional government, and the army commanded by Paul von Hindenburg and Wilhelm Groener. Both Rosa and Karl were regarded as being highly undesirable in the immediate post-war Germany. Even the government of the day could not uphold the fabricated official version of the murders, so a trial was arranged to be held for Lt Kurt Vogel and a trooper named Otto Runge, both accused of the deaths of Rosa and Karl. The prosecutor was Jorns, who vehemently stated that although Vogel and Runge had severely mistreated the prisoners, he saw extenuating circumstances in that both men had excellent war records. It is strongly suspected that both belonged to the *Freikorps*, which was the name adopted by a large number of right-wing nationalists in Weimar Germany after the First World

War had ended. The court case concluded in Vogel being sentenced to twenty-eight months' imprisonment for committing a misdemeanour while on guard duty, illegally disposing of a corpse and filing an inaccurate report, Runge receiving a sentence of just over two years for attempted manslaughter. No one was held to account for the murder of Karl Liebknecht, as it was maintained that he had been shot while attempting to escape arrest. It was later disclosed that Karl's body had been transported to a mortuary and eventually disposed of as an unknown person. Rosa's body had been taken to the Liechtenstein Bridge and thrown into the canal, and was not recovered until May 1919. An autopsy confirmed that she had suffered a beating on the head with the butt of a revolver and had been shot in the head at point-blank range by Vogel.

In 1928, following concerns over the case and the leniency of the sentences handed out to Vogel and Runge, an examining court found that Jorns had abetted the assassins during their prosecution case. By this time, however, he had progressed through the judicial ranks and was therefore not held to account. Incredibly, the Nazis would later compensate Jorns for his ordeal in the findings evidenced in 1928. Trooper Runge was also financially compensated for being 'unfairly punished'. In 1933, Jorns joined the Nazi Party and the following year, at the age of 62, became a senior public prosecutor in the People's Court.

In another high-profile case, on 18 February 1935 at 06.00 hours, two women from aristocratic families, Baroness Benita von Falkenhayn and Renate von Natzner, having been convicted of spying, were beheaded with the axe by the executioner Carl Gropler at Plötzensee Prison. Jorns had been engaged in convicting these two women, who had been swept into a relationship with a Polish spy. The case was heard in secret, and little evidence exists of Jorns' involvement other than the post-court and execution news report subsequently published in the Australian Rockhampton newspaper on 20 February 1935:

TWO WOMEN BEHEADED
BETRAYED GERMAN SECRETS typists deceived by Polish Don Juan
REMARKABLE STORY OF ESPIONAGE

BERLIN, February 18
In the grey dawn, behind the high yellow walls of the Plötzensee Prison on the outskirts of Berlin, a grotesque headsman, dressed in full evening dress, wearing white gloves and a cocked hat, to-day beheaded two women, one of whom was related to the war ace Baron Richthofen and the other related to a famous German soldier family of a later day.

Sentenced by the People's Court on charges of having betrayed German secrets to the enemy, the beautiful golden-haired baroness, Benita von Falkenhayn, divorced wife of Baron von Berg and a member of an aristocratic family, Frau Renate von Natzner, were executed with an axe. Although the evening paper is not permitted to publish reports of the affair it was a sequel to Europe's most secret and most sensational year-long after-war spy trial.

Herr Hitler declined to exercise prerogative of mercy, although death sentences of fellow conspirators a Polish Don Juan, Daron von Sosnowski, who for the last week had vainly and desperately made efforts to marry the Baroness Benita in the belief it would make her a Polish citizen and prevent the extreme penalty from being carried out and the 23-years-old Fraulein von Jena, a descendant of Hohenzollerns, were commuted to life imprisonment.

JUSTICE HAS BEEN DONE

The judge of the People's Court and 12 citizens summoned as witnesses gathered in the courtyard to witness the first execution of women in peace time except for murder. Baroness Benita was first led into the courtyard. Dressed in plain clothes with her neck shaved and her long tresses of golden hair tied up, she laid her head on a wooden block and it was severed with a stroke, the head falling into a basket of sawdust. Then the head and body were put into a coffin and carried away through a small drift of snowflakes while the scaffolding was prepared for the second victim.

As each head was severed the executioner turned to the watchers and declared that justice had been done.

Though nothing is published in Germany, it is known that the spies obtained German general staff plans for an invasion of Poland should the necessity arise. Sosnowski, the leader of the gang is an ex-Polish officer and a dashing horseman and motorist, apparently wealthy. He captivated Berlin society and had amazing influence with women, particularly the Baroness Benita, whom I met at a party in 1925 when she was married to Baron von Falkenhayn, son of the famous wartime general of the same name who divorced her. Baroness Benita, when about to marry Sosnowski, found that he was having another love affair and consequently she married Baron von Berg, a former Russia aviator, who later fought with Germany after the Russian revolution and is at present secretary to the director of electoral works in Berlin.

Sosnowski again captivated Baroness Benita, whose mother after the death of Benita's father had married Baron von Richthofen, cousin of the famous aviator and a member of the Crown Prince's staff.

TRAPPED INTO SERVICE

Baroness Benita acted as intermediary between Sosnowski and the girls whom he trapped into the service. They established fashionable customers and threw the gayest parties. Their favourite method was to invite girls connected with the Reichswehr and then, when the party was at its height, to have a flashlight photograph taken of them in compromising positions and then threaten to send the picture to their families unless they revealed the Reichswehr secrets.

Fraulein von Natznier, aged 32, belonged to an aristocratic German family. Three out of her five brothers were killed in the war. She divorced her husband and then became a Reichswehr typist in order to keep herself and her father. The defence urged that the pay was too poor and that she fell as easy prey to Benita's threats and promises of £10 a month. Fraulein von Jena was also a Reichswehr typist. Both allegedly took carbon copies of documents for Benita. Other documents and plans were secretly photographed with apparatus hidden in the women's cloakroom at the Reichswehr headquarters.

MARRIAGE FORBIDDEN

It is believed likely that Sosnowski will be exchanged for three German spies imprisoned in Poland. It is understood that a fortnight ago he refused to be exchanged because Baron von Berg agreed to divorce Baroness Benita and allow Sosnowski to marry her but the prison officials refused to permit the marriage. Sosnowski started espionage when he wrongly believed that the Nazis would adopt a hostile policy to Poland. The Reichswehr plot was revealed when the mother of a Reichswehr typist questioned her about her extravagance.

Before being beheaded the women were blindfolded and led to the block by armed warders.

The executioner's axe was a large tool, heavier and wider than the English axe. Roland Freisler, the repugnant People's Court judge and prosecutor, defended its use and actually issued a response to criticism in the foreign press that axe beheadings were crude. Headsmen such as Gropler and Reindel, both leading executioners in the 1930s, supported the use of the axe, saying it was fast, easily concealed and—in the hands of an expert—a device that cleanly did its work with a single blow. The executioner's block was elaborate, with metal rings through which cords from the victim's hands were passed and then pulled tight to force the victim forward and into the block. Between three and five assistants were employed to secure the block, one of the executioner's assistants pulling the head forward in order to stretch the neck across the block. The executioner would rarely take more than a single fall of the axe to complete his gruesome work.

Prosecutor Jorns was reportedly present at the executions wearing his robes when the two women's heads were severed on 18 February 1935. He continued to serve in the infamous People's Court until 1941, retiring at the age of 70 years. He died in Berlin on 2 May 1942. Unbeknown at the time, Jorns had presided over the last axe beheadings in Germany. It is thought that this high profile and globally reported case led Hitler to instigate the deployment of the Fallbeil guillotine as the means of further executions, and this was put into effect by Reich Minister of Justice Gürtner on 28 December 1936.

Oswald Rothaug

Born on 17 May 1897, Oswald Rothaug served from 1916 to 1918 in the German army and then went on to practise law, having passed the final law examination in 1922 and the State examination for the higher administration of justice in 1925. In December 1925, he began his career as a German jurist, first as an assistant and later as an assistant judge at various courts. In 1927, he became a public prosecutor in charge of criminal cases, and he served at the local court in Nuremberg from 1929 to 1933, becoming a senior public prosecutor in charge of general criminal cases. Rothaug was an ardent Nazi who subsequently became the Schweinfurt Regional Court director in 1937, following which he returned to the Nuremberg Special Courts in 1938, where he became the Chief Justice and a member of the Leadership Corp. Membership at that high level would have reflected his dedication towards the Nazi Party. In addition, this now placed him in a position to allow his court to become a personal method of inflicting terror and fear, and he appears to have particularly sought cases of racial purity.

In 1942, the case against a 68-year-old Jew, Lehman Katzenberger, came before Rothaug in Nuremberg. Lehman was suspected of having a relationship with his much younger German tenant Irene Seiler. Article 2 of the 1935 Law for the Protection of German Blood and Honour prohibited *Rassenschande* ('racial pollution'). The law forbade sexual intercourse between Jews and other German nationals and so Lehman stood trial on 13 March 1942. It transpired that the relationship was one of friendship, with Lehman loaning Irene money and acting as provider for her. Rothaug ordered that the case be transferred from the Criminal Division Court to the Special Court so that he could be provided with the opportunities he sought to condemn another Jew to death. An eyewitness later materialised who stated that Lehman had reportedly been seen leaving Irene's house after dark. This opened the door to the death penalty as the law provided such a sentence when a crime had been committed during blackout hours. Rothaug provided his court with a biased summary that would ultimately lead to his vindictive sentence:

> The national community is in need of increased legal protection from all crimes attempting to destroy or undermine its inner cohesion … The visits by Katzenberger to Seiler under the protection of the blackout served at least the purpose of keeping relations going. It does not matter whether during these visits extra-marital sexual relations took place or whether they only conversed … The Jew's racial pollution amounts to a grave attack on the purity of German blood, the object of the attack being the body of a German woman … the political life of the German people under National Socialism is based on the community. One fundamental factor of the life of the national community is race. If a Jew commits racial pollution with a German woman, this amounts to polluting the German race and, by polluting a German woman, to a grave attack on the purity of German blood. The need for protection is particularly strong.

Rothaug had conducted nothing short of a show trial in which he demonstrated his personal anti-Jewish hate in manipulating the case to create an opportunity to sentence Lehman Katzenberger to death. Irene received a prison sentence of two years for perjury. The verdict, pronounced in March 1942, drew the attention of the media, the Nuremberg newspaper *Der Stürmer* publishing an article about the trial on 2 April 1942:

> Death to the Race Defiler.
>
> When the court re-enters the courtroom to announce the verdict one can already see from the earnest looks of the judges that the fate of the Talmudic criminal has been sealed. As a race defiler and public parasite Katzenberger is sentenced to death.
>
> The co-defendant Irene S. gets two years' hard labour and loss of civil rights for perjury. President of the District Court of Appeal Rothaug points to words in the findings of the verdict which prove to what extent the German judges are imbued with the tremendous importance of the racial laws. The president brands the depravity of the defendant and stamps him as an evil public parasite. Racial defilement is worse than murder. Entire generations will be affected by it into the remotest future.
>
> President of the District Court of Appeal Rothaug in his speech also refers to the guilt of Jewry in this war. If today German soldiers are bleeding to death, then the guilty falls upon that race which from the very beginning strove for Germany's ruin, and still hopes today that the German people will not emerge from this struggle.
>
> In the case of Katzenberger the court had to pronounce the death sentence. The physical destruction of the perpetrator was the only possible atonement.

Lehman Katzenberger was beheaded at Stadelheim Prison, Munich, on 2 June 1942.

Between May 1943 and April 1945, Rothaug was a public prosecutor at the People's Court in Berlin, during which he heard cases predominantly concerning the undermining of public morale in the Reich territory. Post-war, Rothaug appeared at the Nuremberg Trials charged by the Allies with crimes against humanity, for which he was found guilty. He received a life sentence but was released from custody in 1956. Unlike his victims, he died a free man in 1967.

Roland Freisler

Freisler was born on 30 October 1893 in Celle. After the outbreak of the First World War, he joined the German army and served in the 167th Infantry Regiment. In November 1914, he was attached to the 26th Reserve Corps and was wounded whilst fighting in Flanders. After convalescing for several months in Germany, he returned to his regiment which was in the throes of transferring to the northern sector of the Russian front. Russian troops later captured Freisler while he was on a reconnaissance patrol and he was taken to a prisoner-of-war camp north of Moscow. With the success of the Bolshevik Revolution, German prisoners of war were repatriated, and some speculation exists as to whether Freisler may have remained in Russia voluntarily for an additional period of time, having developed an interest in Russian culture and Communism. However, he eventually returned to Germany in July 1920, studying law at the University of Jena and becoming a Doctor of Law in 1922. He opened his own law office in Kassel in 1924, where he witnessed the growth of the National Socialist German Workers' Party.

In July 1925, Freisler joined the Nazi Party and continued to practise law, defending various members of the party who had been in need of legal representation. These actions were drawn to the attention of the Nazi Party hierarchy and just one month after Hitler's rise to the post of Chancellor, Freisler was appointed as the Department Head in the Prussian Ministry of Justice. On 24 March 1928, he married Marion Russegger, and was appointed to the Reich Ministry of Justice in 1934. The People's Courts were then in their infancy, and in 1936 he encapsulated their position within the Nazi judicial system:

> Until the National Socialist seizure of power the so-called lay judges were chosen by lot, risking the possibly very strong elements of chance and the misuse of the choice of lot. The fear of the power of the state led to the proclamation of the most nonsensical choice of judges as the guardians of the liberty of the citizen. National Socialism however selects its own People's Judges according to their personal suitability and special expertise. Upon the suggestion of the Reich Minister of Justice the Führer appoints the People's Judges who come from the Wehrmacht and the Police, the NSDAP and its formations, and who are uniquely suited to make the people itself the bearer of Justice.

Freisler had witnessed the National Socialist judiciary manipulate the law as a political instrument, an example being on 7 January 1942 when the Reich Ministry of Justice actioned separate criminal law for the Poles (who were regarded as 'racial aliens'), and Freisler's importance is well evidenced through being one of the few people selected to attend the notorious Wannsee Conference on 20 January 1942. The conference was held in a suburb of Berlin at a villa by a lake known as the Wannsee. Fifteen people attended, including high-ranking party officials and SS officers. The purpose of the meeting was to outline the newly planned 'Final Solution', which would entail the rounding-up of all Jews throughout Europe. The final protocol of the Wannsee Conference never explicitly mentioned extermination, but within a few months of the meeting, the first gas chambers were installed in a number of the Polish extermination camps of Belzec, Birkenau, Chełmno, Majdanek, Sobibór and Treblinka.

Freisler was instrumental in enforcing Hitler's directives upon criminal activity and the use of death sentences on those accused of what would appear to be minor infringements. Frequently the jurists would make reference to Hitler's speech of

30 September 1942, broadcast from the Berlin Sports Palace, when he advocated 'exterminating criminals'. The People's Court became a tribunal of revenge on all forms of resistance against the Nazi regime. On 20 August 1942, Freisler was appointed by Hitler as the President of the People's Court. He filled the void left by Hitler's appointment of the merciless Otto Georg Thierack to Reich Minister of Justice. In this role Thierack made it legal for Gypsies, Poles, Jews and Ukrainians to be passed directly to the SS rather than being sentenced by regular courts, thus sealing their fate by being sent to Nazi concentration camps in the East.

After Freisler's appointment and the influences of his predecessor Thierack, the number of death sentences increased significantly: 4,457 in 1942 compared to 1,292 in 1941, rising to 9,600 in 1943 and 1944. Freisler created a renowned and feared reputation during his People's Court hearings. Clearly his ego and status had escalated unabated from 1938, and he was responsible for exceptionally harsh sentencing based on unsubstantiated or almost non-existent evidence. He sentenced many hundreds of men and women to death, the sentence being announced after a long barrage of shouting and humiliating rhetoric.

Elisabeth von Thadden was a 53-year-old teacher who had had her permission to run a school withdrawn in 1941, as she was not deemed to be providing suitable National Socialist education to her pupils. In 1943, Elisabeth was actively working for the German Red Cross and had engaged in what became known as the 'Solf tea party group'. On 10 September, she arranged a birthday party in Berlin for her sister Marie-Agnes Braune. This was attended by Otto Kiep, an employee in the Reich Press Office; Hanna Solf, whose late husband had been Kaiser Wilhelm's last German ambassador to Japan; State Secretary Arthur Zarden with his daughter Irmgard; the social worker Anne Rühle; Fanny von Kurowsky; and counsellor Hilger van Scherpenberg. Elisabeth had also invited Dr Paul Reckzeh, who had only recently become known to her but was reportedly active in anti-Nazi politics. Despite Reckzeh being a stranger to the other guests, the group spoke openly, particularly Elisabeth, whose preoccupation was with politics. In view of Italy's surrender the previous day and what appeared to be a hopeless military situation, the guests candidly discussed options for Germany's reform after the end of the war. Reckzeh, a Gestapo informant, created an atmosphere of trust, which led him to offer his services as a courier of messages to German exiles in Switzerland, and Elisabeth subsequently handed a letter to him. However, her trust was betrayed when he immediately delivered it to the Gestapo. Reckzeh had specifically entered the 'Solf group' with the intention of gathering evidence against them.

On 12 January 1944, members of the 'Solf group' were arrested, even though within the group there were people of influence amongst high society. For example, Hanna Solf retained connections with Japan, which needed to be handled with political sensitivity. On 1 July 1944, Freisler took to his stage in the feared People's Court to hear the evidence against Hanna Solf, Arthur Zarden, Fanny von Kurowsky, Hilger van Scherpenberg, Otto Kiep and Elisabeth von Thadden, who were charged with 'High

Treason, Sedition, Defeatism and favouring the enemy'. Freisler used this high-profile case to demonstrate his authority in the court, sentencing Hilger van Scherpenberg to two years' hard labour in prison, and Otto Kiep and Elisabeth von Thadden to death. Remarkably, Arthur Zarden and Fanny von Kurowsky were acquitted. The specific indictment against Elisabeth, who held a relatively low status within the group, was having 'aided and abetted wartime enemies of the Greater German Reich by undermining the war effort and by conspiring to commit high treason'.

German judges undertook a vital role in eradicating the political resistance of anti-Nazi activists who had been detained or arrested by the Gestapo on suspicion of treason (in all probability relating to an attack on the external security of Germany) or high treason (an attack on its internal security). These cases were inevitably processed by the higher court structure. However, Hanna Solf was removed from the sentencing procedure by Freisler and her trial scheduled for 13 December was postponed after further investigations.

Elisabeth, whilst awaiting execution, was subjected to intense interrogations during late July and August 1944, following an assassination attempt on Hitler. The 'Solf group' was suspected of having been involved after Otto Kiep was later implicated in the assassination plot. On 8 September 1944, Elisabeth was taken to the execution chamber at Plötzensee Prison and her head was removed on the Fallbeil. Otto Kiep, however, had been denied a swift death by decapitation: under direct orders from Hitler he had been hanged by a short cord at Plötzensee on 23 August 1944—in effect a death by slow strangulation.

On 20 July 1944, Claus Schenk Graf von Stauffenberg, one of Hitler's high-ranking officers, had placed a briefcase bomb inside Hitler's Eastern Front command post in Rastenburg, Prussia, but the coup attempt against the Nazi regime failed, Hitler sustaining only slight injuries. Freisler, as the most senior judge within the People's Court, was personally responsible for overseeing the subsequent show trials of the conspirators. As a result of the attempt on the Führer's life, the newly appointed chief of staff, Heinz Guderian, demanded the resignation of any German officer who did not fully support the ideals of the Nazi Party. Over the ensuing months he sat with Gerd von Rundstedt and Wilhelm Keitel in the Army Court of Honour that subsequently expelled hundreds of officers suspected of being opposed to the policies of Hitler. This judgment removed those men from any court martial jurisdiction and instead turned them over to Freisler and his notorious People's Court.

Many of the suspects were either executed or committed suicide. Ninety of the suspected conspirators were tried and executed at Plötzensee Prison between August 1944 and April 1945. Hitler had decreed that the ringleaders of the plot against his life should have a slow and degrading death, the presumption being that Freisler communicated directly with Hitler's entourage in order to carry out his directive. Freisler held the first court hearing against eight of the plotters on 7 August 1944, when he quickly pronounced the death sentences, which were carried out with the accused stripped naked and hung. He personally presided over four other court sessions during August, when a further sixteen suspects were sentenced to a similar death, and many hundreds followed in their footsteps during the ensuing months. The final degrading aspect for these victims was the order that following their execution, their bodies were to be burned and their ashes strewn over sewage.

In early 1945, the United States Army Air Forces (USAAF) were capable of undertaking extensive daylight bombing operations with upwards of a thousand Boeing B-17 bomber aircraft. The German defence structure was failing both in terms of equipment and personnel, which enabled these raids to be undertaken with expectations that Allied losses would be reduced in comparison to previously experienced statistics, particularly whilst attacking Berlin. The Allied forces were massing towards central Germany, but the heart of the Third Reich was still capable of defending itself with its flak units and elite Nazi soldiers. The German courts were still very active despite the disruptions by air raids, and Freisler continued to enhance his reputation of ruthlessness. A 60-year-old mother, Terezija Micej, and her 22-year-old daughter had both been arrested by the Gestapo on 1 June 1944, accused of providing lodging and food to Nazi resistance fighters. They had been brutally interrogated for several weeks to reveal the identity of those fighters, and after seven months of imprisonment they finally appeared in the People's Court. They were denied any defence representation at their trial and, unsurprisingly, on 6 January 1945, they were both sentenced to death by Freisler and beheaded by the Fallbeil six days later.

British night bombing operations continued unabated and the American daylight operations intensified during the final Allied push to crush the German Third Reich.

On 3 February 1945, 1,003 B-17s were sent to attack the railway infrastructure in central Berlin. The concept of 'city' bombing had been purposely avoided by the USAAF, operational briefings concentrating on railway targets as identified to the bombardiers or bomb aimers. On this occasion weather conditions were favourable for both the bombers and their P-51 escort fighters, and the individual 8,000 lb bomb loads from each aircraft were to be dropped from between 24,000 and 27,000 feet. The initial aiming point for the bombers was the Friedrichstrasse railway station. However, the commander, Lt-Gen. James Doolittle, knew that such a limited target area was always likely to create a spread of devastation within central Berlin. This particular operation and the others that followed at this time were very important, both politically and militarily, with the Russians closing upon eastern Berlin and Allied unity being fully demonstrated. The approach of the Russians had brought about a huge influx of escaping refugees into what was to be the area of bombardment, numbers far in excess of any air-raid shelter capacities that remained in operation, and the full might of a large and concentrated daylight raid was likely to be catastrophic both to buildings and occupants.

At this stage in the war Berliners were very accustomed to intense bombing and hurriedly responded to any air-raid warnings. The Germans did not just build *Luftschutzbunkern* (aerial protection bunkers) below ground; they constructed *Tiefbunkern* (underground bunkers) and *Hochbunkern* (surface bunkers). Many of these were constructed for air-raid protection from the mid-1930s onwards. Under the *Führer-Sofortprogramm,* Hitler's 'Immediate Programme' of 10 October 1940 construction intensified and these buildings were sub-classified into *Luftschutzhauser* (air-raid protection buildings) and *Luftschutzturme* (air-raid protection towers. Both patterns were very substantial structures of similar construction. Friedrich Tamms was the designer for the Reich Ministry of Armaments and War Production, with bunker construction built to new and never before imagined levels by the Reich civil engineering organisation headed by Fritz Todt, who utilised hundreds of forced labourers from all over Europe. These enormous concrete 'Flak Towers', each one holding four heavy guns, were always accompanied by a further tower that provided the predicting radar and control equipment that made the heavy guns particularly effective. They were manned by expert gunners, and each pair of towers was additionally provided with the smaller and most effective four-barrelled 2-cm light flak guns. These huge complex structures acted as civil defence headquarters and air-raid shelters for many thousands of city dwellers, and their size and solidity was such that even direct hits by Allied bombers were capable of inflicting only superficial damage. Sixteen such structures were eventually completed: three pairs in both Berlin and Vienna, and two pairs in Hamburg.

Substantial buildings like the Chamber Courts of Justice in Berlin were ideally suited to provide their own air-raid sanctuary deep within their own basements. Indeed when the various bunkers were being constructed in the capital under Hitler's directives, the words published by his state secretary in the National Ministry of Justice, Roland Freisler, concerning the conduct of criminal proceedings on the basis of the ordinance 'Against parasites of the people' was still echoing within chambers and courts across Germany:

> Germany stands in a battle for honour and right. The model for every German today more than ever is the German Soldier. Whoever wrongs the people instead of living up to that example no longer has a place in our society. For the ruthless struggle against these parasites of the people the Ministry for the Defence of the Nation has created the necessary legal basis. I expect all judges and state attorneys to apply the ordinance with the same ruthless, rapid, harsh powerful determination and energy with which it was issued. Not to apply the most extreme severity in the face of such parasites would be treason to the fighting German soldiers. Moreover, all participants must assist in ensuring that the crime, the indictment, the trial, and the judgment and the execution follow immediately upon each other with no delay. All participating judges and state attorneys are to transmit this order immediately. 12 September 1939.

On the morning of 3 February 1945, Freisler convened an extraordinary court session to hear the case against Fabian von Schlabrendorff, one of the many swept up in the purge of suspected conspirators against Hitler. This defendant was seen as a significant figure in the July plot against Hitler and had been a pre-war jurist before joining the German army. No doubt Freisler relished the opportunity to humiliate the defendant and sentence him to a slow death in Plötzensee Prison. Many of those who faced charges in front of Freisler were made to stand through the proceedings with no belt for their trousers, a concept designed to ensure they had to stand holding up their trousers. Freisler allowed just about anything to humiliate those on trial, with their guilt sealed even before their trial had begun. As the court proceedings commenced, the American B-17 bombers were progressing towards their intended target in central Berlin from the south and south-west at 10.30 hours. Von Schlabrendorff faced Freisler, accused with the most heinous of crimes—an attempt to murder Hitler—but with little chance of a fair hearing.

Within Freisler's court, all defendants stood in legal isolation attempting to maintain their dignity and inevitably being denied almost any opportunity to speak. Freisler relished the chance to insult defendants and to politicise his statements to them, but on this occasion he was denied the ultimate sentencing to death of von Schlabrendorff as the air-raid sirens blasted their warning of an impending Allied bombing raid. The B-17s were preparing to drop their bomb loads onto central Berlin, and although marshalling yards and railways were the primary objectives, the Reich and Party Chancellery, Air Ministry and Chamber Courts of Justice were subjected to bombardment. It appears that Freisler was either reticent to leave his court or was delayed in his evacuation to the shelter. Whatever the reason, the delay meant that he received fatal injuries when the court was hit by bombs dropped at the start of the raid. Several accounts exist in relation to his exact position within the court building at the time of impact; he was either crushed by falling masonry or caught by the bomb blast. What is not in doubt is that the USAAF had inadvertently killed the most abhorrent and repugnant upholder of Nazi judicial ideology.

Rather ironically, the American bombing raid was led by the highly decorated pilot Robert Rosenthal, who before the war had been a young lawyer. He survived a most eventful career in the air force, and post-war served as an assistant to Robert H. Jackson, the US prosecutor at the Nuremberg Trials. As part of his duties during the trials, Rosenthal interviewed the top German general Wilhelm Keitel, and Hermann Goering, commander of the German air force and the second highest ranked Nazi during most of the war.

Prior to the February raid, Fabian von Schlabrendorff had been brought before the People's Court on 21 December 1944. Amongst his co-accused was Franz Kempner, who during Gestapo interrogations admitted to having many reservations about National Socialism. In the early years of the Weimar Republic, Franz had worked as a state secretary in the Reich Chancellery from 1925 to 1926. Because the court was unable to hear all the cases that day, Franz's case was rescheduled for 12 January 1945, and it was on that day that he, along with several other conspirators, was sentenced to death. Franz was executed on 5 March in Plötzensee Prison, along with Hasso von Boehmer, a colonel-general in the General Staff.

On the day of the assassination attempt on Hitler, von Boehmer's superior, Gen. Bodewin Keitel, brother of Field Marshal Wilhelm Keitel, was on an inspection tour. In his capacity as Keitel's first officer, von Boehmer received the conspirators' telegrams that arrived from Berlin. Keitel heard about the unsuccessful assassination attempt on the radio and von Boehmer was immediately arrested that same day. Alongside him at the gallows was Ernst von Harnack, an attorney who had argued clearly against National Socialism in speeches and articles. He was not directly involved in the assassination plot but had been arrested on 28 September 1944, Freisler sentencing him to death on 1 February 1945, a victim of the Nazi judge's frenzied retribution.

It is remarkable that Fabian von Schlabrendorff survived Freisler's terror, and without doubt the Allied bombing raid on 3 February 1945 was a most fortunate set of circumstances for him. However, he had not escaped the People's Court and was once again rescheduled to appear on 16 March at a hearing presided over by Freisler's deputy, Wilhelm Crohne. Good fortune continued to favour von Schlabrendorff, as he was provided an opportunity to address Crohne with evidence of his torture, which ultimately secured him an acquittal and resulted in his release. The current state of the Allied advances towards Berlin may well have been an influencing factor; that said, the Gestapo immediately detained him and transported him to Flossenburg concentration camp in the Oberpfalz region of Bavaria, near the Czech border. This long-established work camp housed criminal and political prisoners sentenced to hard labour quarrying stone, and inmates were subjected to executions and cremations as in other such camps. Several of the July plotters had met their deaths in Flossenburg, and it was intended that von Schlabrendorff would follow them. However, with orders issued to evacuate the camp in order to avoid the advancing Allied forces, he was saved once again, although he was to face the horrors of Dachau concentration camp. His remarkable escape from the gallows was complete with his liberation from that death camp on 29 April 1945.

Hanna Solf had experienced similar circumstances, with at least two postponed court appearances. With her fate in the hands of Freisler, the raid of 3 February undoubtedly also saved her life, as she had been due to appear in front of Freisler five days after his death. It appears that she was released from custody in April 1945 during the downfall of the Reich, and despite atrocious treatment she joined von Schlabrendorff in having survived against all the odds. Sadly, that was not the fate of the last prominent figure prosecuted in the People's Court, Ewald von Kleist-Schmenzin. His trial had commenced on the day that Freisler had met his death. Von Kleist-Schmenzin, a prominent man who owned significant holdings of land, had consistently spoken out against Hitler and had been provided with details of the July plot against the Führer. Wilhelm Crohne also took over this belated hearing, on 23 February, and sentenced von Kleist-Schmenzin to death on 15 March. He was decapitated in Plötzensee on 9 April 1945.

Harry Haffner

On 12 March 1945, Harry Haffner was appointed to succeed Roland Freisler as the last President of the People's Court. During the final throes of Nazi judgments he precariously presided at hearings while Russian artillery shelling was clearly audible within his court. The Allied forces were squeezing their military fronts towards central Germany and the Third Reich was slowly crumbling, yet its judicial processes were still being implemented.

Haffner was a relatively young man, aged 44, when he secured his presidency. He had completed his law studies, achieving average grades, in 1926. Employed as a prosecutor, he joined the Nazi Party in 1933 and in the following year was appointed as a prosecutor in Celle, Lower Saxony. In 1936, Haffner was promoted to the position of senior prosecutor to the Prosecutor-General of Kassel. Once again he served for a period of two years before a further promotion in 1938, when he became the General Prosecutor in the industrial district of Hamm. He achieved the position of General State Prosecutor in Kattowitz in 1944 and was prolific in handing out numerous death sentences. Reputedly, he at one time visited Auschwitz concentration camp during his tenure in the Upper Silesian province. Little doubt exists that Haffner would have witnessed the severity of Hitler's courts during his long tenure within the confines of the Nazi judicial system.

As President of the People's Court, Haffner sat in the Potsdam courts to hear just two cases, both connected to high-level civil servants who reportedly left their positions to escape the Russian advance. One was 65-year-old Max Draeger, a fellow jurist and past president at the regional court of Konigsberg (now Kaliningrad), who in disputed circumstances was apparently detained in a vehicle with another high-ranking civil servant, state attorney Gen. Fritz Szelinski, fleeing westward in a vehicle around the outskirts of Berlin. Both were arrested and put before the court. Draeger's companion committed suicide by hanging, whilst Draeger was presented to the People's Court and tried by Haffner. Convicted of desertion, he was sentenced to death by Haffner on 29 March 1945 and taken to Brandenburg-Görden Prison where he was executed a few days prior to the liberation of the prison by the Soviets on 27 April.

With Haffner himself facing the situation of impending death or imprisonment by the advancing Soviets, in unknown circumstances he disappeared with his wife during those last weeks of the war, escaping westwards and eventually surfacing under the name Heinrich Hartmann within the Allied-held territories of West Germany. He had sufficient funds organised to allow him to start a small business, well aware that he was listed in the central register of suspected war criminals. He began trading as a supplier of clothing and produced cloth buttons, buckles and belts, an ironic situation given that it was later reported that in July 1944 he had sentenced to death a Polish citizen in Kattowitz for trading in buttons and haberdashery without authority.

Haffner remained a wanted suspect during the immediate post-war years, but despite investigations he was never formally discovered and as such never faced any form of legal action. In 1953, however, he turned himself in to the authorities, but by that time the investigations against him had been dismissed. He lived the rest of his life under his correct name and received his civil servant's pension with the rank of Chief Prosecutor from the state in Germany until his death in 1969.

Paul Reimers

Born in Bremen in 1902, Paul Reimers was the son of a farmer. His career in law had commenced whilst studying at the University of Marburg. Reimers voluntarily supported the Nazi Party movement in its infancy and became a member of the NSDAP in early 1933. On 7 April that year, the Nazi regime enacted the Law for the Restoration of the Professional Civil Service, which enabled the exclusion of political and racially 'unreliable' individuals from teaching positions. As a result, more than 1,700 faculty members lost their positions across German universities. The vast majority of those dismissed were Jewish, along with individuals who were deemed to have left-wing tendencies. For example, the Dusseldorf Medical School lost half of its faculty, and this was by no means exceptional.

In 1934, Reimers qualified to sit as a judge in the Berlin District Court and after the outbreak of war he served in the Special Court at Berlin. By natural progression he was elevated to the People's Court, where he became known as the 'Bloody Judge', a title that appears to have sat comfortably with him. Reimers became a notorious judge, condemning more than a hundred individuals to death in the German courts. The following cases provide examples of his rulings and sentencing during 1944.

Karl Grabs, a 65-year-old livestock dealer, appeared in the People's Court on 26 February charged with 'defeatist propaganda', having uttered to an acquaintance, 'We must not win the war, for that would be much worse for us than if we lost it.' Several high-profile judges chose to issue verbal statements of significance from their courts in the knowledge that they would be reported and used to support the Nazi strategy of rule, as did Reimers in this case, adding:

> The accused fulfils the requirements of undermining the war strength and at the same time of helping the enemy. For he has continually and openly tried to paralyse the will of another person to warlike assertions of himself in this fateful struggle of the Fatherland, and thus simultaneously contributed to the enemy cause to the detriment of the Reich ... For there could be no stronger inducement to another person to give up working for victory than to say to him that we should and could not win, because it would be worse than if we lost ... Through his actions he has for ever deprived himself of the honour of belonging to the German nation and has himself pronounced his own sentence, which can only be death.

During September and October 1944, Reimers was engaged with the prosecution of several members associated with the Saefkow resistance group, a small group of individuals employed as forced labour in German war factories, who were engaged in agitation and incitement to commit sabotage. The Saefkow group were remotely associated with the plot to assassinate Hitler in July of that year but, that said, there were many fringe elements at that time. The 'Bloody Judge' Reimers sat in the People's Court with similar authority to that of Freisler and in this particular instance sentenced to death ten Czech patriots: Alois Mach, Franisek Strasik, Franisek Medlik, Tuma and Stanislav Zverina, Vaclav Priban, Vaclav Krizek, Malos Gadil, Karel Kapek and Vaclav Satran, all of whom had been convicted of high treason. Additionally he sentenced to death Heinrich Werner, Erwin Freyer and Hedwig Hartung, three German citizens who were suspected of collaborating with the same group of activists.

Reimers later sentenced to death Josef Höhn, Egmont Schultz and Rudolf Seiffert, all forced labourers in Berlin, who were charged with high treason. Once again they were reputedly connected to the Saefkow resistance group. The following summary was issued by the judge:

In 1943 some earlier communist functionaries, including Anton Saefkow and Franz Jacob, began to build up their communist organisation again in Berlin and in Mark Brandenburg. This organisation called upon 'antifascists' and especially on communists with the usual slogans and on other opponents of National Socialism but with the programme of the so-called 'National Committee of Free Germany' ...
In their undermining work Saefkow and Jacob called specially upon workers in big factories and armament works in Berlin. In addition they addressed themselves in letters direct to the soldiers in the front. They did not even halt before direct contacts with Russians, French and Serbian war prisoners. Prompt action by the Police succeeded in defeating this dangerous organisation ...they have dared in this fifth year of the war to give extensive support to a dangerous communist organisation. They were themselves fully aware that they attacked our fighting German soldiers from the rear and tried to rob us of our victory. Anyone who wants Bolshevism, our deadly enemy, to conquer us withdraws himself from our fighting people longing for victory; there is no place for him in our ranks ... The accused Höhn, Schultz and Seiffert are therefore condemned to death and to the loss of civic rights for the rest of their lives because of their dishonourable attitude.

Two Czech professors, Vojtech Jezek and Vaclav Patera, both from Pilsen, also appeared before Reimers in late 1944 charged with 'alleged preparation of high treason'. Both men were condemned to death on 8 December. Also amongst those sent to the Fallbeil by Reimers were German citizens Hermann and Emma Kurras and Otto Potschka, who were beheaded on 22 December, simply because they had given shelter to several Jewish children who had escaped from a concentration camp.

After the war Reimers served in the criminal courts of Germany and subsequently sat as a judge in the provincial court in Ravensburg. In 1960, efforts were made to indict him for crimes he was suspected to have committed as a judge during the Third Reich. That process of indictment failed and he eventually retired three years later. It should be noted that around this time other areas of injustice were being explored by other parties. In 1959, nineteen medical doctors who had themselves been inmates within Auschwitz concentration camp submitted an appeal to the German Medical Council demanding the suspension of doctors who committed crimes in the camps. They put on record that these doctors, whose duty it was to save human lives, in most cases arbitrarily and without regard for professional procedure designed death and that in spite of these horrifying abuses, these men continued to practise as doctors. It was argued those who had been responsible for wholesale murder in concentration camps should not be permitted to bear the title of doctor and helper of mankind.

The process of lawful prosecution sought against Reimers continued, and, for only the second time in West German history, a Hitler-era judge was indicted on charges of judicial murder, in 1984. The 82-year-old Reimers was charged by West Berlin prosecutors with handing down ninety-seven unjustified death sentences from Nazi Germany's infamous People's Court. The negative publicity about the People's Court in the mid-1960s did, without doubt, accelerate the early retirement of many judges of the Third Reich who had continued in service unchallenged after the war within the new West German court system. However, after retirement, men like Reimers all received comfortable state pensions. Many thousands of victims had been sentenced to death in trials devoid of the most elementary standards of evidence and impartiality and Reimers had personally been indicted with almost a hundred deaths. With the inevitability of a criminal trial for his actions and the weight of evidence against him, Reimers decided to take his own life, committing suicide on 5 November 1984.

Johann Reichhart

Alongside the infamous judges of the Third Reich were apathetic individuals prepared to carry out the death sentences and earn a living as executioners. Johann Reichhart was born in 1893 into a family of executioners going back eight generations. He was employed as a butcher and was later called upon to serve in the German army during the First World War. He witnessed the terrible fighting in the trenches at Verdun and was fortunate to survive unscathed. On 23 March 1924, Reichhart applied to the Bavarian State Ministry of Justice in Munich for the position of executioner. Although his execution experience was not significant at this time, his knowledge on the subject was formidable, having spent his life surrounded by the subject, and he understandably looked to follow his family tradition. His application to undertake the role was accepted and publicly announced, the statement reading, 'From April 1,

1924, Johann Reichhart takes over the execution of all death sentences coming in the Free State of Bavaria to the execution by beheading with the guillotine.'

His career as a professional executioner began when he carried out two beheadings in 1924. After four years, Reichhart left Germany and moved to The Hague where he opened a successful vegetable market; he was, however, still available to the Bavarian government to perform his duties as its appointed executioner. With Hitler's rise to power in 1933 and execution numbers increasing, Reichhart returned to live in Germany. He became a member of the Nazi Party in 1937 and with the declaration of war, was provided with a financial income which surpassed that of previous generations of his family who had traded in the sombre business.

Reichhart was a formal man and meticulous about his appearance and manners. He imparted these qualities to his assistants and insisted that they, like himself, should refrain from drinking alcohol twenty-four hours prior to any executions. He distanced himself from the other executioners working at the same time, considering himself professionally superior and regarding the others as incompetent. His historical connections with executions saw him undertake his work wearing traditional attire, a full black coat, white shirt and gloves, black bow tie and a top hat. By 1942, Reichhart had accumulated significant wealth and purchased a home near Munich. His finances were further increased by means of travelling expenses incurred by commuting between several prisons to supply his services.

From the evidence available regarding executions during the Third Reich, Reichhart put to death 3,165 people, the majority of them during the period from 1939 to 1945. According to his own calculations, 2,876 men and women were executed by him, the vast majority being decapitated with the Fallbeil.

With the Allied victory over Germany in 1945, Reichhart, as a member of the Nazi Party and suspected of having been engaged in suspicious multiple deaths, was arrested and interviewed. However, he was neither charged nor tried for administering the judicial executions in the Third Reich, but was detained for what was known as 'denazification', a process designed to remove active members of the former National Socialist Party from official public offices or from influential positions in Germany. Ironically, he was employed by the Occupation Authorities in November 1945 to help execute convicted Nazi war criminals by hanging. Records indicate that he hanged twenty-one condemned men at Landsberg Prison, which was under the control of the Americans, but he was not involved in any way with the executions at Nuremberg.

In May 1947, Reichhart was taken to the civilian internment camp at Moosburg, an old German prisoner-of-war camp in which many British air crews had been imprisoned during the war. Many high-ranking SA and SS members convicted by German denazification courts were detained in Moosburg, including Emmy Goering, the wife of *Reichsmarschall* Hermann Goering and known to Hitler as the First Lady. She was convicted of being a Nazi and was sentenced to one year in jail. The considerable wealth she had accrued during the war was confiscated on her release and she was reduced to living in a modest apartment.

Investigations were conducted into Reichhart's behaviour and activities during his membership to the Nazi Party, and his financial status was also investigated. As a result of the denazification ruling, court proceedings against him began in December 1948. On 29 November the following year, a tribunal confiscated significant funds from Reichhart and sentenced him to a period of hard labour. He was also forbidden from ever voting, holding public office or engaging in politics. After serving two years, Reichhart was released and retired to humble accommodation in Deisenhofen in Bavaria. He had been ordered to pay 26,000 marks for the cost of his trial, which caused his financial ruin. In addition, his marriage had failed and one of his three sons, Hans, had committed suicide in 1950.

Reichhart spent his time breeding Schnauzer dogs whilst showing no remorse for his actions during the Third Reich, professing to have done his duty as a civil servant, just like the judges, prosecutors and postmen. He died in a nursing home near Erding, Bavaria, on 26 April 1972, following which his body was cremated and the remains interred in the family grave where his uncle and mentor, the Bavarian executioner Franz Reichhart, had also been laid to rest.

Manfred Roeder

Roeder was born on 20 August 1900 in Kiel. At the age of seventeen he enlisted into the German army and served during the First World War, surviving relatively unscathed and subsequently gaining civil employment at the Charlottenburger Water and Industrial Works in Berlin. He later turned to the study of law and, having qualified, served as a junior barrister in Lüneburg and Hanover. In 1934, Roeder once again entered military service and became a legal officer before transferring to the Luftwaffe and serving within the Military Courts. He was made a military judge in the Luftwaffe when war broke out in 1939, later seeing service in the Luftwaffe field courts in Berlin.

In April 1942, Roeder was attached to the Reich war courts, and it was here that his torrid reputation was formed. Serving in the highest wartime court, the Reich Court Martial, Roeder appears to have been specifically selected to investigate and later oversee the prosecution of the Soviet resistance group, the Red Orchestra (see Chapter 9). He shared in the responsibility for dozens of death sentences being handed down by the Reich courts on members of the Red Orchestra. Prior to these trials, Roeder had been the prosecutor in several high-profile cases, and his ruthless reputation had come to the attention of Hitler, who had been clearly impressed.

Germany's defeat at Stalingrad gave great impetus for the People's Court to issue large numbers of death sentences against Communist plotters and activists. By this time, Roeder was renowned for his cynicism and brutality, frequently demanding the death sentence as the chief prosecutor for the Reich. Wearing his military dress uniform, complete with sword and ornate silver sleeve insignia, Roeder was present at the executions of the Red Orchestra defendants on 22 December, personally witnessing the slow strangulations on the gallows of Harro Schulze-Boysen, Arvid Harnack, Kurt Schumacher and John Graudenz, and then the following 'more humane' decapitations with the Fallbeil inflicted upon Horst Heilmann, Hans Coppi, Kurt Schulze, Libertas Schulze-Boysen and Elisabeth Schumacher.

Roeder was appointed as the chief judge and legal official within Air Fleet Command and was awarded 'The German Cross in silver' by Hitler on 20 April 1945. He continued to serve the Reich until his arrest by Allied forces on 8 May 1945.

As a military prosecutor, Roeder was known as one of the hardest and most loyal military judges and after the war he was treated as a war criminal, initially being regarded as a witness in the Allied war crime tribunals but then himself being charged and prosecuted for war crimes.

His criminality was evidenced by surviving members of the Red Orchestra group. As a defendant, Roeder was retained in custody awaiting trial. He consistently claimed that he was ordered to prosecute the Red Orchestra defendants by Hermann Goering, the supreme leader of the Luftwaffe, but this was later disproved as he had sought to undertake the case himself and had been promoted as a result of his performance in the matter.

The ensuing post-war tensions escalated and witnessed Roeder being further interrogated by the Allies with the intention of gathering intelligence on Soviet activities. The American occupation forces subsequently found no justification for trying Roeder, but they denied Russia access to him and so he was handed over to the German authorities in the western zone of occupation, who were supposed to investigate his war activities. In June 1948, an appeal was placed for information against 'Judge Advocate Colonel Manfred Roeder' for crimes against humanity. It was hoped that evidence would be forthcoming whilst Roeder remained in the Neustadt internment camp. However, by 1949, sufficient evidence was still not available and the political divide across Germany was an all too consuming factor at that time. Roeder was therefore released from custody and returned to his home in Neetze, near Lüneburg. By 1951, any hope of prosecuting him ebbed away and was lost.

The immediate post-war period witnessed not a single judge or prosecutor convicted for involvement in the judicial travesties that were so prevalent within the many Nazi courts. Incredibly, many judges who had served Hitler were once again empowered to serve within the post-war courts in the Allied zones. Roeder died on 18 October 1971.

Ernst Kanter

In 1936, Ernst Kanter became appointed to Hitler's newly established Military Courts and experienced a surge of power within that judicial arena. Born in 1895, he had served in the First World War as a volunteer and later as an officer between 1914 and 1921.

Kanter studied law and qualified to practise, entering the profession in 1925. His promotion within legal chambers saw him acting as an auxiliary judge and as a district and regional court adviser in several geographical locations within Germany. He ventured into the Military Courts in 1934, and became a member of the Army Judiciary Service two years later. A staunch supporter of the Nazi Party, Kanter became responsible for the transfer of judges into the Military Courts. His influences were deep and intensely impactive, and his judicial sentencing of military defendants and civilians alike was ruthless, in line with the Military Justice Decree of 17 August 1938, which stated:

The following are subject to military justice …

4. All other persons in regard to
a) Espionage
b) Franc-tireur activities [A soldier operating outside the laws of war]
c) Offences against decrees promulgated by the commander in a foreign territory occupied by the Wehrmacht for the security of the Wehrmacht or for war purposes
d) Subversion of military strength.

Kanter's true notoriety came from his appointment as the Chief Justice in occupied Denmark. In February 1943, he assumed further duties as legal adviser to the staff of the commander-in-chief of German troops in Denmark. In that capacity, Kanter pronounced many death sentences and ordered the execution by firing squad of numerous young soldiers. He also regarded Military Courts over which he presided as being competent to sentence Danish civilian patriots. The 1940 Decree of the Army High Command explicitly gave him full power to decide whether the investigation and prosecution of such cases should be made by the Military Court or left to the other judicial courts. This led to a demonstration of outrageous sentencing against accused Danish civilians, and in particular against Danish resistance fighters who fought the Nazi occupation. In the main, these individuals were placed before the Military Court within the provision of Section 3 of the Military Penal Procedure, which clearly stipulated that they were competent to 'punish foreigners for all punishable offences committed by them within the operational area'. The post-war Committee for German Unity documented that Kanter, as the chief military judge in occupied Denmark, was responsible for the deaths of 498 Danish people, thus demonstrating his power to decide on life or death for many Danish resistance fighters.

The tone of the German occupation of Denmark changed in 1943. While there had been some resistance to the Germans during the first years of the occupation, acts of sabotage became more prevalent as the resistance movement gathered strength. Rather than yield to Kanter's new demands for Military Courts to try saboteurs, the Danish government resigned on 28 August 1943. Martial law was declared and German authorities arrested Danish civilians, Jews, non-Jews and Danish military personnel. The Germans took direct control over the Danish military and the civilian police with the aim of eradicating resistance in Denmark completely. All four German Military Courts that functioned in Denmark where prosecutors asked for death penalties or imprisonment for more than three years required Kanter's sanction. In 1944, some 1,500 Danish police officers were sent to Buchenwald concentration camp as they were regarded as a potential threat, having displayed loyalties to the previous Danish government.

The 'Shellhus', a large six-storey building which was (and still is) near the centre of Copenhagen, was occupied by the Gestapo as its headquarters, the Germans having applied a camouflage of green and brown paint in an attempt to break up the unique configuration of this important building. Although the majority of prisoners detained before trial were in the city's Vestre Prison, the Germans also constructed prisoner cells in the 'Shellhus' and high-value resistance suspects were detained there for extensive interrogation and torture. Their interrogator, Frederick Haupt, was renowned for undertaking tooth and fingernail extractions on his subjects. Additionally, the Gestapo gained some satisfaction from the thought that the known detention of prisoners on the top floor of the building would prevent it from being attacked by the RAF. The resistance in Denmark were suffering significant losses as a result of the Gestapo's aggressive offensives, and the courts were securing many convictions resulting in executions. Despite many men being held in the 'Shellhus', the resistance requested that a daring operation be undertaken by the Allied forces.

On the morning of 21 March 1945, a special force of Mosquito aircraft from No. 140 Wing took off from RAF Fersfield in Norfolk to participate in 'Operation Carthage'—the attack upon the 'Shellhus'. Individuals likely to be within the building were Dr Karl Hoffman, the country's Head of Gestapo and his supporting staff, Eric Bunke and Hans Hermannsen. At the time of the operation, information from Maj. Lippman of the Danish Military Intelligence indicated that an estimated thirty-six captured members of the Danish underground movement were in the building, all of whom were likely to be executed. The RAF precision raid struck the building with great accuracy and as a result of the explosions, the building was set alight. A number of prisoners managed to escape in the unfolding events. Several were forced to jump from the fourth floor, a decision that ultimately caused their deaths, but many other agents and detained resistance operatives were able to escape. One SOE agent, Poul Borking, had previously parachuted into Denmark but was captured by the Gestapo. Although he was being interrogated at the time of the attack, he successfully escaped. Two other men who escaped were Mogens Ludolf Fog, who had helped to set up *Frit Danmark*, an illegal non-partisan resistance newspaper, and Professor Poul Brandt Rehberg, who been engaged in the transport of refugees to Sweden. He became a valued witness in the war crime trials that took place in 1946.

It appears that Kanter escaped any post-war accountability and later served in the newly appointed judicial courts of Germany. Documentation held within the UK Parliament's Written Answers Archive confirms that on 16 February 1959, Mr Arthur

Lewis MP asked the then Secretary of State for Foreign Affairs whether he would ask the Committee of Investigation appointed to inquire into allegations and charges that 596 jurists who served Hitler's Special Courts are now back in office, to inquire into the case of Ernst Kanter, the former Judge-General in the Nazi Wehrmacht, Chief Justice in Nazi-occupied Denmark, who was at that time (1959) presiding judge in the Third Senate of the West German Supreme Court in Karlsruhe. The response of the Secretary of State for Foreign Affairs was as follows:

> It is for the Federal German Government to decide what inquiries are to be carried out. They have, however, informed us that Dr. Kanter's case has been investigated and that no evidence has been found to justify his removal from the German judiciary.

Ernst Kanter died in Cologne on 20 November 1979.

CHAPTER 4

The Tegel Fallbeil and Execution Methods

In Germany the word 'guillotine' was not adopted in direct translation, but 'Fallbeil' literally translates to 'drop-axe' and was a reference to the device used to decapitate individuals sentenced to death. Over the years, the Fallbeil evolved from the traditional large high-standing guillotine into a shorter device constructed almost entirely of wood and metal. Prussia used a German-designed Fallbeil from 1856 to 1933, but this device still required the large and bulky permanent scaffold that included a trap hatch allowing the body to be dropped into a box in the void below. This guillotine was used in an estimated eighteen executions from 1856 to 1917. After this time, executions became more frequent, even more so when the Nazis took power in 1933, with Fallbeils claiming far more victims than the guillotine had achieved during the years of the French Revolution.

When Hitler refashioned the German judicial system, many additional new crimes became capital offences. The administration of the legal system by the People's Court resulted in a drastic increase in the number of executions undertaken, primarily for opposition to the Nazis in the Reich. To meet this new demand for 'Hitler's justice', specific prisons across Germany and the occupied territories were designated as execution sites and provided with their own 'Tegel Fallbeil'. Sixteen prisons were designated as execution venues by 1942, the Fallbeils delivered to these sites having been built by the inmates of Tegel Prison in Berlin, hence their name. The design and construction was changed to include a geared winch in order to reduce the force required to raise the sledge that held the angled blade, and a hinged sheet-metal shield was fitted to protect the executioner from the inevitable blood splatter. The crude bench structure that held the full body of the individual upon the device was made of wooden planks with four robust wooden legs, a characteristic of the original Tegel design which was required to steady the device. Several modifications existed where bracing bars were further fitted to enhance the stability.

When the Nazi justice ministry 'standardised' the Tegel Fallbeil throughout the Reich as the official death penalty method for execution, an intention existed for older wooden guillotines to be retired from use and replaced by the new Tegel design. These hideous devices were adapted and changed at various times, but the concept and standard structure remained generally consistent. The Fallbeil was around 8 feet tall, with a heavier blade than the larger conventional guillotine—a necessity in order to produce the required force. The condemned person was made to lie face down on the simple bench; once severed, the head fell into a metal basin or other type of receptacle attached to the frame. Later a tipping board known as a bascule was used to speed up the execution process, and one of the German executioners, Johann Reichhart, designed a device for rapidly clamping victims to this tipping board. He later abandoned the bascule, as it took too much time when carrying out the large number of executions required. His assistants simply slid the condemned prisoner under the blade and held him there until the blade fell. Other modifications were the addition of ducting to funnel the blood into a floor drain, and a head-rest in the surround splash guard. The victim rested his forehead on the restraint, which in turn helped to keep his neck straight; the neck was always laid bare of hair. Evidence exists that the Fallbeil blades frequently suffered damage to their leading cutting edges, and any chips and blunting of their edges needed to be addressed immediately in order to prevent unsatisfactory decapitations. During the manufacturing process the blades required metal tempering to ensure their quality, and this appears to be an area that was at times found to be inferior to requirements. The executioners on occasions undertook their own maintenance on the blades, which inevitably required sharpening after several beheadings.

On 12 March 1938, Germany took over Austria (termed the *Anschluss*), an offensive action that was specifically disallowed in the Treaty of Versailles signed by Germany after the First World War. In Vienna, the Special Court or People's Tribunal condemned 1,377 people to be executed by the guillotine, and when Czechoslovakia was annexed as the Reich Protectorate of Moravia and Bohemia in 1938, the Fallbeils were aggressively deployed there. Between 5 April 1943 and 26 April 1945, more than a thousand people were executed by the infamous executioner Alois Weiss in Pankrac Prison, Prague. Most of the victims were Czech citizens, primarily political prisoners resisting the Nazi occupation. The majority of those victims had their remains taken to the large crematorium in Strasnice that had been built in 1932 and was capable of processing many corpses. The Nazis also used this venue to dispose of the many Czech victims who were shot dead at the Kobylisy firing range.

Detailed records of the executions were compiled at Pankrac Prison, some of which have survived. The Pankrac execution book registers a total of 1,079 names. Of these, 1,075 were beheaded, and four shot at Kobylisy firing range. The entries were handwritten by the appointed executioner Weiss. However, before the Pankrac Fallbeil was installed in the prison, condemned prisoners there were transported to Dresden's Münchner Platz Prison for their death sentence to be carried out.

The entry columns in the book are all written in sequence: the execution number, followed by the condemned person's full name, date and place of birth and the offence for which sentenced, sentence date, execution date, and time of execution. The first entry was made on 5 April 1943 at 16.30 hours. It was the first use of the Fallbeil in the prison, and five people were beheaded. Four further execution sessions took place during that month, making a total of twenty people beheaded. The average time between each execution was approximately two minutes. Bearing in mind the gruesome task of removing the torso and severed head, combined with the management of the significant blood loss and the resetting of the Fallbeil's blade, this is quite remarkable.

The previously mentioned Kobylisy firing range in Prague was a military range, and between May 1942 and May 1945, 470 men and 76 women were executed there, shot by the Nazis. Notably, four Czech soldiers were publicly executed at Kobylisy. Records reflect that these men showed no fear towards their execution, and their actions dissuaded the Nazis from conducting further public executions of military personnel at that location. The four soldiers refused to be blindfolded and loudly called out freedom slogans until they were cut down in a volley of bullets. Weiss recorded these soldiers' names in the Pankrac execution book—Frantisek Rajmon, Frantisek Famfulik, Josef Bojas and Jan Jirasek. Many of the Kobylisy victims were executed in retribution for the assassination of the infamous Nazi Reinhard Heydrich in May 1942. The youngest victims at Kobylisy were two boys who were barely fifteen years old. The Nazi purge after the assassination of Heydrich also struck at Pankrac Prison where sixteen people were beheaded by the Fallbeil.

As the war came to an end, the executioner Weiss and his assistants dispatched their last five victims on 26 April 1945, their Fallbeil having been operational for just over two years with approximately forty executions a month undertaken. Bozena Steidlova was the first in that final group to be executed, and notably was the last female to be beheaded on the Pankrac Fallbeil. Steidlova was thirty-four years of age and had been arrested on 18 January 1945 for providing assistance to resistance operatives in Prague.

Fearing potential Allied reprisals and war crime investigations, the executioners along with officials attempted to dispose of the Fallbeil and deposited some of the equipment into a river. One of Weiss's assistants, Antonin Nerad, had been reputedly engaged in Nazi collaboration activity and was thought to be responsible for exposing many individuals to arrest and ultimately imprisonment or death. After the liberation of Prague, however, the Fallbeil's remains were retrieved from the river and the gruesome device was reconstructed from the parts recovered. The Pankrac Fallbeil is currently displayed in the original execution room within the prison, preserved as a memorial to the victims of the Nazis, and it is now regarded as a highly revered symbol representing the sacrifices and hardships endured by the people of Czechoslovakia during the war.

The Tegel Fallbeil in Kattowitz was named the 'Red Widow' by the populous and was used to decapitate 550 accused and convicted civilians of various resistance activities against the Nazi occupation. At the close of the war the Fallbeil was reputedly removed from its confines and sometime later was rebuilt. It now resides in the Auschwitz-Birkenau Holocaust Museum. The Vienna Museum of Criminology additionally has a Fallbeil on display that had been utilised by the Nazis and had claimed the lives of many victims. It was used in the prison of Wurzburg in Germany before the Soviets captured and secured it. That Fallbeil is now exhibited at the War Museum in Kiev.

Some 800 people were executed in the last period of the Third Reich and during the first few months of 1945, and it is estimated that over 400 of them were German citizens. Several Fallbeils had been captured by the Allies, one device being put back into operational service and retained in the British sector of Berlin. The Allies reinstituted pre-Nazi legislation—the German Penal Code of 1871, the Court Organization Act of 1877, and the Code of Criminal Procedure of 1877—and all Nazi laws and sections of laws that reflected Nazi ideas were revoked. This enabled the German judicial process to continue functioning in some capacity during the immediate post-war period, and the task of administering the reinstituted laws was left to the German courts to implement. For a period of four years after the end of the war the death penalty remained prevalent in the courts in West Germany, and some additional Fallbeils were constructed by the company of Fritz and Otto Tiggeman. The Allies permitted the use of Fallbeil executions for German nationals but, unlike the Nazis, only after a fair judicial process had taken place. West Germany abolished capital punishment in 1951, their last guillotining taking place on 11 May 1949. East Germany continued to use the guillotine until 1967.

CHAPTER 5

Execution Propaganda

The judicial authority imposed by Hitler cast its terror across a spectrum of society which grew to fear the capital punishments widely publicised in bright red notices that were pasted, pinned or otherwise secured for public display in order to intimidate the populace. The notices varied in format but always contained the name of the court that had delivered the sentence and the name or names of those condemned to death. As an example, a seventeen-year-old Polish forced labourer, Walerjan Wróbel, was decapitated in Hamburg at 06.15 hours on 25 August 1942, over 250 execution notices having been posted across the city of Bremen prior to his execution. In this instance, as he was a forced labourer, the notices were no doubt proliferated as a warning to the massed numbers of that repressed labour force.

Walerjan was born in Poland in 1925 and had been selected by the Germans for forced labour in early 1942. He was sixteen, poorly educated and physically frail in stature, the result of an impoverished upbringing. Dauntingly, he was sent away to work on a German farm near Bremen from which he tried to escape a few days later but was spotted by a labourer working on an adjacent farm and returned. Towards the end of April that year, in his naivety he set fire to a farm shed, thinking that he would be sent home. The fire did not take hold and caused only minor damage, and despite Walerjan assisting in putting out the fire, he was arrested and interrogated and then sent to the Neuengamme concentration camp where he remained for nine months. The camp at Neuengamme was established in 1938 by the SS in the Bergedorf district of Hamburg. After the Allies began bombing cities in Germany in late 1942, the SS deployed large numbers of prisoners from Neuengamme to clear the streets of rubble and to remove unexploded munitions from the streets of major cities such as Hamburg and Bremen. Between 1939 and 1945, at least one-and-a-half million Polish citizens were transported to the Reich for forced labour, many of whom were teenage boys and girls. Germany also used forced labourers from Western Europe along with other Eastern European citizens who were viewed as inferior and subjected to harsh discriminatory measures. They were forced to wear large identifying purple letter Ps sewn on their clothing, subjected to a curfew, and banned from using public transportation.

Walerjan was eventually tried by the Special Court in Bremen on 8 July 1942, having been charge with 'arson' and 'impairing the Third Reich', for which he was found guilty and sentenced to death. On 15 August an appeal for a reprieve was rejected and the execution was duly carried out on 25 August.

Walerjan's execution is without doubt an example whereby the occupying Nazis chose to publicise the sentence widely in order to control and influence the significant numbers of people whom they had subjected to forced labour in both rural farming and industrial factory work. The age of Walerjan, his intellectual abilities and the minor nature of his alleged offence appear to have been given little if any consideration against the wider objectives of inducing fear. It was not until some forty-five years after his execution had elapsed that the Bremen Regional Court declared his trial and sentence null and void.

It was not only the young Polish forced labourers that suffered. Boleslaw Swietek, aged 31, was deported for the purpose of working as an unskilled labourer for the building firm of Berger. It appears that he was reported to the authorities, who presented him before the judicial court for a case of 'non-fulfilment of his duty to work'. Judge Rosner heard evidence that he had not worked well and was regarded as lazy. He was sentenced to death on 19 January 1943 because he had opposed the necessary discipline. This was yet again a sentence that was obviously intended to serve as a warning to others, the judge stating:

> His attitude has seriously damaged the reputation and well-being of the German people ... and he has made public his crudely anti-German feelings ... In the interest of maintaining internal order, elements of this sort cannot be tolerated. For this reason a death sentence was necessary.

Other examples of Nazi execution notification posters were printed in a slightly larger format to facilitate the information being printed in two languages, as was the case for the execution of six Czechs sentenced to death for supporting the enemies of the Reich by sheltering them. Three women and three men were to be executed in Pankrac prison on 29 June 1944: Frantisek Blazek, Marie Blazkova, Anezka Vachova, Frantisek Koblie, Jindriska Hermuthova and Antonin Lank. The execution notice was printed on the customary bright red paper with both German and Slovak text, and at the bottom of the notice was the authorisation by the District Court in Prague. The names of these brave people, who were decapitated by the executioner Alois Weiss, are recorded for posterity in the execution book, as well as a small number of the propaganda notices issued in their names by the Nazi judicial system.

On 7 December 1941, Hitler issued the 'Nacht und Nebel' (Night and Fog) Decree under the provisions of which opponents of the Nazi regime were to be arrested and either shot or spirited away clandestinely. Many families experienced the disappearance of individuals who vanished without trace. It was not an uncommon experience for news of an execution by the publication of a notice to be the first indication of a missing person. This accounts for why several notices were recovered and remain to this day, retained by these distraught families who subsequently suffered the indignity of having to pay for the execution of their loved one. Instructions were issued to the Gestapo by *Reichsführer-SS* Heinrich Himmler stating:

> After lengthy consideration, it is the will of the Führer that the measures taken against those who are guilty of offences against the Reich or against the occupational forces in occupied areas should be altered. The Führer is of the opinion that in such cases penal servitude or even a hard labour sentence for life will be regarded as a sign of weakness. An effective and lasting deterrent can be achieved only by the death penalty or by taking measures which will leave the family and the population uncertain as to the fate of the offender. Deportation to Germany serves this purpose
>
> …

Victims of the decree generally came from Belgium, the Netherlands and France. They would be arrested in the middle of the night and transported hundreds of miles away from their homes to be tortured and interrogated. If they survived this barbaric treatment they would be placed into the concentration camps of Gross-Rosen or Natzweiler.

CHAPTER 6

British Psychological Warfare

At the outbreak of war the British government established the Political Intelligence Department as a covert Foreign Office Department, the Political Warfare Executive (PWE) being formed in August 1941 with objectives that included undermining enemy morale and resistance with various forms of propaganda. During the war the RAF delivered over one-and-a-half billion leaflets to eleven different European countries, but most significantly to Germany.

The first operational penetration of German airspace in the Second World War to undertake a leaflet raid took place during the first night of the conflict, on 3 September 1939. Dropped from around 12,000 feet, the bundles of leaflets would become loose and separate in the air, taking more than an hour to gently flutter to the ground to cover an immense area over Germany. The quality of the printed leaflets, known to the RAF as 'nickels', increased as more resources were applied by obtaining better paper, and 'Propaganda Newspapers' consisting of a folded sheet creating four pages evolved in order to deliver more detailed information. The physical presence of Allied leaflets was significant to civilians who were being oppressed and starved of the truth by the Nazis.

The printed caption on the RAF *Luftpost* documents commenced with 'Prohibited everywhere the truth is forbidden'. Ordinary people would secretly collect and read the leaflets, despite the threat of the death penalty if found in their possession or if they attempted to redistribute them. Particularly in Germany, where citizens were restricted to an incessant diet of censored and distorted news of every form, the leaflets became more intriguing, their truthful reporting resonating more as the war progressed. German civilians were reminded of the growing hardships they faced with ever-increasing food shortages. Some leaflets actually reproduced anti-Nazi material created by internal resistance groups from within Germany, such as the university students of the White Rose group whose young leaders were beheaded in February 1943, having been caught spreading anti-Nazi literature. Their original leaflets were smuggled out of Germany and reproduced by the Allies, who dropped them over Germany in late 1943.

Other leaflets did not allow the German people to remain ignorant of the inhuman behaviour of Himmler's infamous SS in the occupied countries. The typographer Ellic Howe, a specialist in German fonts, having resided in Germany between 1934 and 1937 to study German printing techniques and typography, worked in the PWE and created a specific propaganda newspaper on the barbaric atrocities that had taken place during September 1941. The RAF *Luftpost* or Air Mail newspaper was titled 'Himmler's henchmen at work, twenty-eight days of German domination between 1 and 28 September in the occupied territories.' This newspaper divulged the SS hierarchy across the Nazi-held territories, illustrating images of those notorious figures and documenting 317 Nazi executions that had taken place within the occupied countries, and went on to illustrate the frequent acts of sabotage, riots and strikes. This was factual information collated from the resistance networks and other sources. Clearly the Nazi practice of posting notifications of executions was known within those court districts, but the publication by the Allies of these early statistics would have been a revelation to civilians who would eventually see and read of such enhanced judicial terror being applied elsewhere. This particular *Luftpost*, dated 30 September 1941, was No. 20 within the series of newspapers dropped over Germany, and referenced EH510/20. Once printed, this edition was dropped across Germany by the RAF over a period of ten days from 10 October. Some RAF bombing crews undertaking operational training were engaged on specific 'nickelling' operations whereby navigation to specific locations took place simply in order to drop the propaganda, whilst others were dropped during actual bombing operations. Disseminated statistics later disclosed that during 1941 one *Luftpost* document was dropped for every 632 people in Germany.

In the later stages of the war, information from the Allies based on true events did their work for them, causing discontent and unrest to both civilians and troops who dared to read the publications despite the risk of a death sentence. On 8 February 1944, August Ulrich, a 53-year-old mechanic from Duisburg, appeared before Judge Makart because he had passed a leaflet dropped by the RAF to a fellow worker. The judge gave the following summing up in his case:

> He was aware of the destructive effect of propaganda leaflets dropped by the enemy, and in passing this leaflet on he wished to work not only against the war, but also, in a communist sense, against the Reich and its Führer. If there remains the slightest doubt of this, it was dispelled by his way of speaking to the witness Isbanner. These statements were politically quite clear and prove that the accused, even in the fourth year of the Great German Liberation Struggle, saw salvation solely in Communism and expected only evil for the German people if they should win the war and continue on their way to the future under the leadership of the NSDAP … The punishment, according to section five of the Special War Criminal Code, is to be interpreted under the section which threatens the most severe punishment, the death penalty—the only punishment which fits the crime of such a traitor to the people as the accused. The Senate has accepted this. At the same time the accused forfeits all civic rights for life in view of the dishonourable attitude which his actions show.

Archive document 8J 222/43-3L 106/42 fails to disclose August Ulrich's place of execution.

CHAPTER 7

The Executioners

Carl Gropler was the leading executioner across a large geographical area of Germany in the pre-Nazi era and although his duties were providing him with additional income alongside his laundry business in Magdeburg, he was not earning very much from the gruesome executions, all of which were conducted by his skilful deployment of the hand axe. At the time of the Nazis' seizure of power, Gropler had been in office for more than a quarter of the century, but his laundry business had failed by this time and having become entirely dependent on the income from his activities as an executioner, he had to revert to his previously acquired skills as a horse butcher in knacker's yards. Minimal execution work came his way during the last years of the Weimar Republic, but Gropler signed a new contract in April 1924 which gave him a monopoly over all executions carried out in Prussia and in practice throughout the whole of northern Germany. Despite this, he was not gainfully employed and in his early fifties he was struggling to maintain a stable lifestyle.

However, the rise in power of the Nazi Party and the coming of the Third Reich changed Gropler's livelihood and he was re-employed under contract as an appointed executioner for the new ruling power of Germany on 19 February 1933. He was to receive an annual retainer of 1,500 Reichsmarks and an additional 50 marks per execution, depending on the geographical location. Gropler was not slow to demonstrate his loyalty to his new employer and used the Nazi salute at every opportunity. His reputation went before him, as he had executed several serial murderers during the pre-Nazi era, but his advancing years went against him and he was forced into retirement in 1936.

From 1937, there was a three-man team of executioners within the Reich: Johann Reichhart (see Chapter 3) was responsible for southern Germany and Berlin, with Ernst Reindel and Friedrich Hehr working in western and northern Germany. One of Hehr's official assistants, Gottlob Bordt, was added to the list of official executioners in 1940 and was made responsible for Posen (Poznań).

In a Circular issued by the Reich Ministry of Justice on 25 August 1937, the duties of the Reich executioners were made clear by the President of the People's Court, Roland Freisler:

The role of executioner is at the request of the judicial authority within the whole Reich territory to inflict capital punishment by decapitation or by performing hanging.

The Empire Justice Administration reserves the right to allocate executions to individual executioners in certain prisons.

The executioner must be readily available to the Service.

He is obliged to carry out the orders given to him on time and in connection with an enforcement order giving instructions to follow. If it is longer than 24 hours away from his home or he is prevented by illness or other circumstances, he shall inform the competent public prosecutor for his residence immediately.

The executioner is obliged to enforce the orders given to him and the strictest secrecy must be observed in their execution before and after the enforcement.

He has to wear appropriate clothing and the administration of justice requires that the execution will be flawless in every respect.

The executioner has the necessary support to its agents, the number of which shall be set at three and the number of agents requires the approval of the competent public prosecutor's jurisdiction.

The assembly and disassembly of the execution device is up to the prison.

The executioner is required:

a) To examine the device for its usefulness before each execution.

b) To clean up the device and the place of execution after each execution.

c) To place those executed into a coffin box.

Benefits received by the designated executioner amount to 3,000 Reichsmarks a year in monthly instalments of 250 marks on the first of the month and paid in advance. Furthermore, he and his assistants for each execution receive a special allowance of 60 RM. The special allowance is increased to 65 marks if the execution is at a prison facility which is more than 300 kilometres from the residence of the executioner.

When the executions are outside the residence of the executioner the travel costs, 3rd Class, including the use of a Sleeping Car requires the executioner in each case to gain the approval of the resident competent public prosecutor.

Each of the three executioners was given clearly defined areas:

- Reichhart to the Bavarian death sentences in Munich Stadelheim. For its operations in Dresden and Weimar he was instructed to use the Munich guillotine.
- Reindel undertook the transferred executions in Berlin-Plötzensee, Breslau and Konigsberg.
- Hehr undertook the death sentences in Hamburg, Hanover, Cologne and additionally in Butzbach, Hesse.

Reindel tendered his resignation during the autumn of 1943, but prior to this the Ministry of Justice had employed under contract Karl Henschke, one of Bordt's assistants, who was taken on during 1942 and given the responsibility of undertaking executions in Konigsberg. In addition, one of Hehr's assistants and one of Reichhart's team were added to the growing strength of appointed executioners. As we have seen, Reichhart's assistant, Alois Weiss, became the executioner at Pankrac Prison and subsequently beheaded a significant number of people, mostly Czechs.

With newly build execution sites and the increase in the number of executioners, the responsibilities and geographical areas of the executioners changed from time to time. In February 1943, Reichhart was ordered to travel to Berlin to be informed by another newly appointed executioner, Willi Röttger, concerning the technical aspects of hanging, and to view the new hanging provisions. Like many of the Third Reich executioners, Röttger had served in the First World War, having negotiated a diverse employment from a ship's stoker in the navy to an executioner supporting the Nazi judiciary. Röttger would later hang a great many of the 20 July conspirators.

Towards the end of 1943, Fritz Witzka was contracted to ply his deadly execution trade in Vienna, which became so overburdened with scheduled executions that both Weiss and Reichhart were also used at the same location. By the end of the year, Johann Muehl was added to the list of executioners and appointed to Cologne, and finally, during 1944, Alfred Roselieb, another of Hehr's assistants, was added to replace Reindel. These men and their assistants were responsible for all the hangings and beheadings carried out by judicial orders in the twenty-two appointed German prisons that sat within ten large districts. As executioners for the Reich Ministry of Justice, they were employed as servants to the Public Prosecutor's Office and, as executions almost without exception heralded the presence of a public prosecutor, they worked hand in hand alongside each other.

For all executioners, the process of beheading was the same. The vast majority of executions were carried out in the early mornings, but from 1942, due to increased demand, they were conducted at any time, day or night. Likewise, initially the announcement of the enforcement (execution) was made at least twelve hours in advance, but this later became six hours and was then reduced to just two or three hours.

At the end of the Third Reich's judicial reign of power the appointed executioners had carried out approximately 26,000 executions. Dr Thomas Dehler established that the vast majority were by beheading on the Tegel Fallbeil.

CHAPTER 8

Civilian Executions

Condemned for Uttering Jokes

Political jokes, at times uttered with little purpose, frequently led to citizens being sentenced to death by the People's Court. A Catholic clergyman was one such citizen who having been reported for uttering such a joke provided an opportunity for Freisler to criticise the priesthood with anti-Catholic comments. The joke was about a dying soldier who had asked to see those for whom he had to die. A picture of Hitler was placed on one side of the soldier and a picture of Goering on the other, whereupon the soldier said that now he was dying like Christ. Hearing the case, and fully understanding the reference to Christ dying between two thieves on the cross, Freisler announced his judgment on 1 October 1943, stating:

> …with his authority as a priest he has directed the most vulgar and dangerous attacks against our confidence in the Führer, an attack which can reduce the readiness of our people to risk its life for the life of the Volk [People] and he did not do this only once, because what he has said before us points in the same direction! … and he did it while we are engaged in the gravest of battles.
>
> Such behaviour is not only an irresponsible misuse of the authority of a priest, it is more than that, it is treason to Volk, Führer and Reich. Such treason causes external loss of honour. To deter others anxious to do the same, such an attack on the morale of our war effort can be punished with nothing other than death …

With a simple joke interpreted in the courts as treason, the judicial processes saw to it that the penalty was death by beheading. The same sentence was imposed on a young German war widow, Marianne Elise Kuerchner, on 16 December 1943. Evidence of jokes uttered by her included an example of Goering and Hitler sitting on top of the Berlin broadcasting tower with Hitler saying that he wanted to do something to put a smile on the Berliners' faces. Goering replied, 'Why don't you jump?' Freisler announced the sentence, adding:

As the widow of a fallen German soldier, Marianne Kuerchner tried to undermine our will to man defences and dedicated labour in the armaments sector towards victory by making malicious remarks about the Führer and the German people and by uttering the wish that we should lose the war … She has excluded herself from the racial community. Her honour has been permanently destroyed and therefore she shall be punished with death …

In Prague, a Catholic professor of religion, Karel Kratina, appeared before a Special Court presided over by Judge Ludwig and Judge Johannes Dannegger. He was condemned to death on 6 December 1944 for offences of sabotage by 'continued malicious utterances' and for having told political jokes. The court summary appears to be particularly vindictive:

In view of the serious and disreputable nature of the act perpetrated by the accused and in consideration of his person, the penalty prescribed by the law in cases of grave sabotage, namely the death penalty, appears as a just atonement for his conduct. Disseminators of political poison, who as a clergyman subscribe to the idea of stabbing the German Reich in the back in time of war, have not deserved any other fate than their eradication from the community of their people. The dishonourable character of the accused also justifies loss of civic rights for the rest of his life.

The prosecutor in this case was Dr Von Zeynek, who argued for the death penalty against the Catholic clergyman. Among his evidence was the joke uttered by Father Kratina:

A man in a railway compartment is reading a book by the Führer, *Mein Kampf*. Suddenly he begins to laugh. Asked why he was laughing, he read aloud—Give me the government for ten years and you will not recognise the Reich—this is a mockery of the events which have come about as a result of the war …

Father Kratina had allegedly also said that the reason Germany would not win the war was because it fights the CSR, an abbreviation for the Czechoslovak Republic but the letters also stood for the names Churchill, Stalin and Roosevelt. Little doubt exists that the cleric would have been beheaded in Prague almost immediately following his sentence.

The Lübeck Martyrs

Catholic priests Johannes Prassek, Hermann Lange, Eduard Müller and Lutheran pastor Karl Friedrich Stellbrink all worked together amongst the parishes in

Lübeck. Karl was employed in the lesser known Lutheran branch of Protestantism that historically identifies with the theology of Martin Luther, a German religious reformer in the sixteenth century.

The Catholic priests worked at the Sacred Heart Church in the centre of Lübeck where their chaplain was Johannes, who was ordained in 1937. The assistant minister was Eduard, with Hermann serving as the vicar, having joined the Sacred Heart Church in 1939. Karl was an isolated pastor at the nearby Lutheran church. The four became close friends, exchanging sermons and scripts, and occasionally inserting a little information into such sermons gathered from foreign radio broadcasts. They all shared in their rejection of the Nazi Party, and earnestly served the needy within their large parishes.

Karl, aged 47, was the elder statesman. He had served in the German army during the First World War and sustained a serious debilitating injury to one of his hands, leading to him being medically discharged in 1917. He chose to study and eventually became ordained into the Lutheran Church in 1921, the same year in which he married Hildegard Dieckmeyer. They took a ship from Hamburg to Brazil, where Karl served as an overseas pastor for eight years, his wife giving birth to four girls during that time, before they finally returned to a parish in Thuringia. In 1929, Karl ventured into politics and joined the Nazi Party, believing in the hope promised by the party to the people of Germany. Five years later, he took up the position as the pastor in Lübeck, but his beliefs and his friendships with Jews brought him into direct conflict with the Nazi regime. Following an investigation he was forced to resign in 1937. Discontented, Karl felt deceived by Hitler and he formed a strong friendship with the three like-minded Catholic priests.

The chaplain Johannes frequently commented against the National Socialist ideology and was offered guidance to avoid doing so by his elders within the Catholic Church. However, he did not let himself be influenced on the matter, believing in the importance of stating what he believed to be the truth. The four clergymen were active in their anti-Nazi activities, speaking out against the regime and discreetly distributing pamphlets to close friends and their congregation. In 1941, Johannes was befriended by a young Protestant, Hans Luers, who unbeknown to him had been instructed by the Gestapo to gather intelligence about him and his associates. While taking part in church discussions and expressing an interest in converting to the Catholic faith, Luers made notes of the individuals who attended, passing details of their conversations over to the Gestapo who were building a case against them all.

The RAF bombed Lübeck on 28 March 1942. It was the night of Palm Sunday and there was a full moon, so visibility was good for the 234 bomber aircraft dispatched from various airfields by Bomber Command. Lübeck was a city with many narrow streets constructed of half-timbered houses and a large military port complex of industrial buildings. Nazi submarine oxygen equipment was being constructed and supplied from this district. Many bombs fell throughout the built-up area, and incendiary bombs started a great many fires. German records indicate that 1,425 buildings were completely destroyed, while over 8,000 buildings were damaged to varying degrees as well as 246 commercial buildings being destroyed, no doubt temporarily removing them from Nazi war production. Over 300 people were killed in the raid, and a further 600 were injured. At this stage in the war, these were the worst casualties suffered in Germany from an Allied bombing operation.

Karl experienced the trauma of this intense raid, tending to the many injured people as best he could. In his church sermon the following day he attributed the bombing to 'divine punishment' and referenced that 'God had spoken in a loud voice and that the people of Lübeck will once again learn to pray'. His outspoken opinion resulted in him being arrested a few days later, on 3 April, following which his church commenced disciplinary proceedings. Karl was imprisoned at Lauerhof. The intelligence gathered by the Gestapo spy Luers was used to arrest the other priests. Johannes was detained on 18 May and taken to Marstall Prison, and Hermann on 16 June, joining Karl in Lauerhof. Eduard was arrested on 22 June and was likewise removed to Marstall Prison. Why they were not all swept up in one purge remains unexplained, but they were imprisoned for over a year before eventually all moving into the Holstenglacis Prison in Hamburg prior to being presented to the People's Court in June 1943. Ernst Lautz, the Reich's Prosecutor-General, signed the indictment against the priests and eighteen people also arrested by the Gestapo, including church employees Adolf Ehrtmann and Robert Koster.

Wilhelm Crohne, the Vice-President of the People's Court, was summonsed to attend Lübeck and try the case. The duplicitous Crohne assured Bishop Wilhelm Berning of the Catholic Church on the day prior to the trial commencing that there was no need to fear a death sentence. Karl, however, appears to have had no direct support from his church and efforts were under way for them to distance themselves from him. The proceedings began on 22 June 1943, with Crohne presided as the deputy to Freisler, who adopted an aggressive stance against the accused despite the best defence possible being provided by their appointed representative.

The four defendants were found guilty and sentenced to death for 'broadcasting crime (listening to enemy broadcasts), treasonable support for the enemy, defeatism and demoralisation of the Armed Forces'. During sentencing, Crohne criticised Karl for being a Lutheran cleric who had allied himself with a representative of the Catholic Church that fights against Protestantism. The criticism levelled at him illustrates the anti-Christian slant of the People's Court prosecutions.

The following day Crohne sentenced the remaining defendants. Adolf Ehrtmann received a five-year sentence, and Robert Koster was given one year's imprisonment. The others were released as they were deemed to have served their sentence, having been in captivity for a year prior to trial. The four condemned priests were removed from the People's Court and returned to the Holstenglacis Prison in Hamburg, a facility equipped with a Fallbeil, where they were to be executed by beheading. That task would be performed by the executioner Friedrich Hehr from Hanover, a man who had been additionally charged with the task of undertaking death sentences in Hamburg.

Bishop Berning, who had previously been appointed to the Prussian State Council in 1933 by Hermann Goering, took responsibility for the three Catholic priests and wrote a plea for clemency. This was rejected. Karl received less support, fellow Lutheran clerics appealing for clemency but describing him as being mentally deranged. Upon his conviction, the Lutheran Church excommunicated him from its Holy Orders. His wife Hildegard tried in desperation to save her husband, sending a petition for mercy to Hitler. Karl did receive some help from the resident Catholic priest at Holstenglacis, Bernhard Behnen, who had been the prison chaplain since 1928. He visited Karl and the other prisoners, administering the sacraments, and before their execution he prayed with them and escorted them to the guillotine room. He was prevented from accompanying them on their final walk to the Fallbeil, which took place on 10 November 1943. Following the official identification of the condemned men, the executioner decapitated all four priests at intervals of just three minutes. Their headless corpses were removed from the prison and cremated. The remains of both Karl and Hermann were later returned to their respective churches, having been cremated at Ohlsdorf, whilst Johannes and Eduard were cremated at Neuengamme and their ashes scattered within the camp. Hildegard received a letter from the Prosecutor-General's office and believing it to be a reply to her request of clemency she opened the letter only to reveal a request for payment from her for 1,550.70 Reichsmarks, the fee required to cover her husband's court costs, imprisonment and execution.

Fifty years later, the Evangelical Lutheran Church, successor to the Lutheran church body, initiated court proceedings to clear Karl's name and admitted their inadequacies at how he had been treated. In November 1993, the German courts officially overturned the guilty verdict against Karl Friedrich Stellbrink. Remarkably, in 2004, Prof. Peter Voswinckel, a historian at the Federal Archives in Berlin, located the original letters written by the condemned men prior to their execution. The People's Court had directed that they were not to be sent, considering their content to be dangerous. These touching letters fittingly now remain in the care and custody of the Federal Archives and are acknowledged to the 'Lübeck Martyrs'. That same year, 2004, Hamburg's Archbishop Dr Werner Thissen initiated the process of beatification of the three Catholic priests, which concluded successfully in 2010.

Communist Youth Federation

The Communist Youth Federation had been formed in 1920 from the Free Socialist Youth Movement, which created active programmes to further their beliefs. In the early years the group confined themselves to 'ideological schooling' amongst themselves, reading and debating as well as hiking and camping. Liselotte Herrmann from Berlin joined the Communist Youth Association of Germany in 1928 whilst studying chemistry and biology at the Technical University in Stuttgart and later at the University of Berlin. However, as a result of having joined the German Communist Party (KPD) in November 1931, she was expelled from university in July 1933. Liselotte married, but her husband and fellow communist Fritz Rau received fatal injuries during a Gestapo interrogation.

In May 1934, Liselotte gave birth to a son and returned to her parents in Stuttgart in September that year. She began work as a stenographer in her father's engineering office but remained interested in Communist politics. Liselotte subsequently made contact with the then illegal KPD, where she met Stefan Lovasz, head of the group in Württemberg, and where she later became active in gathering intelligence about Germany's secret rearmament programme. Her activities were divulged to the Gestapo by an informant and Liselotte was arrested on 7 December 1935, almost immediately being detained in solitary confinement for eighteen months. On 12 June 1937, Liselotte appeared in the People's Court where she was sentenced to death for 'treason and acts preparatory to high treason'. Treated as a Communist spy, she remained in isolation and no doubt was subjected to repeated interrogations. Some of the information held by her had been supplied by a man named Goritz, which included details of a secret underground munitions factory near Celle. In June 1938, Liselotte was finally transported from her isolated prison cell to Plötzensee Prison where, on the 20th of that month, she was executed together with other members of her group, including the informant Goritz, the KPD group leader Lovasz, and Josef Steidle.

Amongst many other members of the Communist Youth Federation was a young girl, Ursula Goetze from Berlin. As a high school student in 1933, she had been arrested and detained for a short period for being a member of the federation. After graduating from school she became a shorthand typist. Ursula voluntarily helped racially and politically persecuted individuals affected by the Nazi Party and, in May 1942, she decided to post literature voicing opinion against the 'Soviet Paradise' exhibition. She became aware of the intense activity of the Gestapo but had no reason to suspect that she would be apprehended. However, several months later, in October, she was arrested by the Gestapo for her rather insignificant involvement, and placed before the People's Court in January 1943. Ursula was to become another victim of the intense judicial actions undertaken against those who had reportedly taken action against Nazi exhibition propaganda: she was sentenced to death and executed in Plötzensee Prison on 5 August 1943. Amongst the other females murdered that day was 33-year-old Maria Terwiel, who had been found guilty in the People's Court of assisting Jews by providing food ration cards and identity papers, and the Red Orchestra operative Liane Berkowitz who had also been engaged in flyposting.

From the end of 1941 onwards, the Communist John Sieg regularly distributed *Die Innere Front* (The Inner Front) leaflets. The documents, containing information about the war and details of the transmission frequencies of Radio Moscow as an inducement to get people to listen to the Communist broadcasts, were printed in Berlin by Herbert Grasse, and were written in German and other languages in the hope that they would reach the many enslaved forced labourers. Grasse, who had joined the Communist Youth Federation and later the German Communist Party, had been involved in the production and distribution of an earlier illegal newspaper. As a result of this activity he had been arrested and sentenced to two and a half years' imprisonment. After his release in January 1939, he was able to re-establish contact with his friends and moved back into Communist resistance circles that centred around Sieg. Grasse secretly produced printed leaflets and helped to duplicate Sieg's illegal publication. He distributed leaflets for various resistance circles until his inevitable arrest on 23 October 1942. The next day he committed suicide to avoid interrogation by the Gestapo in Berlin. Sieg had also been arrested a few weeks previously, on 11 October, and he too had taken his own life by hanging himself in his cell four days later. Many more young men and women who had been members of the Communist Youth Federation would follow them to the Nazi People's Courts and thence lose their lives either to the Fallbeil guillotine or the gallows.

Hitler Youth Movement

In 1927, the Hitler Youth made their first public appearance in Nuremberg when 300 members marched next to 30,000 Nazi storm troopers. Three years later, on 20 March 1930, the Hitler Youth gathered in Berlin for their first solo mass rally, which featured inflammatory speeches by Joseph Goebbels and the Hitler Youth Leader, Kurt Gruber. The Hitler Youth movement was beginning to achieve the goals that Hitler had sought, believing vehemently that he must control the youth in order to control Germany. In January 1933, the Hitler Youth movement had expressed its hostility to Scouting, claiming that the Hitler Youth alone represented the youth of Germany. On 17 June 1933, the Scout movement was prohibited, and on 26 May 1934, a subsequent decree forbade any federation or connection to any Scout movement. The decree stated that it 'had become a place of refuge for the young enemies of the new state'.

In August 1933, the World Scout Conference had been held in Hungary and had voted in favour of a resolution entitled 'Political Propaganda', which stated:

The Congress once again invites attention to the fact that any political propaganda of any character, direct or indirect, national or international, must not be permitted in any camp or scout gathering in which representatives of other nations are invited to participate.

Despite these intentions, the fate of Scouting in Germany had been sealed, and this action was to be hugely significant to the life of Helmuth Hübener, one young Boy Scout in Germany.

The Scout movement was aggressively opposed to the actions being taken in Germany. In November 1937, a meeting was arranged between the influential founder of the movement Lord Baden-Powell and Jochen Benemann and Hartmann Lauterbach, officials of the Hitler Youth movement, after consulting with Joachim von Ribbentrop, the German ambassador to London. That same year the World Scouting Organization responded to the prohibition of Scouting by the Nazis by passing a resolution entitled 'Patriotism':

> The Conference resolves that the International Committee be requested to do all that it can to ensure that Scouting in all countries, while fostering true patriotism, is genuinely kept within the limits of international co-operation and friendship, irrespective of creed and race, as has always been outlined by the Chief Scout [Baden-Powell]. Thus, any steps to the militarization of Scouting or the introduction of political aims, which might cause misunderstanding and thus handicap our work for peace and goodwill among nations and individuals, should be entirely avoided in our programmes.

These actions were to prove pointless and it is interesting to reflect upon the subsequent Nazi invasion plans for Britain, prepared in 1940 by the SS General Walter Schellenberg, who foresaw the arrest of about 2,800 prominent British citizens, amongst whom were Lord Baden-Powell and the main leaders of the organisation's International Bureau, men who had sponsored opposition to the Hitler Youth movement. The Nazis believed that since Lord Baden-Powell had been an intelligence officer in the First World War, the Scout movement he had created in 1907 had been only for the purpose of espionage for the benefit of Britain and that commissioners of various international organisations had as their sole mission to prepare monthly and quarterly reports on the political, economic and social life of their country for the International Bureau. The portion devoted to Scouting was also an illustration of Nazi racism, with Hubert Martin, director of the International Bureau, being described as 'half Jewish'.

Hitler's youth movement was designed to instil Nazi philosophy from a young age. As soon as members of the Hitler Youth reached the age of 18, they were forced to join the Nazi Party. Girls became members of the BDM, *Bund deutscher Madel* (League of German Girls), where identical values were imposed. By the end of 1933, the Hitler Youth had grown to over three-and-a-half million members, and the organisation continued to grow due to the authoritarian power of the Nazi Party. By 1936, a law was passed that made it mandatory for all German youths to be educated in National Socialism through the Hitler Youth, except for Jews. Parents who would not allow their children to join the organisation were punished following appearances in Hitler's Special Courts.

Through the coercive persuasion of the Hitler Youth movement, the young people of Germany were beginning to regard Hitler as a god-like leader and were willing to die for his cause. On 10 September 1938, over 80,000 members marched into the city stadium at Nuremberg and performed a military-style parade. The following year saw the Hitler Youth become the largest youth organisation in the world, with over 7.3 million within its ranks. A law was issued on 25 March 1939, conscripting any remaining youth into the organisation amid warnings to parents that unless their children were enrolled they would be forcibly removed and placed in the custody of state-run orphanages.

Helmuth Günther Hübener was born on 8 January 1925 and grew up in Hamburg. In 1931, he attended the primary school in Luisenweg and thence the upper level at Brackdamm School, until April 1941. His family were Mormons, members of the Church of Jesus Christ of Latter-day Saints, where he was proudly a member of their Boy Scout group. When Germany banned Scouting, Helmuth had been forced to join the Hitler Youth, enrolling on 20 April 1938. He and his friends would eventually carry the issued dagger with the words 'Blood and Honour' etched onto the blade and the uniformed brown shirt, shoulder belt and neckerchief. After he finished his middle school education in 1941, at the age of sixteen he began an apprenticeship as an administrator for the executive civil service in Hamburg. Around this time, he located his brother's short-wave radio that had been hidden in his home and began to secretly listen to the BBC, despite knowing that it was very dangerous to do so. He knew that if he was caught he would be in serious trouble, as it would be considered an act of treason. However, the plight of his Jewish friends within the community and the desire to understand exactly what was happening in the war induced him to listen and what he heard was seriously disturbing.

The only radio permitted to be used at this time was the *Volksempfaenger* or People's Receiver, which enabled the populace to hear only that which the German government wanted them to hear. Helmuth's two best friends were Rudolf Wobbe, a sixteen-year-old apprentice mechanic, and Karl-Heinz Schnibbe, a seventeen-year-old apprentice house painter. He persuaded his Mormon friends to join him in his quest to let more people know the truth of what was happening in the war, the illegal radio broadcasts becoming their primary source of information. At 22.00 hours its feeble tone sounded the first four notes of Beethoven's Fifth Symphony, equated with a signal in Morse code, 'V for Victory', which was always given at the beginning of every British news broadcast given in the German language. The boys were joined somewhat later by Gerhard Düwer, a seventeen-year-old administrative trainee, who most probably worked with Helmuth. Their aim was to correct the lies published in the National Socialist Wehrmacht reports and the fake German news broadcasts. Helmuth became adept at writing the BBC news broadcasts in shorthand and used maps from his atlas to follow the military progress. The information was in stark contrast to the gloriously represented German news.

Helmuth decided to spread the news by creating small leaflets in the form of simple messages left in public places with a request to hand them on to others—a type of chain letter. Later, during August 1941, the leaflets became larger and consisted of factual reports taken from the British news broadcasts. Together the four young men bravely wrote out by hand or typed sixty different news sheets and pamphlets, knowing the dangers they faced, as local newspapers frequently carried accounts of long-term prison sentences and capital punishment for high treason. It proved possible to type up to eight copies using carbon paper on one typewriter, these materials being available to Helmuth at his place of employment. The boys always met at the weekends in the church, and that venue also assisted in the endeavour of locating plain writing paper.

The boys distributed news leaflets throughout Hamburg, using simple methods such as pinning them on bulletin boards, randomly inserting them into letterboxes, and stuffing them in coat pockets. Unsurprisingly and inevitably with such activity, Helmuth was arrested by the Gestapo at his workplace in Hamburg on 5 February 1942, his arrest having come about following suspicions aroused by his work colleagues. His home was searched and the Gestapo located the radio and several previously compiled leaflets, his shorthand notes, and the typewriter with a piece of work in the process of being composed. Subjected to terrible interrogation in an effort to gather as much information as possible, and almost a month after his arrest, he was transported to Moabit Prison in Berlin, one of Germany's oldest prisons, which held its inmates in filthy louse-ridden cells, having previously endured a ferocious imprisonment in the KolaFu concentration camp.

At 10.00 hours on 11 August 1942, his case was tried by Chief Justice Fikeis at the People's Court in Berlin. The panel of judges consisted of Vice-President Karl Engert, National Socialist Motor Corp Brigade Leader Heinsius, Senior District Leader Bodinus, Senior District Judicial President Hartmann representing the Public Prosecutor, State Prosecutor Drullmann, and Secretary of Justice Wohlke. Sitting next to the Chief Justice, wearing his red robe, was a high-ranking SS Officer. In addition, Helmuth was to see in the courtroom the political overseer Mohns from his place of employment in Hamburg. Mohns was to be a main witness against him, it having been his responsibility to watch for anti-Nazi activity and to keep his office free from impure political thinking. It was Mohns who was ultimately responsible for exposing the activities of Helmuth and his friends.

The court was cleared during the actual examination of the leaflets, and throughout his questioning Helmuth confirmed the content to be true. It was exceptionally brave to address the court in that way. However, in typical People's Court style, the accused were berated with abuse. Helmuth was found guilty of conspiracy to commit high treason and treasonous furthering of the enemy's cause. He was sentenced not only to death but also to permanent loss of his civil rights, which meant that he was most probably mistreated in prison and stripped of clothing, with no bedding or blankets in his cold cell in Plötzensee Prison.

Helmuth's solicitor, Herr Knie, and his mother appealed for clemency and were hopeful of his sentence being commuted to life imprisonment, as he had fully confessed in an effort to reduce any sentence upon his friends. However, the court stated that the danger posed by his activities to the German people's war effort made the death penalty necessary. On 27 October 1942, the Nazi Ministry of Justice upheld that verdict. Helmuth was advised of the decision at 13.05 hours that day, the scheduled day of his execution, and he was beheaded by the Berlin executioner, Röttger, at 20.13 hours that evening. Despite being only seventeen years old, he had been tried and sentenced as an adult.

This case was exceptional and was no doubt used as an example to the German people. His two friends, Karl-Heinz and Rudolf, were given prison sentences of five and ten years respectively, and Gerhard was sentenced to four years in a labour camp, based on the fact that no evidence existed to show he had ever listened to any enemy broadcasts. Fikeis additionally ordered all of the defendants to bear the costs of the court proceedings according to the Code of Criminal Procedures.

Helmuth Hübener's decapitated head and body were given to the Anatomical Institute of the University of Berlin in accordance with article No. 39 of the Reich's ordinance of 19 February 1939, and he has no grave of any description. His mother Emma and his grandparents were themselves to become victims of Germany's war when they lost their lives during the RAF attack on Hamburg on 28 July 1943. This was the night of the well-documented firestorm that started through an unusual and unexpected chain of events. Hamburg was tinder-dry and the temperature was particularly high. The RAF bombers dropped their bomb loads with accuracy, and the ensuing fires combined to create a massive firestorm which sucked the air away with great ferocity. Carbon monoxide poisoning caused the death of an estimated 40,000 people, and approximately 16,000 multi-storey apartment buildings were burnt out and destroyed.

Helmut Hirsch

The Nazis executed Helmut Hirsch in 1937, before the Second World War had broken out. His story is not unique amongst those who were decapitated in Germany, but it is significant as his death brought to the attention of the United States of America the grim reality of what was taking place within the Nazi movement across Germany. Helmut became the first American citizen to be executed under German National Socialist laws.

Born and raised in Stuttgart, Helmut was the elder child of Marta Neuburger Hirsch and Siegfried Hirsch; his sister Kaete was one year younger. Most importantly, before Helmut's birth in 1916, his grandfather had emigrated to the US with his young son Siegfried (Helmut's father) who was educated in the state schools and became a naturalised American citizen. Returning to Germany in 1914, he later married Marta. The family was Jewish and Hitler's rise to power and the passage of anti-Semitic laws designed to keep Jews out of schools and businesses impacted upon them. Helmut was later forced to move to Prague in order to continue his college education. At the age of fifteen, he joined the *Jungenschaft*, a youth group founded in 1929 by Eberhard Koebel. Activities included camping trips and other group outings, and the youth group also encouraged an interest in culture, music, philosophy and politics. The Nazis, keen to suppress any ideology apart from their own, dissolved the *Jungenschaft* and replaced it with their own youth movement in 1934. Helmut, as a Jew, was ineligible to remain in any youth movement, so this would have had an enormous impact upon his life. After he moved to Prague in 1935 to pursue a degree in architecture, he remained in close contact with his *Jungenschaft* friends, in particular Eberhard, who recommended that he should make contact with Otto Strasser, the leader of the Black Front, who was living in Prague. The Black Front was a splinter group of the Hitler movement, with a socialist agenda not shared by the Nazis. Otto opposed Hitler and rather delusively held the belief that he could motivate and educate the German people to overthrow him, although Otto's brother Gregor remained loyal to the Nazi Party, serving as the Reich Organisation Leader of the Nazi Party until 1932. However, having fallen from favour with Hitler, he eventually became one of the many victims of the Führer's treachery. On 30 June 1934, Gregor was arrested by the Gestapo as part of the Night of the Long Knives operation. He was taken to Gestapo headquarters and ruthlessly shot in the back of the head.

The German expatriates and former Nazi Party members who made up the Black Front were particularly dangerous to associate with. The People's Court made a judgment on 20 February 1935, condemning them as highly treasonable group. By the time Helmut's family had followed him to live in Prague in 1936, he had become heavily involved in the underground activities of the group, but he never disclosed his membership of the Black Front to his family or to his girlfriend Vally Petrova. Later that year, Black Front members actively engaged in the planning of an audacious plot to explode a bomb in Nuremberg, the symbolic seat of the Nazi Party.

In December 1936, Helmut advised his parents that he would be going skiing with a friend; however, this was a cover for his plan to return to Germany in order to carry out the bombing at Nuremberg. Unbeknown to Helmut, German agents had been infiltrating the Black Front for some time, and the Gestapo were waiting to arrest him when he re-entered Germany. Helmut was captured in Stuttgart and taken away for interrogation, with his parents having no knowledge of what had become of him, only for him to appear in the People's Court in Berlin during March 1937. Helmut was sentenced to death on or around 20 March for the 'preparation of high treason and the criminal use of explosives, endangering the public'. This was despite the fact that he was not actually carrying any explosives when he entered Germany. The propaganda opportunity was not missed by the Nazis, who broadcast the court's findings, and it was only when his family heard his death sentence announced on the radio that they learned of his fate. Helmut wrote five letters that were posted to his family from Plötzensee, dated between 20 March and 3 June 1937.

Upon hearing of their son's death sentence, Helmut's family immediately began to make appeals for his release and sought the help of relatives and officials in the US due to his American citizenship. It transpired, however, that his father Siegfried's American citizenship had been revoked sometime after he had returned to Europe, so by the time Helmut was born, he and his family were considered to be 'stateless persons'. This was rectified in the April of 1937, when they were officially recognised as American citizens, but this action and the diplomatic efforts of US Ambassador William E. Dodd were not enough to be able to secure Helmut's freedom. Dodd had made a significant effort to get Hitler to pardon Helmut from his death sentence, but it appears that this case was no more than an irritation to German officials, who saw the US effort as an unwarranted interference in internal German affairs. It was all to no avail. On 4 June 1937, Helmut Hirsch was decapitated in Plötzensee's execution cell by the Nazi government. The day before his execution, Helmut wrote this final letter to his family from his jail cell:

Berlin-Plötzensee   June 3, 1937

Dear Mother, dear Father,

I have just been told that my appeal for clemency was turned down. I must die then.

We need not say anything anymore to each other. You know that in these last months I have really found the way to myself and to life. Real beauty must stand before unswerving honesty. You know that I have lived every moment fervently and that I have remained true to myself until the end. You must live on. There can be no giving up for you. No becoming soft or sentimental. In these days I have learned to say 'yes' to life. Not only to endure it, but to love life as it is. It is our own inner gravity, the force by which we have entered life.

It must help you in some way that I know I have finally reached my own inner image and feel complete. And in this feeling is much of our time and our world.

The only way I know how to thank you is by showing you until the last moment that I have used all your love and goodness towards becoming a whole being of my time and my heritage. Do not think of the unused possibilities, but take my life as a whole. A great search, a foolish error, but on the path to finding final truth, final peace.

Please care for Vally as for a child [his girlfriend at the time of his death]. I embrace you, dear mother and you, my father, once more for a long, long time. Only now have I realized how much I love you.

Yours forever,
Helmut.

The day after his execution, *The New York Times* published the story on its front page: 'Germans Execute Hirsch, United States Citizen; Youth of 21 Guillotined, Despite Repeated American Appeals to Hitler for Clemency.'

Helmut spoke no English and had never set foot on American soil, but he was the first American citizen to be executed by the Nazi Party in Germany. The US strove to maintain positive relations with Germany and, in retrospect, the death of Helmut in 1937 might well have soured that relationship, which in effect still remained positive until 1939. Helmut's death imposed by Hitler's People's Court was a glaring case that provided a telling insight into the totalitarian administration of justice in National Socialist Germany.

Knowledge concerning the rise of Hitler and the atrocities committed in his name must not be lost to future generations, and Brandeis University near Boston, Massachusetts, houses a number of special collections that focus on anti-Semitism and the Jewish resistance to persecution. Within the archives is the Helmut Hirsch Collection, donated to the university by Helmut's surviving sister Kaete.

Max Josef Metzger

On 3 February 1887, Max Josef Metzger was born to Anna (née Gaenshirt) and Friedrich August Metzger, a schoolteacher who inspired his family in the Catholic religion. The family lived in Schopfheim in the Black Forest, and Max was the eldest child with three younger sisters. At the age of seventeen, he successfully achieved his ambition to study for a life in the church, gaining a position with the Archdiocese of Freiburg in the university at Freiburg. In 1910, he gained a position at St Peter's Seminary, where he achieved his aim of being ordained a priest in June 1911.

Father Max served as the parish assistant in the industrial district of Mannheim, and following the outbreak of the First World War he volunteered to serve as a front-line chaplain. He found himself attached to the 42nd Cavalry Brigade and became ferociously engaged in the trenches. On 6 May 1915, he was decorated with the Iron Cross for his courageous work, but later that year he developed a severe case of inflammation on the lung and was discharged from the army. There is a likelihood that his condition may have been caused by the deployment of mustard gas or another type of chemical warfare agent used by both factions in the static trench wars of that time.

As part of his religious beliefs, Father Max abstained from alcohol, tobacco and the eating of meat. He was approached by the *Kreuzbündnis* (League of the Cross) organisation, which had been founded in 1896 by a Catholic priest to support alcoholics, alcohol abuse being a particularly prevalent social problem at that time. The position was in Austria and additionally required him to occupy the post as head of the Priests' Abstinence League. In 1916, Father Max toured Austria and Germany delivering lectures on alcoholism and gained great satisfaction in developing the German Catholic youth organisation named Quickborn. He wrote passionately about this subject, publishing many articles and booklets, which eventually brought him to the attention of the infant Nazi Party.

Although the Catholic Church was opposed to the Nazi Party on both theological and moral grounds, by 1933 a number of Catholic priests had joined the party.

Amongst them was Father Max's bishop, Conrad Gröber, who openly supported Nazism. In May 1933, at a time when it was dangerous to do so, Father Max voiced criticism of the party and published a very direct editorial pamphlet, 'Die Kirche und das Neue Deutschland' (The Church and the New Germany). Later that year, he wrote another pamphlet, which he intended to send to the deans of every chapter of Catholic priests throughout Germany. Father Max wanted the matter of Catholics in the church working alongside the Nazi government to be discussed, but before he could distribute the pamphlets the Gestapo intercepted them and he was arrested in January 1934. His typewriter was seized, as well as other writing materials. Having served a short period of detention, he returned to his activities undeterred, steadfast in his concerns about the Nazi Party, which were heightened further when, on 16 March 1935, Hitler proclaimed to Germany that compulsory military service was to be reintroduced and would increase the peacetime size of the army to more than 500,000 men. In addition, a rearmament programme would commence. Father Max responded to this announcement by publishing a pamphlet proclaiming, 'Give us peace Lord in our days!' He continued to write various works against the Nazi regime right up to the beginning of the Second World War.

Predictably, Father Max was arrested in 1939, during the months of September and October. He was subjected to more robust questioning than previously and once again his writing materials and equipment were confiscated. He was again arrested in November and this time was imprisoned without charge between 9 November and 4 December. This may well have been as a result of the material seized by the Gestapo on his arrest. Reflecting in his prison cell, Father Max wrote to the Pope, believing that the Gestapo would allow the letter to be sent, and following his release from prison he returned to church duties and continued to travel as best as possible, lecturing throughout 1940. In the summer of that year, he moved to Berlin, where he erroneously concluded that he was safer from the Gestapo, but unbeknown to him, he was being watched and in 1941 his residence was searched. However, no incriminating evidence was found. In Berlin, Father Max joined the circle of friends around Hanna Solf, the widow of diplomat Wilhelm Solf. All were opponents of the Nazi regime, and as we have seen, several of them lost their lives following show trials in the People's Court conducted by Roland Freisler. Father Max had been invited to inform the circle about the Una Sancta Brotherhood, his concept for bringing Catholics and Protestants together for theological discussion and prayer, which had been founded in 1938. Unbeknown to the Solf circle, it had been infiltrated by a Gestapo informant who was ultimately responsible for the death of its members. Father Max had fortuitously distanced himself from that particular individual as he had doubted his integrity.

Having witnessed the Nazi persecution of the Jews and indeed the eventual offensive stance taken against the Catholic Church, Father Max had good reason to fear the Gestapo, who were very much aware of his activities. However, in 1942, he felt empowered to write to Hitler, believing that he could provide a rational reason for the Führer to make way for another government that would be able to negotiate an honourable peace settlement. No doubt as a result of heeding good advice, he never actually proceeded with that approach, but he did undertake another form of written correspondence relative to the state of the war, and this was to have significant ramifications for him.

In early 1943, Father Max had decided to seek the assistance of his friend, Archbishop Eidem of Uppsala in Sweden. The purpose of writing was to make the archbishop aware of the predictable consequences of Germany's defeat in the war and thus, at an opportune time, to ensure that the document would be passed to the English Church, which would in turn present it to the British government in an attempt to gain a mitigated peace settlement for Germany. Father Max sought the help of a Swedish convert to the Catholic Church whom he trusted to deliver the document, a courier named Dagmar Imgart. Having disclosed the content of the document to her, she agreed to carry the papers to the archbishop on her next trip to Sweden. When Father Max met with Dagmar in Berlin in June 1943, he had no reason to suspect anything was untoward and handed over the document. A short time later, Dagmar reappeared in company with what were obviously the Gestapo, who searched her and located the documents and then arrested them both. This was nothing other than pretence, because Dagmar was in fact a Gestapo agent who had infiltrated the Catholic Church and had been engaged in assessing the network of friends that surrounded Father Max, even having successfully engineered meetings with cardinals in Berlin and Munich as well as infiltrating other areas of interest as directed by her Gestapo 'Religious Education' controllers. She was also responsible for other personnel within the wider church movement of the Una Sancta Brotherhood being arrested. For example, Ernst Christoph Steiner, an outspoken pastor from Vienna, was betrayed by her work. He died following brutal torture by the Gestapo and before a trial in the People's Court could take place. Dagmar Imgart was a married woman with a daughter, and her husband Otto was a member of the SS who served at Bergen-Belsen concentration camp, where he contracted typhus and died in 1945.

Father Max was taken to the infamous Gestapo headquarters in Berlin on Prinz Albrecht Strasse, where he was held in the basement cells. On 11 September 1943, he was transferred to Plötzensee Prison, which had recently been damaged by RAF bombing. He was forced to wear prison clothing and had no access to any scriptures, embarking on weeks of petitioning in order to obtain a copy of The New Testament.

The trial against him for conspiracy to commit high treason and aiding and abetting the enemy was held in Berlin People's Court on 14 October 1943, presided over by Roland Freisler. Despite the 'public' that filled the courtroom being made up of many invited Nazi Party members, Father Max's secretary Sister Judith Maria and Sister Gertrudis were able to obtain admittance before the courtroom was closed. His trial was due to commence mid-morning and was one of six cases to be tried that day. Eventually his case was presented to the court in mid-afternoon, three cases having already received death sentences. There were five judges, two jurists and three laymen. The jurists and the prosecutor wore their red satin robes, while the lay judges wore Nazi uniforms. After a trial lasting not much more than an hour, the prosecutor read the indictment, which charged Father Max with 'conspiracy for high treason' and 'giving aid and comfort to the enemy' according to section 91 of the criminal code.

The judgment was then given and Father Max was condemned to absolute loss of honour and death. Freisler added to the sentence:

> Max Josef Metzger, a Catholic diocesan priest, who, convinced of our defeat, in the fourth war year attempted to send a 'Memorandum' to Sweden to prepare the way for an inimical pacifistic-democratic, federalistic 'government', with the personal defamation of the National Socialists. As a traitor of the people, forever without honour, he will be punished with death.
>
> Everyone must submit to being measured by the German National Socialist norm, and that norm clearly dictates that a man who so acts is a traitor of his own Volk.
>
> Metzger, who through his behaviour has forever lost his honour, must therefore be condemned to death.
>
> Because he is condemned, Metzger must also pay the costs.

When asked if he had anything to say, Father Max replied:

> I would only like to say once again that before God and my people my conscience is clear—I sought only to serve them.

With his hands chained behind his back, he was led out of the courtroom and back down to the cells. Along with the other prisoners condemned to death, he was transferred from Plötzensee to Brandenburg-Görden where he actively corresponded with his Sisters of Christ from his solitary confinement. Unbeknown to him, Archbishop Gröber wrote to Bishop Wienken on 25 October, requesting that the bishop personally appeal to both the Reich Minister of Justice and State Prosecutor to have the sentence commuted. However, all appeals for clemency were refused and Father Max remained in solitary confinement at Brandenburg-Görden until shortly after midday on 17 April 1944, when he was advised that he was to be executed that afternoon. He was removed to a holding cell closer to the execution chamber and shortly after 15.00 hours was led to the place of execution. At 15.26 hours, Max Josef Metzger was beheaded.

The news of his execution brought forward plans previously made by Sister Judith Maria for his body to be released to the Church for burial, and she immediately travelled to Brandenburg where she was able to obtain the permission of the local authorities to bury Father Max in the local cemetery. Although a change of rules had been forwarded preventing the release of bodies, she simply hoped that the

Brandenburg officials would know nothing of this new regulation and would keep to their agreement. On 21 April 1944, at eleven o'clock in the morning, Father Max was buried in the old city cemetery in Brandenburg next to Father Alfons Maria Wachsmann, who was also from the Freiburg diocese where Father Max had previously served. Father Wachsmann had spoken out against National Socialism and during the Gestapo's operation against Catholic priests in Pomerania, had been arrested on 23 June 1943, sentenced to death by the People's Court on 3 December, and decapitated in Brandenburg-Görden Prison on 21 February 1944. Sister Judith Maria received an account from the Ministry of Justice with charges to be paid for the punishment imposed upon Father Max. The execution fee was 300 Reichsmarks, and expenses incurred were prison costs for 293 days of confinement charged at 1.50 Reichsmarks per day (439.50 Reichsmarks) and an additional 12 pfennigs for the cost of the stamp in sending the charges.

On 18 September 1946, Father Max's body was exhumed and moved to St Hedwig's cemetery, the oldest catholic cemetery in Berlin. A further exhumation subsequently took place and he was finally laid to rest in Meitingen cemetery on 27 April 1968. On his gravestone is an inscription of the words he uttered as his death sentence was being pronounced: 'I have given my life for peace in the world and unity in the Church.' On 6 March 1997, the Berlin Regional Court lifted the death sentence against Father Max Josef Metzger, acknowledging that his death had been unlawful. He was honoured as a martyr and recognised as a pioneer in ecumenism.

Irena Bobowska

Irena was born in 1920 and was struck down by polio at the age of two, thereafter being able to move only with the assistance of leg callipers and a wheelchair. Educated in Poznań, she was destined to be a most gifted poet, and as a result of her passion for literature Irena initiated the establishment of the first youth library in Poznań. Irena was frequently seen with her young friends being pulled in a cart. She accepted her disability and enjoyed belonging to the Polish equivalent of the Girl Guide movement. In the summer of 1939, when she was nearly nineteen, her country was barbarically invaded by Germany and she became a highly motivated person, desperately wanting to serve her country. She joined a secret organisation, a Polish resistance group, and busied herself distributing their secret newspaper in order to do what she could for her oppressed homeland. In early 1940, the resistance group developed and Irena in all probability took to writing propaganda material which was being distributed across Warsaw. The military and political situation of Poland was central to the material created, with the belief that Poland would rise again after the Allied forces overcame the invading Germans.

Inevitably, on 20 June 1940, Irena was arrested by the Gestapo. She was initially imprisoned in her local district of Poznań but later transported to a prison in Wronki, the largest in Poland and one used by the Germans to hold political prisoners. The conditions were particularly unpleasant, severe overcrowding creating extremely harsh conditions for the prisoners. However, Irena was eventually moved to the infamous Plötzensee Prison and throughout her imprisonment the Germans treated her with great suspicion, assuming her disability was false, and her treatment required bravery of the highest level as without her leg supports or wheelchair she was reduced to pulling herself along the unkempt prison floors using just the strength in her arms and shoulders. The reality of appearing in the People's Court, and the likelihood of a capital sentence, was not lost on Irena. On 24 August 1942, she was sentenced to the death following her defence speech of thirty minutes, during which she made no plea for mercy nor offered any justification of her acts, but instead listed atrocities committed by the Nazis in the Second World War.

The Fallbeil in Plötzensee Prison would once again be used, and her execution took place on 27 September 1942. In justification of the verdict upon the 22-year-old Irena, it was written:

> From January till May 1940 Irena Bobowska had written articles about the political and military situation, expressed her opinions that the bad situation of Poland would get better when England and France overcame Germany, that Poland would gain a victory and that Poland would be resurrected again.

Irena's physical disability would have prevented her from a dignified journey from her cell to the execution room, and no evidence exists as to her wheelchair or callipers being available to her, so the horrific circumstances of the manhandling of her paralysed body onto the Fallbeil can only be imagined, thus creating a truly undignified end to her life. It must be speculated that her remains were the subject of specific interest in the city's anatomical institute.

Her bravery now recognised, Irena Bobowska has become a named patron of the Kraków Girl Scouts troop and is remembered most appropriately amongst the youth group that she so enjoyed in her early years. Her legacy also includes the many poems she wrote during her short but important life.

Otto and Elise Hampel

Otto and Elise were a working class couple who had married in 1935 and lived in Berlin. A veteran of the First World War, Otto worked tirelessly in a factory as a labourer whilst his wife worked as a domestic. Elise became greatly affected when her younger brother was killed in action during the German invasion of France, and her devastation led the couple to become anti-war activists.

Jointly and completely in isolation from any other individuals, Otto and Elise created handwritten postcards on which they criticised the Nazi regime. The postcards were also composed with messages urging the German people not to serve in the army and to resist requests to donate money to the various war appeals. With no political motivation, the postcards were all simply written and contained general anti-war scripts.

Both Otto and Elise came from humble backgrounds, and during the composition of the cards and a few larger leaflets they consistently displayed grammatical errors and spelling mistakes. The couple targeted mailboxes in stairwells to avoid detection during the distribution of the cards, a concept that was designed to facilitate a recipient finding the card and showing it to others. This was, however, a flawed concept, as the vast majority of recipients were in fear of being in possession of such anti-Nazi material and the majority of the 200 handwritten cards were immediately handed into the police or residential block supervisors. For two years their campaign thwarted the Gestapo, who wrongly thought they were trying to trace a larger group of activists.

Eventually, the Hampels were tracked down by the Gestapo and both were arrested in October 1942. It was clearly a surprise to the authorities that the material had been created and distributed by a married Berlin couple, and it must be assumed that the Gestapo went to ruthless means to establish the evidence needed to confirm that the Hampels were acting alone. Both Otto and Elise were duly presented to the Berlin People's Court to be judged by Roland Freisler.

In accordance with Freisler's usual practice, the married couple were humiliated and degraded in court. Both were sentenced to death for the preparation of high treason, agitation, and demoralising the German troops. They were taken from the court in Berlin, separated, and imprisoned in Plötzensee Prison. On 8 April 1943, Otto, aged 45, and Elise, aged 39, were taken to the execution chamber and were both beheaded. The remains of Elise were almost immediately subjected to the rigours of dissection at the hands of Hermann Stieve at the Institute of Anatomy in Berlin.

Ignatz Kaczmarek

Halemba was a small farming community in Poland, situated close to the German border, which had been overrun by the German army. The Nazi controls implemented in relation to food production and sourcing were difficult, and small groups of trusted individuals engaged in livestock dealing amongst them. Ignatz, a 63-year-old farm labourer, had hidden a radio receiver on his farm and listened cautiously to the British news broadcasts on a regular basis, keenly aware of the consequences of doing so.

In March 1943, he met with a livestock dealing acquaintance and began negotiations over the acquisition of a pig. In what he thought was a secure environment, Ignatz spoke of having listened to the radio and said he believed that Poland would rise again and Germany would be crushed. This matter was reported to the authorities, who told Ignatz's acquaintance to continue the negotiations over the pig in his house and that they would listen to the conversations. A further meeting took place, this time with the police listening, and once again no doubt coerced, Ignatz spoke of listening to the radio, going so far as to say that the Russians had an excellent tank that was superior to the German machine.

Inevitably, Ignatz was arrested and interrogated. No doubt the radio was recovered, but it seems not to have featured in any documentary evidence. On 27 June 1944, he appeared in court addressed by a judge named Wedde. He was charged with undermining the war effort, and swiftly found guilty, the judge stating in his court summary:

> Ignatz Kaczmarek had uttered that nobody wanted the war, but Germany had started it and invaded Russia. The Bolshevists who were not wild beasts at all, were according to his account friendly and hospitable; they were only angry and defending themselves like lions ...

He was sentenced to death and decapitated at an unknown penal facility, as evidenced in the research document No. (19) Js 15/44 (35)/44 Committee for German Unity.

Helene Kafka, Maria Restituta

Anton Kaflak was a humble shoemaker in Brno, Czechoslovakia, married to Marie, who on 10 May 1894 gave birth to their sixth child, Helene. Life was exceptionally hard, so in 1900 the family moved to Vienna where they lived in the 20th District. Helene found work at an early age in a tobacco shop, but the opportunity to work as a nurse in the Lainz Hospital situated soon followed. The Franciscan Sisters of Christian Charity were engaged with the hospital, Helene becoming part of their nursing team. On 25 April 1914, against the wishes of her parents, she joined the convent of the Franciscan Sisters and received her habit on 23 October 1915. She would forthwith be known by the name Maria Restituta, after a virgin Roman martyr of the third century, St Restituta.

From 1919, she served in the Mödling Hospital in Vienna where she became a most competent surgical nurse. Sister Restituta was recognised for her professional attitude and individual personality, and although her medical competency was as an anaesthetist, she never lost the desire to help the poor and those persecuted by the growing unrest in Austria. Witnessing the rise to power of the Nazi Party, and with Hitler taking over Austria, she made her feelings known, verbally labelling Hitler a madman even though the hospital had been put under the control and administration of personnel loyal to the new Nazi government.

The Roman Catholic Church was suppressed throughout the conflict by the Nazis, particularly in Poland because historically the Church had led Polish nationalist forces fighting for the country's independence from outside domination. The Germans treated the Church harshly in all annexed regions, systematically closing places of worship and either killing, imprisoning or deporting many priests. Of her own volition, Sister Restituta placed crucifixes on the walls of a newly constructed section of her small hospital in an attempt to reaffirm her religious freedom. Her refusal to remove them brought her into direct conflict with the authorities, who threatened to remove her from the hospital should she not comply. Unbeknown to Sister Restituta, the resident SS surgeon, Lambert Stumfohl, informed the Gestapo about her activities, which included reportedly having written a poem mocking Hitler. The poem was in fact simply a previously published soldier's song that spoke of democracy, peace, and a free Austria.

On 18 February 1942, having completed her duties in the hospital operating theatre, Sister Restituta was arrested by the Gestapo. She was searched and a pamphlet concerning the German Catholic youth was found. As all Catholic societies and youth organisations had been disbanded under the Nazis, this would have been seen as significant evidence of her anti-Nazi activities.

Sister Restituta was taken to the Provincial Court of Vienna on 6 March and remanded pending a trial in the People's Court. Although she endured significant hardship in prison, she expressed concern for those around her and even forwent her meagre food ration to share with other, needier prisoners. Seven months later, on 28 October, she was tried and found guilty of 'aiding and abetting the enemy in the betrayal of the fatherland' and for 'plotting high treason', for which she was immediately sentenced to death along with the loss of all her civil rights for life. No doubt the wearing of her habit as a Franciscan Sister would have provided her with some strength, and many Sisters and Brothers appeared in their Catholic dress for the trial, all of whom were visibly shocked at the death sentence. After returning to her squalid quarters of imprisonment she was offered her freedom, with the proviso that she would vow to leave her religious congregation, but she refused to comply.

Her prosecution and sentencing brought forth an immediate request for clemency to Hitler's confidant, Martin Bormann, a man who had previously announced that there was no place for a Christian church in Germany, stating that the power of the church 'must absolutely and finally be broken'. Unsurprisingly, Bormann rejected the request for clemency on the ground that he felt the execution of the death penalty was 'necessary for effective intimidation'.

On 4 December 1942, representation was made from Sister Restituta's Order to the court for her body to be returned to them after the sentence had been carried out. Additionally, representation was made to the Nazi judiciary from the highest possible levels, including Cardinal Theodor Innitzer, the Archbishop of Vienna. Regardless of these significant interventions, the execution status remained and additionally the request for Sister Restituta's body to be returned or made available to her Holy Order was refused, stating, 'It is to be expected that the dead body will be used for propaganda purposes and for glorification of the convict as a martyr.'

An estimated 487 decapitated bodies were delivered from the Provincial Court to the Anatomical Institute in Vienna in 1943, but their capacity to hold corpses was restricted. Other bodies were secretly taken to the central cemetery where large shafted common graves were dug to hold around forty executed individuals at a time. Following the Allied victory over Germany, the Catholic Church instigated the recovery of Sister Restituta's body. On 27 August 1946, an exhumation took place at the central cemetery in Vienna from one of the common graves thought to contain Sister Restituta, so that her body could be transferred to a grave within the community of her Holy Order.

In September 1957, Father Johann Ivanek, the pastor at the Provincial Court of Vienna, responded to a letter sent by Sister Immakulata Kandler concerning the events surrounding his work at the Court and his knowledge of Sister Restituta's last moments. This exceptional letter, which uniquely explains the duties undertake by the pastor at the prison, is quoted here by permission of the Silesia Restituta:

Reverend Mother,

I have been away for a spiritual retreat in Melk and thus unable to reply to your letter of December 23 any earlier. I did not meet Sister Restituta until her very last hours, as I usually helped out the deceased Monsignor Köck on execution days only. Officially I was suffered at the Provincial Court for the non-German-speaking foreigners, unofficially though Monsignor Köck would pass me the hard-nosed sinners who did not want to know about the priest. Thanks be to God I was able to make good catches this way, not on my account I will admit but on account of the sacrifices and prayers of our congregation. It was the Most Reverend Köck who took care of the good and saintly, not I. Now what I know of Sister Restituta I will gladly tell you.

In May 1942 about sixty truly innocent Czechs [women, young girls about nine of them, the rest were men and boys] had been condemned to death. The Reverend Köck asked that I start hearing their confessions right away. So for three days I went from cell to cell, from morning till night. When I got to the women's section on the third day the women imprisoned there told me about this Nun who was showing great kindness to everyone and giving them succour in their distress. It was six o'clock at night already and I had to make it in time for the seven o'clock May Sermon in St. Ulrich, so I had no time left to visit Sister Restituta after I had taken care of the Czech women. It was impossible for me to otherwise enter the prison wing without an official pass (the death cells were all facing the other way). Only during Lent or Advent were we allowed to hear the prisoners' confessions in the chapel or the prison hospital.

Thus it was on March 30, 1943 that I first met Sister Restituta in her death cell. When I got to the pastor's office Monsignor Köck assigned me my duties: to take care of non-German-speaking foreigners and, as I said before, the obdurate ones who refused to see a priest. We began our work at one o'clock in the afternoon and had to hear everyone's confession about one and a half hours before their execution. That day the Monsignor said to me, 'It is the Sister's turn today.' I was surprised because Dr. Gürtler had on one occasion before shown himself confident that

Sister Restituta's case would be settled favourably in Berlin. When we had finished with confessions we secretly took the Blessed Sacrament from the prison chapel so nobody would see us. Because nobody else in the prison was to know there was going to be another execution that evening at six o'clock. Sister Restituta shared cell number one with a girl and another woman. We set out to give their absolution and the viaticum, starting in cell forty-seven. Finally we arrived at cell number one. I pointed out to the Reverend Köck that members of religious orders before their last Holy Communion usually renew their vows. Sister Restituta recited her formula of profession aloud and then in her own words prayed for the repentance of the enemies of the Kingdom of God. Her pleas took some time and then she received the Divine Bridegroom, under the species of bread. I first spoke to her when she had received the papal blessing. She expressed her delight at being allowed to meet a Father from Maria Stiegen yet. She told me that when she was young she would often come to our church. She also asked me to give her greetings to her fellow sisters in the convent (which Reverend Köck has already done officially for I had to keep silent about all this or other death candidates might not have had a priest to speak to in their own language). Finally she asked me to pray for her so her purgatory would not be an extended one. I quickly replied: 'You won't need to go there at all. You have nothing left but your life. If you sacrifice it for the love of God you will go to Heaven straight away.' She seemed content with what I said. The young girl joined her in this. It was the last hour and I had to go and see the prisoners entrusted to me, to speak and pray with them and accompany them on their last journey to the guillotine. When the women were taken to be executed I stayed behind in the corridor as it was my break and I wanted to say goodbye to Sister Restituta. Reverend Köck was her pastor. When sister saw me she said: 'Father please make a sign of the cross on my forehead,' which I did; then she was taken to the high court—a few seconds and we could tell by the heavy, dull blow of the blade that Heaven had received another God-loving soul. We immediately blessed the bodies of the executed while the executioner wiped the blood from the guillotine next to us.

This is all I can tell you. Maybe her lawyer, Dr Gürtler, has more to say about her year in prison. Did Monsignor Köck not leave behind any records? Perhaps the Archbishop's Office has an idea of where Reverend Mother might turn to for more information.

God's blessings for this work which is no doubt agreeable to God—letting the world know about heroic virtues of his transfigured devotees must surely be equal to a homily for the people of today!

Faithful to the most sacred of hearts

Father Johann Ivanek, C.SS.R.

Some fifty years after Sister Restituta's exhumation, an application from her Holy Order and her relatives was submitted to the Vienna Regional Court for Criminal

Matters. They subsequently decided by judicial decree that the verdict pronounced on 29 October 1942 by the German People's Court, shall be deemed to be 'not stated'. This officially proved the illegality of Sister Restituta's death sentence and thus she was totally rehabilitated. This important legal process led to the Catholic Church announcing on 21 June 1998 at the Heldenplatz in Vienna, the location where Hitler had announced the annexation of Austria in March 1938, that the blessed Maria Restituta had become the 'First martyr of the Archdiocese of Vienna and the first female Austrian Martyr'.

The Purple Triangle

The Jehovah's Witnesses, also known as the International Bible Students Association and the Watch Tower Society, were founded in 1870. They professed their loyalty only to Jehovah, and in that belief they refused to serve in the army of any nation or to give their allegiance to any government. In Germany they were uniformly disliked for their opposition to the First World War, but despite this, in the aftermath of the conflict Jehovah's Witnesses increased their numbers within Germany. Their stance on condemning anti-Semitism brought their faith into greater criticism, and once the Nazis came to power in 1933, drastic changes occurred that led to Jehovah's Witnesses being persecuted in Nazi Germany until the outbreak of the Second World War. The words uttered from Hitler's mouth in 1933 must have been echoed in many homes occupied by Jehovah's Witnesses across Germany. 'If there are still those in Germany today who say: we will not submit, then I respond: you will disappear—and after you will come a youth that will know nothing else.'

The Hitler salute, which became law in 1933, required all German citizens to raise their hand or arm and to utter the words 'Heil Hitler!' Germans would offer the salute at numerous times in the course of a day; schoolchildren were required to do so on starting and finishing their daily education and similarly adults on entering and leaving work. Repeating the salute affirmed everyone's belief that Hitler was the saviour of Germany. Jehovah's Witnesses recognised the unmistakably religious overtones of the salute and refused to use the greeting, as the word 'Heil' in the German Bible is connected with 'salvation' by the Christ or Messiah (cf. Acts 4:12). Many lost their jobs and were eventually banned from civil service positions simply because they refused to salute. Their children faced beatings by fellow students and ultimately expulsion from school, following which they were placed into various Nazi institutions. The individual German states outlawed Jehovah's Witnesses in 1933 as 'enemies of the state' and a national ban followed two years later. The Nazi establishment took away their rights, confiscated their private property and suspended or removed their pensions.

In 1936, the Gestapo formed a special unit to combat Jehovah's Witnesses and orchestrated mass arrests that succeeded in dampening their underground religious activity. This persecution became state policy, and several thousands of them were sent to Nazi prisons and camps. Within the infamous early concentration camps, they were identified by their own camp uniform symbol, the 'purple triangle', which they were required to wear on their clothing. The SS had instigated visual marking on concentration camp clothing, various triangles being deployed in several colours. Under the prisoner classification system, Jehovah's Witnesses wore the purple triangle with an 'IBV' symbol, an abbreviation for the official name of their organisation in German, *Internationale Bibelforscher-Vereinigung* (International Association of Bible Students). The purple triangle could have an additional triangle fixed to create a star symbol, which would identify further status; for example, a purple inverted triangle superimposed upon a yellow one indicated a Jehovah's Witness of Jewish descent.

Because Jehovah's Witnesses refused to serve in the German military or give allegiance to the Nazi government, hundreds were to eventually lose their lives through executions, while an estimated 10,000 were sent to numerous concentration camps. The Special Courts and People's Courts tried a great many German Jehovah's Witnesses who had been charged with various offences, often minor but always resulting in a severe sentence. Those who had merely attended bible study lessons received a few months' imprisonment, whereas leading figures received five years. Sentences imposed upon Jehovah's Witnesses varied greatly between the different courts, and to add further pressure, Wilhelm Crohne from the Reich Ministry of Justice subsequently stressed that maximum sentences were not being imposed often enough by the judges. The German judges responded accordingly, which resulted in many receiving a death sentence inflicted by the Fallbeil. Between August 1939 and September 1940, a significant number of Jehovah's Witnesses appeared before the highest military court of the Wehrmacht charged with 'demoralisation of the armed forces' by not serving their country. More than a hundred were executed, usually by beheading. The practice of the removal of the children from their parents was an attempt to cleanse them, a policy designed ultimately to eradicate the next generation of Jehovah's Witnesses.

The German military machine required both military and industrial commitment from its population, and conscientious objectors such as Jehovah's Witnesses received severe punishment for refusing to perform the most menial military service in the factories or other production lines. On 15 September 1939, August Dickmann, a 29-year-old Jehovah's Witness and conscientious objector, was executed by firing squad in Sachsenhausen concentration camp. Heinrich Himmler, head of the SS (*Schutzstaffel*), Hitler's elite guard, personally approved the death sentence on what was thought to have been the first public execution of the war. Himmler's assumption that this execution would induce compliance was sorely misplaced. August Dickmann, who had been interned in the Sachsenhausen concentration camp in 1937, died in front of his fellow inmates, who had been ordered to watch the spectacle. His brother Heinrich was present and was made to handle his dead brother's body after the execution. Now, on the site of the concentration camp, a memorial stone stands dedicated to the life of August Dickmann.

Jehovah's Witnesses, being prisoners of conscience, were unique because they could have avoided their fate, unlike Jews and others targeted by the Nazis. They were given the opportunity to buy their freedom by simply signing a declaration card that renounced their faith and pledged allegiance to Hitler. Few took up that offer, which was frequently placed before them in the courts, prisons and concentration camps:

Translation of Declaration Document

Department II
DECLARATION, I the ....
Born on .... in
....
Herewith make the following declaration:

1. I have come to know that the International Bible Students Association is proclaiming erroneous teachings and under the cloak of religion follows hostile purposes against the State.
2. I therefore left the organization entirely and made myself absolutely free from the teachings of this sect.
3. I herewith give assurance that I will never again take any part in the activity of the International Bible Students Association. Any persons approaching me with the teaching of the Bible Students, or who in any manner reveal their connections with them, I will denounce immediately. All literature from the Bible Students that should be sent to my address I will at once deliver to the nearest police station.
4. I will in the future esteem the laws of the State, especially in the event of war will I, with weapon in hand, defend the fatherland, and join in every way the community of the people.
5. I have been informed that I will at once be taken again into protective custody if I should act against the declaration given today.

................................., Dated ....

Signature ....

Gregor Wohlfahrt was an Austrian who had served and been wounded in the Austro-Hungarian army during the First World War. He converted from Catholicism to become a Jehovah's Witness during the late 1920s. When Germany annexed Austria in 1938, Gregor led his congregation in a boycott of the ratification against Austria's union with Germany, and because of his anti-Nazi stand, the mayor of his town brought about his arrest on 1 September 1939. As a result of his opposition to military service, he was sent to Berlin to be tried by a military court where he was sentenced to death. On 7 December 1939, Gregor was executed by guillotine in Plötzensee Prison. During the war, Gregor's entire family was arrested for refusing to co-operate with the Nazis. He had three sons, two of whom were subsequently executed—one being beheaded in Plötzensee Prison, whilst the other was shot. The oldest son Franz was sentenced to five years' hard labour in Germany.

Helene Gotthold was born in Dortmund in 1896. Helene and her husband were both Jehovah's Witnesses. Her husband was arrested in 1936, followed shortly afterwards by her own arrest. Helene was brutally beaten and later tried by a Special Court, which sentenced her to eighteen months' imprisonment, a similar sentence to that given to her husband. However, in February 1944, Helene and her husband were rearrested and imprisoned once more. Whilst in prison, Helene and five other Jehovah's Witnesses were charged with undermining the nation's morale and sentenced to death for illegally holding bible study meetings. Mercifully, she was allowed to send a letter to her husband and children before her execution on 8 December 1944.

Wolfgang and Wilhelm Kusserow became Jehovah's Witnesses when infants. Their entire family were known to the German authorities, their home being the headquarters of a congregation of Jehovah's Witnesses. Even after the Nazis arrested Wolfgang's father and oldest son Wilhelm, the Kusserow family, including Wolfgang, continued to host bible study meetings in their home. Wilhelm's arrest had been for refusing to serve in the German army. The judge and prosecutor at his trial offered to rescind his execution order if he renounced his 'evil and destructive' beliefs. Wilhelm refused and the court sentenced him to death. According to his defence counsel, Wilhelm 'died in accordance with his convictions'. He was shot by firing squad in Münster Prison on 27 April 1940. Wolfgang also refused to be conscripted into the German army and was arrested in December 1941. He was to spend several months in prison before being tried in court. Wolfgang did eventually appear before a judge and, like his brother, was subsequently sentenced to death. On the night before his execution, he wrote to his family to assure them of his devotion to God. Wolfgang was beheaded by guillotine in Brandenburg Prison on 28 March 1942. Both of the Kusserow brothers were twenty years old when they were executed. More than 200 male Jehovah's Witnesses were tried by the German War Court and executed for refusing to undertake military service.

Axel Rudolph

An author who published works not only under his own name but also using at least two pseudonyms in Germany from 1932 to 1943 in order to increase his income potential, Axel Rudolph created some fifty publications. These included crime and adventure novels set across several continents and including Germany as well as his country of origin, Denmark.

Having left a failed marriage behind him and forging a new life for himself in Rathenow, a small village in the Brandenburg district of Germany, in 1933 Axel met Gertrude, to whom he became engaged three years later. As a struggling author he witnessed the Nazi rise to power and the regime's restrictions on popular literature, in particular the manipulation of rhetoric by the Nazi propaganda minister Joseph Goebbels. Axel had previously experienced the Brownshirt Nazi storm troopers who were nothing more than bullying enforcement troops for the Nazi Party. They had intimidated his friends and himself, having clearly been identified as an undesirable author amongst the Jews and Communists who were being targeted.

University students across Germany were being manipulated by the Nazi Party, which dictated whether a certain piece of literature was acceptable or not. Jewish staff and other undesirables in the various universities were being dismissed and at the same time many internationally recognised authors were deciding whether to leave Nazi Germany for their own safety. Literature, art and music suffered greatly as a result of Nazi policy, many authors being sidelined for others who wrote about the glorification of war, the importance of the Aryan ideal and the glorification of Hitler. The Führer was acutely aware of the power of authors on civilian morale. As early as May 1933, he took the decision that literary freedom had to be controlled and that authors must write only in a manner approved by the government. On 10 May, the German public witnessed the first mass book burning ceremony, organised by Propaganda Minister Joseph Goebbels. Men from the SA heaped 'unacceptable' and 'undesirable' books into a vast pile opposite the University of Berlin. They then used torches from their torchlight parade to set the books alight. SA members continued feeding books into the fire as the rally was addressed by Goebbels. His long political speech was recorded for posterity and his words were reported widely, this short section alone demonstrating the meaning behind the action taken that night:

> The old past lies in flames; the new times will arise from the flame that burns in our hearts. Wherever we stand together, wherever we march together, we want to dedicate ourselves to the Reich and its future.

At this time, the famous German poet and playwright Bertolt Brecht made the decision to leave Germany. He quoted a short but very profound sentence, written by the nineteenth-century author Heinrich Heine, after the first book burning ceremony. 'Where they have burned books they will end in burning human beings.' Brecht would have had no conception at the time that those few words would eventually evidence the truth of what the Nazis actually did.

Not all book burnings took place on that particular night. The majority of burnings were facilitated by the German Student Union, which arranged others across some thirty-four university locations. Widespread newspaper coverage and radio broadcasts brought the speeches and promotion of Aryan culture to the masses across Germany. All public and private libraries and book retailers were purged of books written by Jewish and other 'undesirable' authors.

The remaining authors in Germany, including Axel Rudolph, were required to comply with the Department of the Ministry of Public Enlightenment and Propaganda, a department that had full authority and control over all the publishing houses across Germany. However, by 1939, a significant proportion of authors had left Germany, and those who remained would have been very aware of the consequences of writing anything of which the Nazis disapproved. The department's most important task was to promote Hitler's book *Mein Kampf*, which was regarded as the highest form of literature, and more than six million copies had been sold by 1940.

Authors who were acceptable to the Nazi state and were under the control of the Ministry of Public Enlightenment and Propaganda were restricted to writing articles or books about only four mandatory subjects. The first category was 'Battle Front Experience'; the second was 'World View', which promoted the views of Hitler; the third category was 'Regional Novels', which showcased the various regions of Germany; and the final category was 'Racial Doctrine', which emphasised the greatness of the Aryan race when compared to Jews or any of the others regarded by the Nazis as *Untermenschen* or inferior people.

Axel continued to write for his living even though he was bound within the 'Regional Novels' category, which was not ideal or likely to be very productive. In 1943, he married his fiancée Gertrude, but a former lover of his, who was the daughter of a Nazi Party leader, exposed several letters he had previously written, knowing them to contain derogatory comments about the Nazi regime. The Gestapo investigated the matter and on the last day of December 1943 they arrested both Gertrude and Axel, subsequently searching for additional evidence within his manuscripts and papers to incriminate Axel whilst he and his wife remained in prison in Potsdam until May 1944. After five months of detention, Gertrude and Axel were taken to central Berlin. Little if any evidence had been secured against Gertrude, but on 18 July 1944 they both stood before the infamous Roland Freisler in the Berlin People's Court. They were found guilty of 'demoralising the German People and aiding the enemy', another report indicating that they should both be found guilty of 'contempt of the Nazi Party'. Gertrude was sentenced to three years' imprisonment, which was to be followed by attendance at an education camp. Axel received no leniency. He was sentenced to death, a sentence that was carried out on 30 October 1944, when he was beheaded in Brandenburg Prison.

Karl-Heinz Becker

Karl-Heinz Becker came from an intellectual Austrian family, his father being a public prosecutor and his grandfather having been a professor of law. However, Karl-Heinz did not follow in their footsteps, qualifying as a pastor in the late 1920s and taking his first parish in Franconia, eastern Germany, during the mid-1930s.

Having married and being regarded by his parish as a successful pastor, Karl-Heinz witnessed the gradual rise of the Nazi Party and the oppressive impact it was having on German civilians. He was opposed to National Socialism and voiced that opposition by writing to several ecclesiastical associations across Bavaria as well as submitting articles to newspapers. Although these were published in various forms, none appeared to draw the support he sought from his church. He was forced into adopting a differing strategy by publishing academic studies that touched upon subjects that the Nazi Party would no doubt object to, but written under the guise of historical accounts. They were printed in Romania or Hungary at his own expense, as some of the material was directed at anti-National Socialism and would have been impossible to get printed in Germany.

In 1937, as a result of his activities, his licence to teach religion was revoked for misuse of the pulpit. However, this had little effect on him. He was called up to serve in the Wehrmacht and undertook military duties during the invasion of Poland and the Low Countries. Promoted to the rank of an officer chaplain in the Wehrmacht, he served at several European locations where he witnessed increased civilian oppression by the Nazis. Karl-Heinz's Christian beliefs and fervent opposition to the Nazi Party forced him to continue with publications that he endeavoured to distribute throughout the church. His works concentrated on his opposition to the Nazi state and its judicial stance, evidencing that the Gestapo had based its power on the 'Emergency decree for the protection of the Nation and State from February 1933, a decree which placed the German people in a legal situation towards its government which was fully unprecedented in history through the suspension of fundamental rights'. He also made reference to the legal consequences that would result for the Wehrmacht from the crimes committed by the SS against civilians and Jews.

Karl-Heinz knew his actions were placing him in a very perilous position, but even so, he distributed his publications to a handful of people in confidence. The news of the failed assassination plot against Hitler in July 1944 seriously concerned him. He was serving as a chaplain in a military hospital in Hungary at the time, and even though the Gestapo were redoubling their efforts to eliminate those opposed to Hitler, he continued in his endeavour to get a publisher to print his works, declaring them to be academic publications. Karl-Heinz managed to circumvent the restrictions on printed material and secured sufficient resources for his needs. By October 1944, he was serving in Vienna, but a German pastor came across one of his publications and immediately denounced him to the Gestapo. As a serving member of the German army, Karl-Heinz was informed that on the orders of Heinrich Himmler he was to be court-martialled. He was detained and interrogated, and a charge levelled against him of calling the legitimacy and development of the Nazi judicial system into question.

On 16 January 1945, a military judge ruled that there was no evidence of misuse of the pulpit and high treason, but Himmler immediately responded by withdrawing the case from the Military Courts in Vienna and passing it to a higher court capable of dealing with a German serving officer who was still a member of the Wehrmacht.

1 SA 'Brownshirts' posting notices on Jewish premises. Of note is the young civilian supporting a Nazi armband assisting them. The posters read, 'Germans defend yourselves against Jewish atrocity propaganda. Buy only at German stores. The Jewish owners would eventually be driven out through lack of business by this Nazi persecution policy. (*United States National Archives and Records Administration, College Park, MD*)

2 The Reichstag building destroyed by fire on the 27 February 1933. Adolf Hitler used the incident to implement extraordinary powers in Germany having convinced the German president, Paul von Hindenburg, to declare a state of emergency. (*Bildarchiv Preussischer Kulturbesitz*)

3 The young Dutch Communist Marinus van der Lubbe who was arrested at the scene of the Reichstag fire. He was successfully tried in a high profile court appearance and convicted of setting the fire for which he was sentenced to death. This image of him bearing the extensive restraints clearly illustrates the manner in which he was treated despite suffering from a mental impairment. Three Reichstag proceedings took place. The first judicial phase was a preliminary examination of evidence, with the objective of compiling a dossier to bring formal charges. This phase was under the control of Judge Paul Vogt, a loyal Nazi who ordered the defendants to be held in chains. (*Public domain image issued by a German federal or state authority or court*)

4 Hermann Göring standing defiantly in the examination of evidence against Marinus van der Lubbe. Göring was a witness called to give evidence due to his attendance at the fire scene. To his left behind the judicial bench stands a large plan of the Reichstag building. (*The Bavarian State Library Bayerische Staatsbibliothek, BSB Munich*)

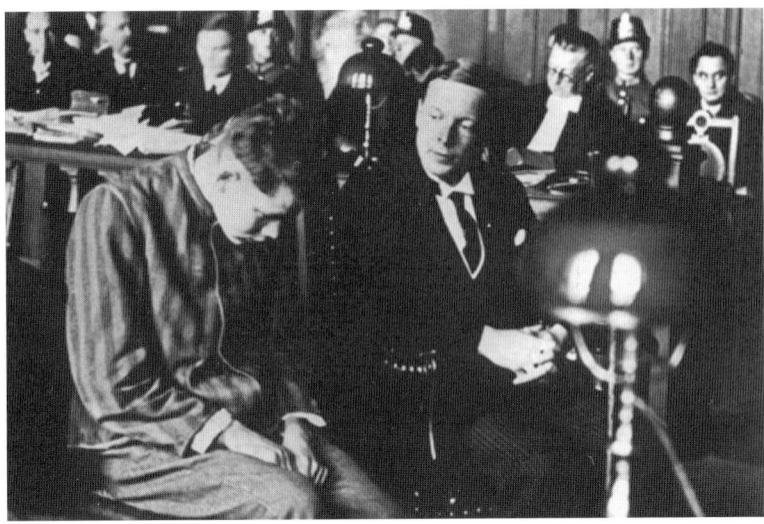

5 The third proceeding on the 21 September 1933, the criminal trial opened in Leipzig. On 10 October the proceedings moved to Berlin in order to observe the Reichstag premises and later returned to Leipzig. Marinus van de Lubbe is shown sitting in the German Supreme Court during his trial, head bowed and apparently overcome by the traumatic experience. His counsel, Dr Seuffert offered comfort towards him having to wipe the drool from his mouth on occasions. There were four other defendants, German and Bulgarian communists who had been acquitted. Presiding Judge Buenger finally pronounced the verdict on the 23 December. (*Public domain image issued by a German federal or state authority or court*)

6 Adolf Hitler was appointed Chancellor of Germany on 30 January 1933. Hitler is seen bowing to the heavily decorated President von Hindenburg on the 21 March 1933. This image was widely published and no doubt purposely managed to illustrate Hitler as a loyal subject in civilian clothing in order to manipulate the public and press. (*Bundesarchiv Bild 183-S38324*)

DAS *Andere* DEUTSCHLAND

FÜR ENTSCHIEDENE REPUBLIKANISCHE POLITIK / KEINER PARTEI DIENSTBAR

Berlin, Sonnabend, den 11. März 1933

Der Polizeipräsident
Landeskriminalpolizeiamt (?)
I³ 35ᵐ 191. 33.

Berlin, den 3. März 1933.

VERBOT.

Auf Grund des § 1 der Verordnung des Reichspräsidenten zum Schutze von Volk und Staat vom 28. 2. 1933 (RGBl. I S. 83) verbiete ich hiermit im Interesse der öffentlichen Sicherheit und Ordnung das Erscheinen der Wochenzeitung

„Das Andere Deutschland"

auf die Dauer von 3 Monaten.

Zuwiderhandlungen werden nach § 4 der Verordnung bestraft.

I. V.
gez.: Diels.

An den Verlag
„Das Andere Deutschland"
Berlin W 57

Für richtige Abschrift:
gez. Dommitzsch
Kanzleiangestellte.

7 *Das Andere Deutschland* [*The Other Germany*] was a weekly pacifist policy newspaper established in Germany in 1925. The newspaper was shut down by the Nazi party on the 11 March 1933, less than two weeks after the Reichstag Fire. (*Public domain document issued by a German federal or state authority or court*)

Above left: 8 Hitler in 1933 standing in company with Ernst Röhm who carried facial scars from injuries received during his service in the First World War. Röhm was head of the infamous SA 'Brownshirts' and his men were used to round up communists after the Reichstag building fire. Hitler would eventually turn against Röhm imprisoning him in the large prison in Stadelheim. The prison was famously associated to Hitler himself when he served a short period of imprisonment occupying cell 70 in 1922. Ernst Röhm died in that same cell in 1934 when he was shot whilst in custody. (*Bundesarchiv Bild 146-1982-159-21A*)

Above right: 9 The Berlin Police. These were the men of the Orpo (Ordnumgspolizei) who were also known as 'Die Blauen'—the Blues. Their shako or Tschako Police helmets were worn during the 1920s and until 1945—a most distinctive piece of uniform. The Prussian shield as worn in this image was replaced by the Nazi national eagle and swastika, a feature immediately identified as being worn by the Police in The People's Court and Special Courts instigated by Hitler. (*Bundesarchiv Bild 183-C00772*)

10 The first Peoples Court in Berlin with the opening speech by the Justice minister in 1934. The German Chancellor Adolf Hitler had been dissatisfied with the outcome of the Reichstag Fire Trial and so he created what were to become viciously offensive courts which sat in session until the end of the Second World War. (*Public domain image issued by a German federal or state authority or court*)

11 The farmer Carl Wentzel is standing before Roland Freisler during his trial. Wentzler's brave defiant face projecting that of a man filled with contempt against the Nazi regime who would order his life to be taken for supporting the plot to kill Hitler. (*Bundesarchiv Bild151-53-30A*)

12 Hitler attends a memorial ceremony for the victims of Georg Elser's unsuccessful assassination attempt on Hitler. Eight other people died in the attempt and a further sixty-three were badly injured. A bomb had exploded in the Burgerbraukeller beer halls on the 8 November 1939 where Hitler had been giving an anniversary speech to the surviving veterans of his failed rebellion in 1923. Hitler's last minute changes in his speech schedule undoubtedly saved his life from a well planned and executed plot. The Dias where Hitler had been standing a few minutes earlier was crushed beneath several feet of roofing timber, bricks and rubble. The failed attempt had been the work of just one man, an unassuming carpenter Georg Elser. Elser was later arrested trying to escape into Switzerland and found with incriminating evidence which connected him to the assassination attempt. Hitler, believing him to be connected to a deeper plot ordered that Elser be indefinably detained for a show trial. However, in 1945 Himmler saw to it that Georg Elser was executed a short time before he would have been liberated by the advancing Allied armies. (*Public domain image issued by a German federal or state authority or court*)

13 The dejected figure of an elderly Ulrich von Hassell, the former German Ambassador to Rome being tried for high treason in The People's Court. *(Bundesarchiv Bild151-22-35)*

14 Roland Freisler and Otto-Georg Thierack shaking hands in 1942 following their respective promotions within the Nazi judiciary. Thierack was promoted from the Presidential position to that of the Reich Minister of Justice and Freisler was appointed into the Presidential position. *(Bundesarchiv Bild 183-J03230)*

Sterbeurkunde

(Standesamt Berlin -Charlottenburg   Nr. 3117/1944

Die Rotekreuzhelferin Elisabeth von T h a d den

– evangelisch,

wohnhaft in Berlin-Charlottenburg, Carmerstraße 12,

ist am 8.September 1944 um 16 Uhr 47 Minuten

in Berlin -Charlottenburg, Königsdamm 7, verstorben.

D ie Verstorbene war geboren am 29.Juli 1890 – – – –

in Mohrungen/Ostpreußen – – – – – – – – – –

(Standesamt – – – – – – – – – Nr. – – – – – –

Vater: Adolf von Thadden – – – – – – – – – –

– –

Mutter: Ehrengard von Thadden, geborene von

Gerlach, beider letzter Wohnort nicht bekannt.

D ie Verstorbene war — nicht — verheiratet . – – – – – –

– – – – – – – – – – – – – – – – – – – –

– – – – – – – – – – – – – – – – – – – –

-Charlottenburg   , den 7.Mai   1948

Der Standesbeamte   Ad

In Vertretung

Ramin

(Siegel)

Todesursache: Enthauptung.

Stand II C 20. Sterbeurkunde
Mat. 2904 ● Din A 5. 150 000. 9. 47 ⊗

15 Post war death certificate for Elisabeth von Thadden evidencing her death at precisely 16.47 hours on the 8 September 1944. (*Public domain image issued by a German federal or state authority or court*)

16 From left to right—General Hermann Reinecke a Nazi officer charged with political propaganda in the Wehrmacht alongside the Presiding Judge Roland Freisler, and The People's Court Judge Lammele who acted as associate judge sitting on the trials of those who plotted to assassinate Hitler. The Nazi leadership used the failed coup as an opportunity to eliminate other enemies through arbitrary arrests which led to pre judged trials and executions. These Gestapo investigations continued until the end of the war. An estimated 1,500 persons were arrested and 200 executed during a Nazi frenzy of offensive deployment against those that were assumed to be involved. (*DIZ Muenchen GmbH, Sueddeutscher Verlag Bilderdienst and Bundesarchiv Bild 183/64425/001*)

17 Hitler addressing the Reichstag on the 11 Dec 1941 during which his lengthy rhetoric speech engaged some 12,000 words declaring war against the United States of America. The original Reichstag building was unusable after the Reichstag fire and so the Kroll Opera House was modified into a legislative chamber. (*Bundesarchiv Bild 183-2004-1001-501*)

18 Manfred Roeder, the Nazi Judge and Prosecutor against the 'Red Orchestra' Resistance Group photographed in the Nuremburg War Crime trials where he was deployed as a prosecution witness. (*US Army Public Relations image OMT-111-W-72*)

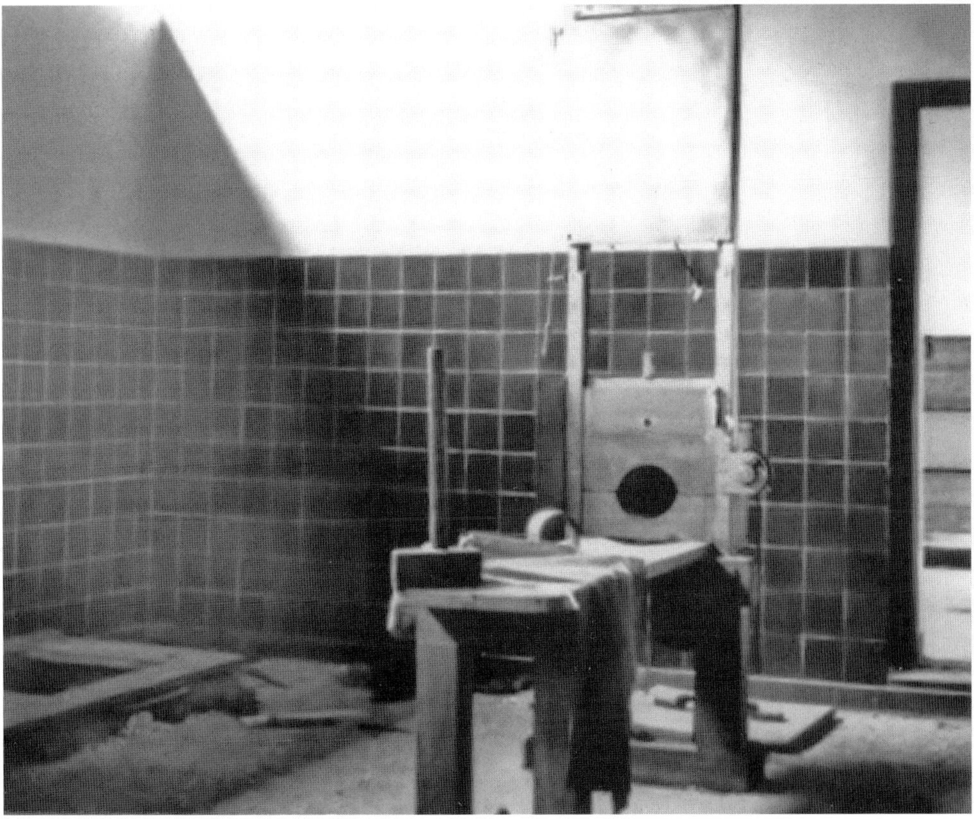

19 The Tegel Fallbeil in Poznan execution chamber where the high tiled walls can be clearly seen. Various items are strewn about the room which had been left in disarray prior to the prison being liberated by the Russians. (*Image presumed to have originated by the Soviet forces*)

20 The Katowice Fallbeil, an image taken by the Polish historian and Staff member of the Auschwitz-Birkenau State Museum, Adam Cyra where the device accompanies many other exhibits, evidence of the persecutions imposed on humanity by the Nazis. (*Adam Cyra*)

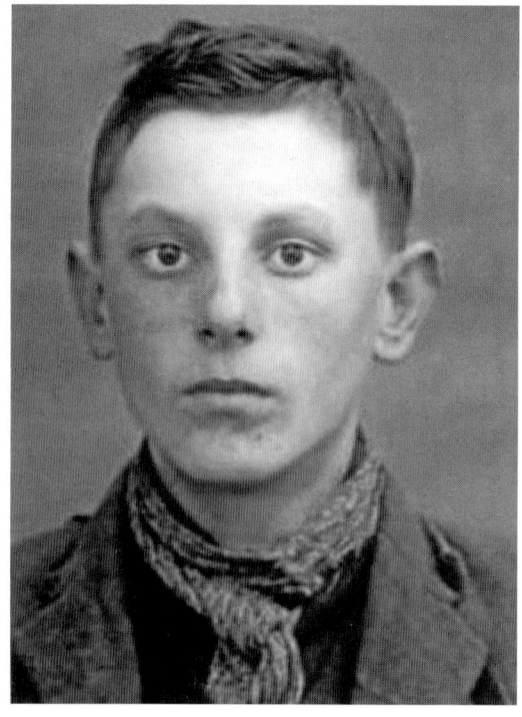

21 Walerjan Wrobel was forced to undertake work on a farm against his will. At just sixteen years of age, he sought to be returned to his home by setting a small fire at the farm. Instead he was tried for arson and beheaded by the Nazi judiciary who had convicted and sentenced him. (*www.holocaust-mahnmal.de/ jugendwebsite/p_walerjan/index.htm*)

Beglaubigte Abschrift.
==========================

In der Strafsache gegen den vom Sondergericht in
Bremen am 8. Juli 1942 als Volksschädling wegen
Brandstiftung zum Tode verurteilten

Walerjan W r o b e l

habe ich mit Ermächtigung des Führers beschlossen,
von dem Begnadigungsrecht keinen Gebrauch zu machen,
sondern der Gerechtigkeit freien Lauf zu lassen.

Berlin, den   15. August 1942

Der Reichsminister der Justiz

In Vertretung

(Siegel)   gez. Dr. Freisler
                    ————

Mit der Urschrift gleichlautend:
Berlin, den 17.August 1942

als Ministerialkanzleiobersekretär.

22 The certified copy document signed by Roland Freisler rejecting a reprieve of sentence for Walerjan Wrobel and authorising the original death sentence to be carried out forthwith. (*Public domain image issued by a German federal or state authority or court*)

Am 29. Juni 1944 sind die durch das Sondergericht in Prag zum Tode verurteilten:	Dne 29. června 1944 byli popraveni:
Franz Blažek aus Birkicht, geboren am 14 März 1899.	František Blažek z Březiné, narozeny 14. března 1899.
Marie Blažek geb. Toman aus Birkicht, geb. am 8. August 1907,	Marie Blažková, roz. Tomanová z Březiné, narozená 8. srpna 1907,
Agnes Vácha geb. Koblic aus Chejnow, geb. am 9. Jänner 1904.	Anežka Váchová, roz. Koblicová, z Chejnova, narozená 9. ledna 1904.
Franz Koblic aus Bradatschow, geboren am 1. Oktober 1896,	František Koblic z Bradáčova, naroz. 1. října 1896,
Henriette Hermuth aus Prag, geboren am 25. Juni 1902, und	Jindřiška Hermuthová z Prahy, naroz. 25. června 1902, a
Anton Lank aus Prag, geb. am 14. April 1904, hingerichtet worden.	Antonín Lank z Prahy, naroz. 14. dubna 1904, jež odsoudil Sondergericht in Prag k smrti.
Die Verurteilten haben einen staatspolizeilich gesuchten Reichsfeind trotz Kenntnis dieses Umstandes längere Zeit beherbergt und ihm sonstige Hilfe geleistet.	Odsouzení poskytli státní policii hledanému nepříteli Říše přes znalost této okolnosti po delší dobu přístřeší a byli mu i jinak nápomocni.

Der Oberstaatsanwalt
bei dem Deutschen Landgericht in Prag.

23 The execution notice printed on red paper publicising six Czechoslovaks sentenced to death for supporting the enemies of the Reich simply by providing them shelter. (*Public domain image issued by a German federal or state authority or court*)

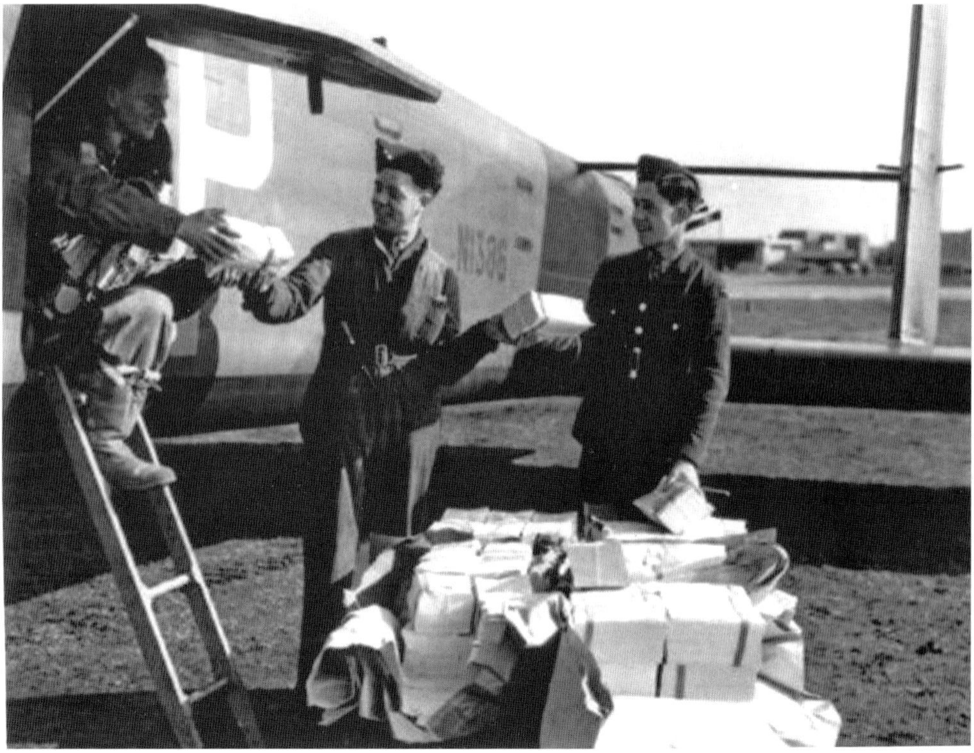

24 RAF ground crew passing bundles of propaganda to the flight crew of the Whitley aircraft who are about to embark on a night raid into Germany in April 1940 where they will drop the printed propaganda over their targets. (*Author's collection*)

LUFTPOST

Von der Royal Air Force abgeworfen

Nr. 20

30. September 1941

Verboten überall, wo die Wahrheit verboten ist

Die SS ergreift die Macht

Himmlers Henker am Werk

DER CHEF: *Himmler*

FRANKREICH: *Stülpnagel*

NORWEGEN: *Rediesz*

CSR: *Heydrich*

POLEN: *Frank*

HOLLAND: *Rauter*

DER Herrenklub-Neurath ist hinausgeflogen. Heydrich, der Mann des 30. Juni, ist sein Nachfolger im Hradschin in Prag.

Das ist mehr als ein Henkerswechsel. Es bedeutet:

1. Einen neuen Sieg für Himmler in seinem Kampf um die unbeschränkte Herrschaft der SS über Deutschland und Europa.

2. Das Eingeständnis der Armeeführer, dass die Verwaltung der besetzten Gebiete durch die vorgeschobenen Quislinge zusammengebrochen ist.

Die deutschen Generale wissen aus der Erfahrung des letzten Kriegs, wie gefährlich es ist, die feindliche Zivilbevölkerung mit militärischem Terror zu bekämpfen.

Aber überall im besetzten Gebiet, von Oslo bis Paris und Prag, haben die Himmlerleute die Verhängung des Standrechts und die Errichtung ihrer Willkürherrschaft erzwungen. Zum ersten Mal in Westeuropa ist durch sie die Erschiessung unschuldiger Geiseln als Verwaltungsmassnahme eingeführt worden.

In Norwegen versucht SS-Gruppenführer Rediesz, der Generaloberst von Fritzsch umlegen liess, durch Massenverhaftungen und Hinrichtungen den Widerstand der Bevölkerung zu brechen. Der Hinrichtung Hansteens und Wickstroems folgten Unruhen in ganz Norwegen.

In Paris hat General von Stülpnagel 59 Hinrichtungen angeordnet. 28 waren Geiseln.

In Holland hat SS-Gruppenführer Rauter seit Anfang September 6 Personen erschiessen lassen. Weitere Sabotageakte und Unruhen in Utrecht, Leyden, Wouw und Groningen waren die Folge.

In Brüssel hat General von Falkenhausen 48 Belgier an die Wand gestellt; 25 davon waren wahllos aufgegriffene Geiseln.

Aber der Terror der SS und der Armee ist in Frankreich und Belgien so wirkungslos geblieben wie in der Tschechoslowakei und in Jugoslavien. Die Produktion der für die deutsche Kriegsmaschine ... den Fabriken geht zurück. Französische Hafenarbeiter haben die ... von U-Booten zugeschweisst.

Serbische und kroatische Freischärlerbanden machen die neue Todstrasse am Balkan zu einer Strasse des Todes.

Neurath vom Herrenklub ist hinausgeflogen. Heydrich von der Prinz Albrechtstrasse wird nicht erfolgreicher sein.

28 Tage deutscher Herrschaft

WAS SICH ZWISCHEN 1. UND 28. SEPTEMBER 1941 IN DEN BESETZTEN LÄNDERN EREIGNETE

(Nach amtlichen Berichten der deutschen Behörden oder der unter deutscher Leitung stehenden Zeitungen und Rundfunksender)

	HINRICHTUNGEN *durch deutsche Behörden vom 1. — 28. IX. ausgeführt:*	SABOTAGEAKTE *vom 1. — 28. IX.*	UNRUHEN UND STREIKS *vom 1. — 28. IX.*
BELGIEN	48 Personen hingerichtet, einschl. 25 Geiseln.	gegen Eisenbahnen ... 2 gegen Rüstungsbetriebe ... 2	Unruhen in Gent, Brüssel, Dixmuiden, Lüttich.
FRANKREICH	59 hingerichtet, einschl. 28 Geiseln; 12.000 Geiseln verhaftet.	gegen Eisenbahnen ca 90 gegen Rüstungsbetriebe ... 5 Brände ... ... ca 20	Unruhen in Paris, Toulouse, Lille, La Rochelle, Somain, Nice, Besançon, St. Cloud, Nancy, Marseille.
GRIECHENLAND ...	12 Hinrichtungen	gegen Eisenbahnen ... 1 gegen Schiffe der Achsenstaaten 2	Generalstreik in Saloniki, Unruhen in Eleusis.
JUGOSLAWIEN ...	126 Hinrichtungen ...	gegen Eisenbahnen ... 7 gegen Rüstungsbetriebe ... 3	Kämpfe in Bosnien, Herzegowina, Kroatien, im Bezirk von Doboj, in Agram und Kralje.
NIEDERLANDE ...	6 Hinrichtungen	nicht näher bezeichnete Sabotageakte 3	Unruhen in Leyden, Wouw, Utrecht, Groningen.
NORWEGEN	Hansteen und Wickstrøm, Gewerkschaftsführer, hingerichtet.	gegen Eisenbahnen ... 1 gegen Schiffe der Achsenstaaten ... ... 7 gegen Rüstungsbetriebe ... 3	Unruhen in Borge, Rolsvey, Trondheim, Kingsvinger, Lillehammer, Gjovik, Stokke, Oslo, Fredrickstad, Egersund, Haugesund.
POLEN	39 Hinrichtungen ...	gegen Eisenbahnen ... 3 Brände 1	Kämpfe um Warschau und überall in den Bergen.
TSCHECHOSLOVAKEI	27 Hinrichtungen	gegen Truppenzüge ... 5 gegen Rüstungsbetriebe ... 2	Streiks in Königgrätz, Prag, Eipel, Politz an der Mettau.

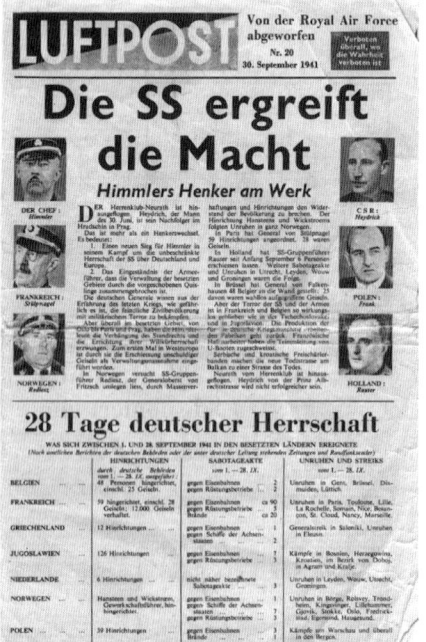

25 An important Luftpost propaganda folded leaflet which was distributed by the RAF across areas of Germany in October 1941. The document advises of the German SS terror which had inflicted executions all across the occupied territories. The readers were provided with the truth about the SS leadership and frightening statistics. (*Author's collection*)

Above left: 26 An early Portrait image of Father Max Joseph Metzger who founded The Una Sancta Brotherhood in 1938, bringing Protestant and Catholics together for theological discussion and prayer. (*An image likely to have originated from the Church* c. *1916*)

Above right: 27 Portrait image of Irena Bobowska. (*Institute Pamieci Narodowej*)

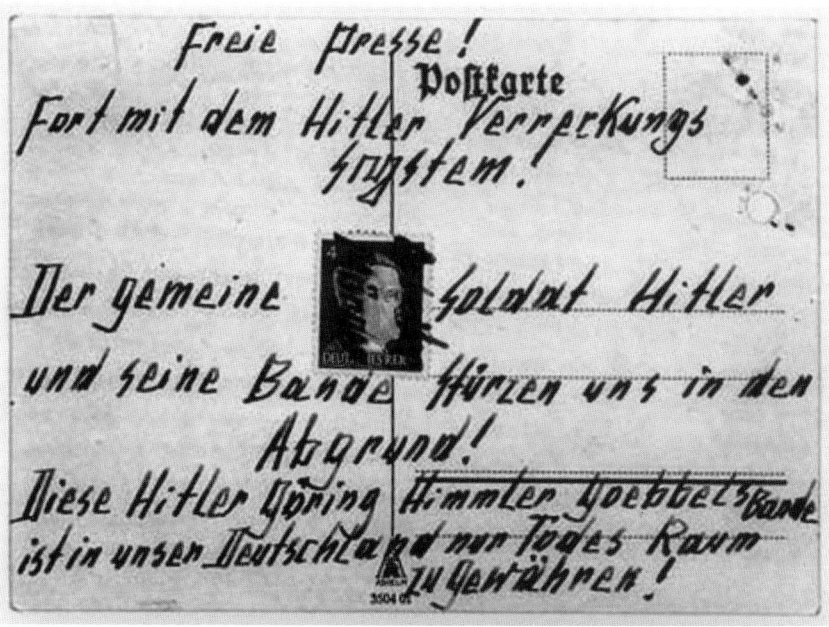

28 One of the many postcards used as evidence and presented to The People's Court during Otto and Elise's trial. The heading on the postcard translates to—Free Press! away with the Hitler dying a wretched death system! The centre of the postcard is a postage stamp bearing Hitler's face, scrawled with the words—worker murderer. (*Public domain image originated from primary evidence utilized by The People's Court*)

29 Otto and Elise Hampel Police portrait images taken after their arrest in 1942. (*Police and People's Court identification photographs*)

30 Portrait of Helen Kafka, Sister Resoluta. (*An image likely to have originated from the Church c. 1920*)

31 Elisabeth Gloeden appearing before Roland Friesler where she admitted knowing the identity of the person being harboured by her husband on the 27 November 1944. Elisabeth and her mother chose to go to the Fallbeil together as a family. Charged and found guilty of treason against Germany, on the 30 November 1944 the Gloeden family were all decapitated at Plotzensee. (*Library of Congress collection: Trials of the men and women involved in the attempt on Adolf Hitler's life in July, 1944*)

32 The Reichstag building shortly after the war. The majority of the bronze lettering cast in Loevy's foundry remains despite the onslaught of Russian munitions that struck the building during the final assault against the fanatical Nazis that defended it. (*Postcard image by Verlag Rudolf, Pracht, Berlin*)

DAS Sowjet-Paradies

AUSSTELLUNG
LUSTGARTEN
VOM 9 MAI BIS 21 JUNI 1942 · TÄGLICH GEÖFFNET VON 9 BIS 21 Uhr

33 Nazi poster advertising the 'Soviet Paradise Exhibition' in Berlin. Organized by the Nazi Party's propaganda office, it was to show the German public the evidence that everyday life under Bolshevism was one of great misery. The propaganda stated to the German people that it was the Jews who were behind the Soviet industrial structure that supplied the arms to fight the war.

34 Wolfenbuettel Fallbeil bolted to the floor in the execution room. This image presumed to have been taken by the Allied forces after the venue was liberated in 1945.

35 RAF Short Stirling displaying the code letters LS allocated to 15 Squadron. This aircraft type was consistently used within the special duties work of the RAF to drop agents into occupied Europe. The Stirling bomber was also the type of aircraft deployed in dropping propaganda across Germany during the early years of conflict. The Stirling was the first four engined bomber which preceded the famous Lancaster that eventually destroyed the might of the German Industrial war factories in the Ruhr. (*Author's collection*)

36 Hans Scholl (left) Sophie Scholl and Christoph Probst, leaders of the White Rose resistance organization together in Munich, Germany. (*United States Holocaust Memorial Museum*)

37 Poznan execution chamber with high tiled walls in what appears to be a small room. This image was taken at the point of liberation in 1945 by Soviet troops, three of which are seen examining the Fallbeil. It appears that the blade is in the shielded upper section of the device and the person on the left is holding the release mechanism. (*Image presumed to have originated by the Soviet forces*)

38 Adolf Hitler narrowly escaped death after a bomb exploded at his command Headquarters in Rastenberg, East Prussia. The image shows Göring surveying the damage. Little doubt exists that had the meeting been held within one of the secure concrete bunkers of Hitler's Headquarters, the explosives planted by Stauffenberg would have most probably killed all of the people present. The blast would have been consolidated and contained whereas in the actual meeting room which was a temporary building, the blast simply forced itself through the flimsy construction. (*Bundesarchiv Bild 146-1972-025-10*)

39 Members of the Kreisau Circle on trial, each defendant being guarded in what appears to be a small court room. Note the shako or Tschako, distinctive helmets of the German Police worn during the 1920s and until 1945. (*Library of Congress collection: Trials of the men and women involved in the attempt on Adolf Hitler's life in July, 1944*)

Above left: 40 Plotzensee Prison—The main entrance which greeted the inmates. The architecture, in particular the window design is replicated in the execution room illustrations. (*Yivo Institute for Jewish research library*)

Above right: 41 The Plotzensee execution room seen from the external viewpoint. The windows immediately identify this perspective to be the rear wall. (*Yivo Institute for Jewish research library*)

42 The Plotzensee execution room viewed from the rear looking towards the entrance door and windows. The Fallbeil with its blade poised stands in the litter strewn room. This image is most likely from the military forces that liberated the prison. Tattered remnants of curtain can still be seen on the rail. The metal door in the wall leads to the anti-room where the corpses would be removed to after the executions. (*Image presumed to have originated from Allied liberation forces via Landesarchiv Berlin*)

43 Roland Freisler sitting in judgement and gesticulating to the court before announcing an inevitable death sentence on an alleged plotter who stands hands clasped and mute before him. The large bust of Hitler was always in the gaze of Freisler atop the ornately robed feature in The People's Court. (*Library of Congress collection: Trials of the men and women involved in the attempt on Adolf Hitler's life in July, 1944*)

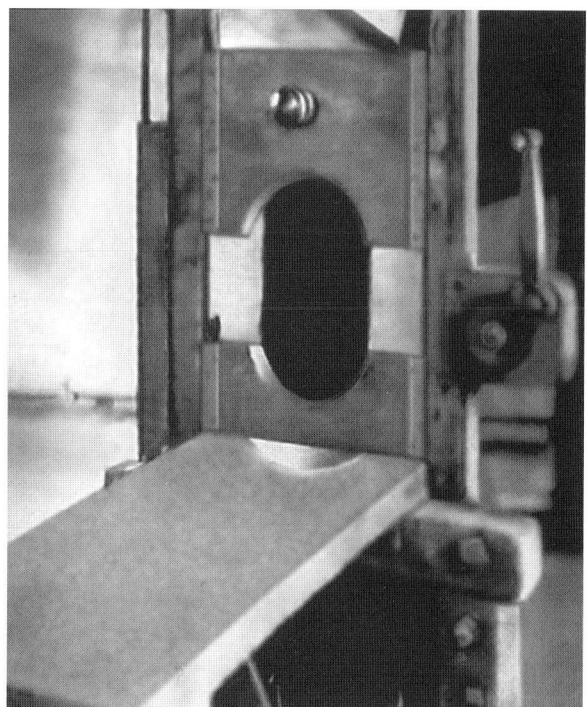

44 The Plotzensee execution room restored as a monument of respect to the many men and women who died in that building. The hanging hooks were installed in 1942 at the request of Otto Thierack, the then newly appointed Reich Minister of Justice and remain as a chilling reminder of that room's purpose. (*Author's collection*)

45 The Brandenburg-Gorden Prison Fallbeil, a stout wooden construction is evident in this image which is presumed to have originated at the close of war. The winching device on the right appears to have had the handle removed to prevent its operation and the tip of the blade appears at the top of the image. (*The* Observer *Newspaper Office of Military Government for Germany, Berlin*)

46 The Wolfenbuettel Prison Fallbeil was initially used in the courtyard where it proliferated in several hundred executions.

47 The Allies liberated Wolfenbuettel on the 11 April 1945 and preserved the Fallbeil. They also secured a significant amount of documentation that evidenced the Fallbeil's use during the war years. The machine had been used within the execution chamber building upon which was adorned an unusual clock tower. Post war the Fallbeil was subsequently maintained by the Allies as a functioning device. The Fallbeil blade can be clearly seen illustrating the size and weight of which was required to humanely sever the head. The bevelled leading edge of the blade was always fitted facing away from the intended victim and this forced the head away from the body and into the receptacle placed to accommodate it after the blade had fallen.

48 Dr Hermann Stieve. From 1938 onwards, he became one of the most prolific anatomists in Europe, simply because he had an abundance of corpses available.

49 Roland Freisler holding court in his robes supporting the Third Reich eagle. (*Bundesarchiv Bild 151-17-15*)

50 Preparing the Palace of Justice primary Courtroom in Nuremburg in November 1945. This view from the public or media gallery discloses the extensive preparations with lighting and seating arrangements. You can see the dock for the prisoners on the left with the elevated Judge's bench on the right. Because of the translation requirements, the court was fitted with a complex translation service which meant that the trial could not proceed any faster than sixty words per minute. The witnesses would respond to a flashing yellow light to notify that he was speaking too quickly, or a red light indicating that he should stop and repeat what he had just said. It proved to cater exceptionally well for the multi-language complexities at Nuremburg. (*Press agency photograph wired to the USA*)

51 Two Nuremburg defendants Hans Frank on the left and Alfred Rosenberg. Following Hitler becoming Chancellor in 1933, he appointed Frank as Minister of Justice in Bavaria and at the outbreak of the Second World War, Frank was appointed as Governor General of Poland. A German lawyer and prominent Nazi, Frank oversaw the segregation of the Jews into ghettos in the larger cities and the use of Polish civilians as forced labour in German war industries. He was arrested by the Allies in 1945 and tried at Nuremburg accused of crimes against humanity. In court when asked to reply to the accusations which had been brought against him in the indictment he replied: To these accusations I can only say that I ask the Tribunal to decide upon the degree of my guilt at the end of my case. I myself, speaking from the very depths of my feelings and having lived through the five months of this trial, want to say that now after I have gained a full insight into all the horrible atrocities which have been committed, I am possessed by a deep sense of guilt. He was found guilty and executed on the 1 October 1946. Alfred Rosenberg was a radical Nazi, in January 1934 who had been appointed as the Nazi Party's chief racial theorist. He had vehemently voiced his opinion on proving Aryan superiority and that the Germans were the 'Master Race'. He was found guilty of crimes against humanity and executed on the 16 October 1946 by hanging. (*Press agency photograph wired to the USA*)

52 Nuremburg prison viewed from the Palace of Justice. The covered walkway was built to facilitate the daily movement of prisoners to the various courts which were in session. This was the closest sector of the prison from which all of the prisoners were escorted on a daily basis. (*Press agency photograph wired to the USA*)

53 Adolf Hitler decreed on 7 March 1936 that the national emblem of the Reich would show the swastika, surrounded by an oak wreath, on the oak wreath an eagle with spread wings.

54 The courtroom in the Hall of Justice at Leipzig. The bench with the presiding judge is in the background and in the foreground a significantly large number of individuals permitted to report and witness the proceedings against theose accused for the Reichstag fire. (*Associated press 29-9-33*)

Karl-Heinz's case would inevitably have been presented to the People's Court in Vienna had it been possible, but the advancing Allies ultimately prevented any further court procedures. Without doubt, the closing stages of the war created disruption that resulted in communication failures between the various authorities—circumstances that were to save his life. As a serving member of the Wehrmacht he was secured and imprisoned by the liberating American forces but eventually released, whereupon he returned to his pastoral duties. Karl-Heinz died in 1968, three years after having retired.

The Russian *Untermenschen*

During the Second World War, the Soviet Union purposely excluded its fighting forces from the protection of the Geneva Convention. As a result, Russian prisoners were subjected to barbaric and brutal treatment by the Third Reich. The death toll in captivity for Russian prisoners during the war has been estimated to be over three million, representing a mortality rate of just over 50 per cent. The Reich labelled all Russians as *Untermenschen*, this term being used repeatedly in writings and speeches directed against Russians, Jews and other racial groups whom the Nazis regarded as inferior. Regulations were issued to all German prison camp commandants during 1941 in respect of the treatment of Soviet prisoners of war, the order being signed by Gen. Hermann Reinecke, chief of the division of German High Command responsible for, amongst other duties, the supervision of prisoner-of-war matters. These orders stated:

> The Bolshevist soldier has therefore lost all claims to treatment as an honourable opponent, in accordance with the Geneva Convention ... The order for ruthless and energetic action must be given at the slightest indication of insubordination, especially in the case of Bolshevist fanatics. Insubordination, active or passive resistance, must be broken immediately by force of arms (bayonets, butts and firearms) ... Anyone carrying out the order who does not use his weapons, or does so with insufficient energy, is punishable ... Prisoners of war attempting escape are to be fired on without previous challenge. No warning shot must ever be fired ... The use of arms against prisoners of war is as a rule legal.

In September 1941, one Russian prisoner, Fyodor Azarov, managed to escape from captivity and during his escape he ventured into the village of Borki, in Konin, central Poland. Josef Augustyniak, his wife Veronika and their nine-year-old daughter were farmers who helped the Russian escapee by providing him with shelter and as much food as possible from their meagre provisions, despite being fully aware of the risks associated with providing such assistance. On 25 November 1941, Fyodor was arrested near the farm. The Augustyniak family had been betrayed, and Josef was arrested alongside several other local Polish citizens. Two months later, Veronika was also arrested, and they were both charged with 'jointly ... during the war against the Reich, aiding and abetting the enemy power and placing the armed might of the Reich at a disadvantage'.

On 28 May 1942, the People's Court sentenced them both to death. An appeal for clemency based on their daughter was rejected by Roland Freisler, who requested that the executions be undertaken with all possible speed. On 15 August, Josef and Veronika Augustyniak were beheaded in the execution room at Plötzensee Prison. The decapitated remains of 42-year-old Veronika were taken directly to the Berlin Institute of Anatomy where her reproductive organs were removed for dissection.

Zygmunt Kucharczyk

At the beginning of the Second World War, almost a quarter of the pre-war Polish territorial areas had been annexed by Nazi Germany and placed directly under German civil administration. Zichenau, now known as Ciechanów, was part of a district incorporated into East Prussia by Hitler's decree of 26 October 1939. The German army had entered the area of Zichenau on 3 September, and in October began destroying Jewish properties, including synagogues that were destroyed on 10 November. The Zichenau Special Court soon developed a reputation for issuing harsh anti-Polish and anti-Jewish sentences, the execution lists of the Ministry of Justice recording that per head of population it was disproportionately and prolifically active. In the annexed eastern territories in 1942 alone, 1,129 death sentences inflicted on the Poles and Jews were registered.

Judge Breustedt of the Zichenau Special Court heard a case against Zygmunt Kucharczyk on 25 January 1943. Document No. KL 32/43 confirms that Zygmunt, a 32-year-old Polish farmer, had previously had an altercation with a German police officer named Wronna on 3 November 1942, during which an impertinent answer offered by the farmer resulted in him receiving a box round the ears. This clearly resulted in a physical exchange between the two men and, seven days later, when the police officer returned to the farm with two colleagues, Zygmunt allegedly offered some form of resistance in what are unknown circumstances. The incident resulted in his arrest, and despite there being no independent witnesses, he was imprisoned for three months. Breustedt subsequently heard the prosecution case against the Polish farmer, and summarised with the following findings:

> He has committed acts of violence against the German Police in that on the first occasion ... he took up a threatening attitude towards the gendarme Wronna and on the second occasion ... offered resistance to the officers ... Through his remarks and in his whole attitude he also damaged the honour of the German Reich. The sentence could only be the death sentence ... A Pole who behaves in such a way to German officials has thrown away his life.

Zygmunt remained in custody until 22 March 1943, when the death sentence was duly carried out in the prison situated in the large port of Königsberg, the furthermost of Hitler's nominated execution facilities. In 1941, in retaliation for the German bombing of Moscow, Joseph Stalin had personally ordered the Soviet air force to bomb Königsberg, which was Germany's easternmost city. In 1945, Königsberg suffered extensively and much of the city was destroyed during the Russian occupation. The Allied agreement concerning the passing of Königsberg and the eastern part of Prussia to the Soviet Union was signed on 2 August 1945 in Potsdam. It was then rebuilt as the Russian city of Kaliningrad.

Breustedt sentenced other Polish subjects just as harshly, including a young servant girl named Rosalie Kulesa. Rosalie was executed simply for protecting herself from blows inflicted by her German mistress, who had struck her about the face with a handbag. The judge survived the war and surprisingly became one of the many men from the Nazi judiciary who sat in the post-war court system, becoming a prosecutor in Giessen, approximately 50 km north of Frankfurt. Breustedt was one of 181 former Nazi public prosecutors employed by the West German government, men who were supposed to have been removed from public office as provided for within the immediate post-war international agreement over the new judiciary.

Ignatz Kazmierczak

The prosecution of the Polish citizen Ignatz Kazmierczak in January 1942 is deserving of recognition as it provides a graphic example of the judicial persecution of his race and the fragility of evidence accepted in Hitler's courts. Ignatz was born on 3 December 1912 in Głuchów, a small town in what is now central Poland. The circumstances of his employment are not known, but in 1942, during the German occupation of his country, he had cause to be engaged in what appears to have been a minor confrontation with German police officers who were accompanied by a dog. Ignatz was arrested and eventually presented before Judge Kowalski, his case being prosecuted by Walter Curth of the Special Court in the area of Inowrocław, which was administered under the military district of Poznań.

The criminal offence laid against Ignatz was that of 'wilfully damaging official property by allegedly wounding the dog of a German policeman behind the ear'. Curth had advocated that the death penalty be imposed for this offence, and Kowalski announced the verdict of guilty, adding:

> The witnesses did not themselves see who wounded the dog, but the dog itself immediately recognised the accused as his enemy… and the accused is quite capable of the offence if one takes his past life into account.

The death sentence was in all probability carried out in Poznań Prison. The court document No. SD 4 KLs 339/41 fails to provide any additional evidence against

Ignatz. Effectively, the defendant was beheaded on the reaction of a dog, and this evidence was acceptable to the Nazi courts administered by the German Ministry of Justice within the occupied territories.

Walter Curth subsequently prosecuted and called for the death penalty against other Polish subjects. In July 1942, Jan Paradowski, a 42-year-old forestry worker, stood in the Special Court sitting in the district of Włocławek. Jan was amongst the many thousands of Polish men forced to work for the Nazis, in his case providing the might of Germany with the endless supply of wood needed for the industry of war. Forestry workers were controlled and guarded by 'Land Guards' and Jan reacted in defence to unwarranted physical blows inflicted upon him by a guard, for which he was later to appear before the Special Court. The court accepted Curth's application for the death sentence and Jan was executed at Poznań Prison on 14 July 1942. The following report is an extract of his execution witnessed by Curth:

> At this point the executioner's assistants took the place of the prison officials. The curtain before the execution room was drawn aside. The condemned man was then, after his shoulders had been bared, led to the execution block behind the executioner and laid on the block. The head of the condemned man was separated by the guillotine from the body. The executioner then reported the completion of the sentence. The condemned man remained calm during the execution proceedings. The corpse of the condemned man was laid in a coffin which stood ready in the neighbouring post mortem room and then handed over to a representative of the Secret State Police in Poznań. The execution covered the following period of time.
>
> From presentation until the handing over to the executioner 15 seconds.
>
> From the handing over to the executioner to the execution of the sentence 5 seconds.
>
> The execution proceedings were completed at 18.19 hours.

Public Prosecutor Curth appears to have been ruthless in his application for the death sentence whilst serving in the German Special Courts and yet impunity appears to have been laid upon his actions. Post-war, Curth served in the West German judicial structure, recorded in documents as a Counsellor of Justice/Prosecutor in Mannheim. The German-enacted Law for Liberation from National Socialism and Militarism in March 1946 put in place procedures whereby quasi-judicial party members' activities were subjected to denazification. The problem, however, was significant as evidenced by a survey in August 1945 undertaken in Bamberg. This revealed that out of 302 judges and court officials, only seven had not been members of the Nazi Party. In addition, more than 1,500 individuals tentatively accepted for employment in the immediate post-war German courts had been dismissed during the denazification procedures.

Erich Gloeden

Born in Berlin in 1888, Erich was the second son of the renowned Berlin foundry owner Siegfried Loevy, responsible for casting many impressive features that adorned several state buildings across Germany. The large bronze dedication above the Reichstag 'Dem Deutschen Volke' (To the German People) was cast in his Jewish family business of S. A. Loevy, each letter being individually cast to adorn the stonework above the main entrance. The building was constructed for the German parliament and therefore the architect, Paul Wallot, considered the German people as his employer. The inscription was originally proposed in 1894, but controversy over the matter existed for more than twenty years until 1916, when the Loevy foundry finally cast the letters from battlefield bounty, most probably cannons and cannonballs, taken in the war with Napoleon in 1813.

The Loevy family were Jewish and that would inevitably lead to the demise of their profitable foundry, the deportation of family members, and for Erich, the changing of his surname to Gloeden, being baptized with his new name at the age of 30. Having studied and qualified in architecture, Erich married Elisabeth Kuznitzky, a qualified lawyer who was fifteen years younger than him, and settled in Berlin, the couple celebrating the birth of their daughter within a year of the marriage. Elisabeth and Erich were jointly opposed to the Nazi movement, and after the outbreak of war he was drafted to serve in the Todt Organisation, a German construction firm founded by Dr Fritz Todt. With Hitler's support it grew into a military-based organisation that became extremely efficient at construction projects associated with the war. A basic uniform was worn by Todt staff, and the company subsequently employed significant numbers of forced labour from across those countries occupied by the Nazis. Erich's duties in the occupied lands allowed him to witness the persecution of Jews and other minority groups, which deepened his dislike for the Nazis even further.

Erich and his wife agreed to offer help where they could to Jewish people in need of shelter from persecution. The couple lived in an apartment with Erich's mother-in-law at 23 Chestnut Avenue, Charlottenburg, Berlin. Within a very close network of friends they became known for their charity and providing temporary accommodation for people in desperate need. Hans Ludwig Sierks, a fellow architect and internationally recognised city planner, was a friend of Erich's. In 1933, the Nazi Party banned one of his books and his protests led him to be imprisoned for a short period of time. Although Hans was connected with the Communist movement, he joined a resistance group identified as the Free German Movement. In July 1944, Erich and his family became aware of the assassination plot against Hitler, the true facts of which were being twisted to suit propaganda created by the Nazi Party in order to illustrate the Führer's ability to survive against the odds. In addition to the significant amount of arrests being made of anyone remotely suspected of any connection with the plot, the Nazi Party offered a large financial bounty for the capture of identified resistance operatives complicit in the attack. Five days after the failed assassination attempt, Hans asked Erich and his wife to shelter Gen. Fritz Lindemann, who was fleeing from the Gestapo.

Fritz Lindemann was a high-ranking German officer who had served in the Great War. During the Second World War he had witnessed German atrocities in Poland, France and the Soviet Union, experiencing enough to convince him that Germany's fate rested with the removal of Hitler, so he had collaborated and engaged in the planning of the July plot to kill the Führer. Gen. Helmuth Stieff, a confidant of Lindemann, had been immediately arrested by the Gestapo on the night of the failed plot and brutally tortured. Stieff held out for several days against all attempts to extract the names of fellow conspirators, which would have included Lindemann. High Command had by this time technically removed Stieff from military service, allowing him to be tried by the People's Court, which sentenced him to death on 8 August 1944. He was executed that same day in Plötzensee Prison.

Lindemann had managed to evade the Gestapo and initially hide with relatives in Dresden prior to being given shelter in Berlin by Erich and Elisabeth. In all probability they had no idea that the man they were sheltering had a bounty of half a million Reichsmarks on his head, as he had been introduced under a false name to them. However, that may well have changed during the several weeks in which he was with them. Erich provided him with full access to their apartment. The Germans had officially discharged Lindemann from the army, and whilst he was in hiding with Erich the Gestapo increased the intensity of their investigations in an effort to find him. Had the plot been successful, Lindemann would have been the person nominated to broadcast the facts of the attack to the German people and act as the official spokesperson for the new government.

Lindemann and the Gloeden family were eventually betrayed, which resulted in the Gestapo bursting into Erich's apartment on 20 August 1944. During the arrest, Lindemann was shot in the stomach and the upper leg as he tried to flee, and Erich was beaten about the face. On 22 September, whilst still under guard in hospital, Lindemann died of his wounds. The Gestapo tortured and interrogated all the suspects captured at the apartment, believing them to have been part of the July plot.

Erich, his wife and his mother-in-law were jointly committed to the Berlin People's Court on 27 November, charged with treason against Germany. Roland Freisler was the presiding judge, hearing a string of cases in which individuals were charged with treason and assumed to be associated with the July plot against Hitler. Many of these trials were filmed and widely reported across Germany. Recognising the severity of the position in which they found themselves, Erich sought an opportunity to tell the court what he had done but to assert that his wife and mother-in-law were unaware of the identity of Fritz Lindemann and should therefore be acquitted. Freisler, however, dismissed his plea and found all three guilty, ruling that both females were to be sentenced to long periods of imprisonment, whilst Erich was to be executed. Elisabeth bravely spoke up, declaring that she did know the identity of the German officer, which was immediately followed by her mother making the same declaration.

Freisler then also sentenced the two women to death, and just three days later, on 30 November 1944, Elisabeth Gloeden was executed in Plötzensee Prison at 11.02 hours, followed by her husband at 11.04 hours and her elderly mother, who was laid upon the Fallbeil just two minutes later.

Today outside the property where Erich's family had provided protection to so many people from the persecution of the Nazis are three small bronze plaques known as 'stumbling blocks', so called because pedestrians are likely to stumble unintentionally across them. They bear the names of Erich Gloeden, born Erich Loevy, his wife and mother-in-law, each plaque being engraved with their dates of birth and death. The plaques are privately funded and several thousands are now in place across many locations in Germany. It is indeed ironic that it was a Jewish-owned family company that produced the symbolic lettering for the seat of government that witnessed the growth of German nationalism and its emphatic opposition to and eventual persecution of the Jews. The fate of the Loevy family was therefore inevitable, just one of many accounts of how an educated and established Berlin family was destroyed by the Nazi movement. Fortunately, some family members survived, having emigrated in time, including the gifted composer Leo Kopf, who had married the daughter of one of the Loevy brothers.

During the Battle of Berlin in 1945, the Reichstag became one of the central targets for the Russian army, most probably for its symbolic significance. It was defended to the hilt by the loyal Nazis who had used the building as a stronghold. The building had been fortified and had to be assaulted across open ground by the Soviets. An estimated 500 Nazi troops died fighting in the decimated building, with all but two of the large bronze letters of the iconic inscription remaining in place.

CHAPTER 9

Atrocities against Resistance Organisations

Vienna Regional Resistance

On 12 March 1938, Hitler ordered the German armed forces to seize and occupy his native homeland, Austria. He had previously evidenced this objective in the first paragraph of *Mein Kampf*, written whilst imprisoned in Landsberg in 1924. The *Anschluss*, the incorporation of Austria into Germany, caused dramatic consequences and many Austrian people joined the National Socialist organisation. However, there was resistance to those events in Vienna, demonstrated mainly by Communist sympathisers, but anti-Semitic feeling was also evident, local Nazis forcing many Jews from within their former imperial capital and making them openly scrub the streets and walls.

The Gestapo headquarters in Vienna, located at Morzinplatz in the 1st District of the city, operated from what was the Hotel Metropol. This building was the embodiment of Nazi terror, the entrance for prisoners being situated off Salztorgasse, from where they were taken directly downstairs into the prison cells. In Vienna the Gestapo were particularly brutal, detained suspects often being tortured for weeks in order to obtain a confession. Many died or committed suicide as a result of this abuse. The Gestapo was led by a native of Munich, Franz Josef Huber, with an estimated staff of 900, a sizeable establishment that reflected the perceived Communist threat. In early 1943, more than forty Communist resistance fighters, many of them Jews who had initially escaped to France, returned to Austria with false documentation and disguised as French 'foreign workers'. In the spring of 1943, the Gestapo arrested one of these individuals and extracted the names of other activists through torture, whereupon they swiftly arrested several others and subjected them to brutal interrogations. As a result of the intelligence gathered, the Gestapo sent a team to France and arrested many of the Austrian resistance fighters located in Paris and Lyon during late 1943 and mid-1944.

Austrian resistance to the Nazi regime during the Second World War was significant; it is estimated that over 2,700 members of the resistance movement were executed by the Gestapo, with many more deported to concentration camps. Much Communist propaganda activity was carried out by members of the illegal

Communist Youth League (CYL) who additionally tried to penetrate the Hitler Youth. This active group distributed a news sheet titled *Rote Jugend* (Red Youth) and sent anti-Nazi letters targeted at young serving soldiers. There was brutal suppression against these young activists, and many of them, barely twenty years old, were executed.

Ernestine Diwisch, born in Vienna in March 1921, was employed as a clerk in an aircraft engine factory in Neustadt. She joined the illegal CYL, where she was engaged in the sending of anti-Nazi letters and creating anti-Fascist pamphlets. Arrested on 25 May 1943, she was subjected to interrogation in the Hotel Metropol before eventually being sent with other defendants to the People's Court in Berlin. At her court appearance on 23 September, the senior prosecutor called for the death sentence as Ernestine had been charged with 'conspiracy to commit high treason and aiding the enemy' through being a member of the CYL. In accordance with common practice for hearings in the People's Court, the cases of defendants accused of similar crimes were heard together. Her co-defendants included Alfred Rabofsky, a young man and fellow CYL member who had participated in similar activities but had been called up to serve in the Wehrmacht and was in the Medical Corps when arrested on 16 June 1943. He was sentenced to death on 2 August 1944 for 'high treason and aiding the enemy' and beheaded in the Vienna Provincial Court seven months later. Ernestine was sentenced to death on 8 February 1944 and executed at the same location by beheading on 24 May. Of the other co-defendants, Sophie Vitek, who had been sentenced to death, received clemency and her sentence was commuted to fifteen years' imprisonment, alongside Ernestine Soucek, who was sentenced to eight years in prison on a charge of 'complicity in treason'.

A leading figure within the Austrian Communist youth movement was a chemist named Walter Kampf. He was betrayed by Gestapo informers, which led to him being executed at the Vienna Regional Court on 2 November 1943. Another leading individual, the Communist resistance and Spanish Civil War fighter Josef Meisel, returned from France to Vienna disguised as a French 'foreign worker' and engaged in anti-Nazi resistance. He was arrested by the Gestapo on 17 May 1943 and interrogated with some force, but was subsequently able to escape from Auschwitz concentration camp where he was being held and establish contact with Polish partisans. The reason Meisel was not presented to the People's Court remains unknown, but serves to illustrate the flexibility of manipulation by the Gestapo in their Vienna district of operations.

The Soviet and British Secret Services collaborated in deploying agents into Austria. They were primarily Austrian Communists who had escaped from the Nazis and agreed to be parachuted back into their homeland. These operations were of the utmost secrecy, many agents being flown from the Special Duties Squadrons at RAF Tempsford in Bedfordshire. Since the Communist resistance groups had been successfully infiltrated by Gestapo informers, most of these parachutists were immediately followed, observed in the field of operations and then arrested, together with their liaisons and supporters, and almost all of them were murdered. Johann Sanitzer, the Gestapo officer in charge of capturing the parachute agents, was able to deploy ferocious interrogation and torture methods to enforce compliance on captured agents in order to establish and maintain radio contacts with their controllers. This practice proved successful as more parachutists were flown into Austria by the Allies and they too were arrested. Rosa Grossmann and her parents Johann and Elise Brunner were arrested by the Gestapo on 25 October 1943 because of their contact with a parachutist, Gregor Kersche, who amusingly chose to wear a small Hitler moustache and was a member of the Communist Party of Austria. To avoid betraying her fellow fighters under torture, Rosa purposely threw herself down a stairwell from the fourth floor of the Gestapo headquarters with the intention of taking her own life, but despite being severely injured, she survived.

One Viennese resistance fighter, Selma Steinmetz, reported in her post-war witness account the abuse she suffered at the hands of Gestapo officer Eduard Tucek in France in June 1944. Tucek, a Vienna police officer, had joined the Gestapo headquarters in 1941, and together with other Gestapo members was sent to France in 1943-44 to trace Austrian resistance fighters based in Lyon:

> Tucek wanted to find out from me by any means the names and addresses of those I had been in contact with and who had worked for the resistance movement. Since we lived there illegally and in a strictly conspirative manner, I knew neither the true names nor addresses of most of them, thus, for the life of me, I wouldn't have been able to reveal anything. I was enchained by Tucek; at first, he hit with his bare fists. Then he helped himself to a bull pizzle [a whip made from a bull's penis] with which he flogged me all over so that my body was full of bloody welts and my skin was hanging in shreds. The following day he applied the bath method. I had to undress down to my underwear, was tied up hands and feet, and put into the bathtub, which was filled with cold water. On and on, my head kept being pushed underwater; when my head emerged from the water, a shower was held to my face so that again I was hardly able to catch air because of the water jet. Then he pulled me up on my tied feet so that my head got again underwater. I thought I'd suffocate at any moment. Tucek carried out these tortures as a quasi training session since several young Gestapo officers were present to whom he explained throughout the demonstration how to go about these treatments to get the prisoners talking.
>
> Witness account by Selma Steinmetz before the police headquarters Vienna, 28 June 1946.

The Fallbeil used by the Vienna Regional Court decapitated several hundred people, many execution sessions consisting of ten to twenty individuals at a time. Amongst the fifteen victims executed on 21 November 1944 was Leopoldine Padaurek, a metal worker in the Siemens-Schuckert factory in Leopoldstadt. She had been arrested on 25 January that year for resistance activities involving the distribution of anti-

Nazi leaflets, and appeared before the People's Court on 27 September, when she was sentenced to death. Leopoldine was beheaded in the Vienna Provincial Court together with three fellow workers, an addition twelve people also being decapitated by the Fallbeil during that same execution session.

Heinrich Maier, an Austrian Roman Catholic priest, was among six people beheaded on 22 March 1945, the last execution session undertaken in the Vienna court, the day before the Red Army's invasion of Vienna. Maier had been heavily involved in the resistance against the Nazis together with the resistance fighters Walter Caldonazzi and Franz Josef Messner. They were able to gather and collate evidence in relation to Nazi armament factories and other military establishments and send the intelligence to the Allies through intermediaries in Switzerland. However, they were exposed by a traitor in early 1944, eight leading members of the group being arrested and placed before the People's Court on 28 October 1944, charged with 'conspiracy to commit high treason'. A total of eight death sentences were imposed against Heinrich Maier, Walter Caldonazzi, Franz Josef Messner, Andreas Hofer, Josef Wyhnal, Hermann Klepell, Wilhelm Ritsch and Clemens von Pausinger. Caldonazzi was beheaded in January 1945 in the Vienna Court, and Messner died in the Mauthausen concentration camp, gassed in April 1945. Josef Wyhnal was beheaded alongside Heinrich Maier in March 1945.

At the Gestapo headquarters in Vienna, enthusiastic Gestapo officers continued their activities against Soviet resistance, and that included within their own army. Wehrmacht soldiers Maj. Biedermann, Capt. Huth, and 1Lt Raschke had formed an understanding with the Soviets to prevent Vienna being destroyed in the Russian advance, and were all executed on 8 April 1945 in the Floridsdorf district of the city.

Of the thirty-one anatomical departments within universities in Germany and its occupied territories during 1933 and 1945, all without exception received bodies of the executed from civil executions. The University of Vienna developed a special hearse that took delivery of the cadavers from the execution chamber of the Vienna Regional Court and carried them to the Institute of Anatomy. Prof. Eduard Pernkopf, the chairman of anatomy in Vienna from 1933 to 1945, left a printed legacy to those many decapitated bodies in the form of a now infamous illustrated anatomy tome. Post-war research has established that many of the incredibly detailed illustrations in Pernkopf's anatomical atlas depict the bodies of victims of Nazi terror. A staunch Nazi, after Hitler's invasion of Austria in 1938, Pernkopf became the Dean of the Vienna medical school. One of his first acts was to purge the faculty of Jews and other so-called undesirable members. Pernkopf's work on the atlas began in 1933, and he attracted a number of gifted Nazi artists capable of capturing his dissections in incredible detail. It is mooted that Pernkopf arranged for the bodies of nearly 1,400 people executed by the Gestapo, mostly for political reasons, to serve as models for the drawings in the atlas, and decapitated heads formed a large part of the meticulous dissections.

Incredibly, the key Nazi personnel involved in the atrocities were dealt with leniently after the war despite their barbaric actions in Austria. Pernkopf spent three years in an Allied prison camp near Salzburg immediately after the war, but was never charged with war crimes. On his release in 1948, he returned to the university and, although he was stripped of all academic titles, resumed work on the atlas, dying suddenly of a stroke while working on the four-volume tome.

Franz Josef Huber, the head of the Gestapo office in Vienna, the largest branch of the Gestapo in the Reich, had participated in Nazi judicial processes and mass deportation of Jews in Vienna. After the war, Huber was arrested by the Allies but was never punished for his actions. He worked in Munich as an accountant until his retirement and his natural death in 1975.

The brutal Gestapo officer Eduard Tucek was sentenced to five years in prison in France in 1947. However, no legal proceedings were ever initiated against him in Austria.

The Gestapo officer in charge of investigating parachute agents, Johann Sanitzer, was arrested and confined in Glasenbach SS prisoner-of-war camp under the control of the American military authorities near Salzburg. He was tried by the People's Court in Vienna and sentenced to life imprisonment for the brutal abuse of twenty-five persons. In 1946, he was transferred to an Austrian prison in the Russian zone. He was released to the Russians for investigative interrogation, as mention had been made during his trial of his order to have a number of Russian officers executed at Mauthausen. In 1955, Sanitzer was returned to Austria, but the Soviet Union, having secured evidence that he had captured a Soviet radio transmitter in Austria and transmitted false information, sentenced him to twenty-five years' imprisonment in Russia. A clemency appeal, however, resulted in considerable publicity for his case and with time served in Russia, Sanitzer eventually gained parole.

Red Orchestra

One of the most prolific groups opposed to National Socialism was the Schulze-Boysen/Harnack Red Orchestra group comprised of Communist sympathisers led by Luftwaffe officer Harro Schulze-Boysen. In the mid-1920s, a Polish Jew by the name of Leopold Trepper established a Communist underground network that enabled him to work as an agent for the Soviet military intelligence service. The network expanded within Western Europe and carried out intelligence-gathering operations in Germany, France, the Netherlands and Switzerland until the early 1930s when the French intelligence service successfully broke up the network, forcing Trepper to escape to Moscow.

Undeterred, in 1939, Trepper and an associate Soviet agent established themselves in Belgium, where they developed several well-organised Communist groups. It was here that they were able to connect with Schulze-Boysen who was employed on the Luftwaffe's General Staff in Berlin. More impressively, as Trepper established greater links across Europe he even managed to infiltrate the German military intelligence service, the Abwehr. Trepper's organisation gained in reputation, so Moscow deployed three experienced officers to work with him in gathering specific intelligence in France, Belgium and the Netherlands. Soviet agents Yefremov, Makarov and Danilov were dropped by parachute and, having permeated into Trepper's network, they subsequently transmitted significant amounts of information back to Moscow over a long period of time.

The name 'Red Orchestra' appears to have arisen from the many investigations undertaken by the Abwehr and Gestapo into groups of Communist sympathisers thought to be engaging in opposition to the Third Reich. Post-war research has identified that Soviet clandestine radio transmitters were referred to as 'music boxes', and radio operators as 'musicians' or 'pianists' because of their dexterity with the Morse code key. Thus the German label 'Red Orchestra' related to these operators 'playing' their instruments—the transmitters.

Harro Schulze-Boysen was born on 2 September 1909 in Kiel and grew up in an upper-middle-class military officer's family known to hold Nationalist sympathies. His paternal great-uncle was the famous admiral Alfred von Tirpitz, whist his maternal great-uncle was the philosopher and sociologist Ferdinand Tönnies. Harro was brought up with politics and developed a personal interest in overcoming class barriers which at that time were prevalent in Germany. He studied law but gained great interest in the world of publishing, becoming the editor of the journal *Gegner* in mid-1932, a publication banned by the Nazi Party in April 1933. Immediately after the National Socialists took power, he wrote an article criticising the new government, following the publication of which he was detained and his editorial offices were searched. Harro was roughly treated, and owed his release from prison to the intervention of his mother. However, his release was tempered with orders to leave Berlin. He gained a place at the commercial aviation school in Warnemünde, which in retrospect was a most fortunate development, as it led to subsequent employment in the intelligence department of the new Reich Aviation Ministry in 1934. Harro later met Libertas Haas-Heye, an assistant consultant in the Reich Aviation Ministry, and together they travelled to Britain and Switzerland where they met several German emigrants. The couple were married in Liebenberg, Berlin, on 26 July 1936.

After the wedding, Harro resolutely gathered a circle of like-minded friends around him. Opponents of National Socialism, they discussed philosophical problems and fundamental political issues. In the confines of their discussions he spoke frankly and his resolve against Nazism increased. A pivotal action took place in 1938, when he passed on information obtained through his work to the Soviet Union. No doubt the involvement of Germany in the Spanish Civil War was fundamental in his actions. The Gestapo later accused him of having exploited his circle of friends and politically influencing them, but this was far from the truth; the group were all political activists. In 1940, Adam and Greta Kuckhoff, members of the discussion circle who also knew Mildred and Arvid Harnack, proposed a meeting. Adam had links to the Social Democratic resistance and collaborated on several Red Orchestra pamphlets in 1941, as well as safeguarding a radio transmitter for the resistance group, so was of central importance to the group's activities. The transmitter was used in communications with Russian operatives, which indicates the depth of contacts available to this particular group. Harro met Arvid at the planned meeting and together they developed the activities of the group, which were evidently based on active opposition to National Socialism. Although the Red Orchestra was an isolated group, Arvid's younger brother Falk was known to have met and actively engaged with members of the White Rose group, Sophie Scholl and Alexander Schmorell, who had visited him in Chemnitz with the intention of recruiting him. Falk had been called up to serve in the German army in 1941, but continued to meet with Sophie and Alexander on several occasions during 1942, as well as meeting Prof. Kurt Huber. Falk was arrested alongside other White Rose participants in early 1943, but miraculously escaped execution after appearing in the People's Court. The German army sent him to fight in Greece, where he deserted; to avoid arrest by the Gestapo he joined the Greek Partisan movement and organised the Anti-Fascist Committee in which he fought for freedom until the end of the war.

The Red Orchestra continued with its meetings, and Falk's brother Arvid came into close contact with an active Communist group centred around the activities of John Sieg. John was born in 1903 into a German-American family. In 1929, he joined the German Communist Party (KPD) and, like Harro, developed an interest in publishing. He met Adam Kuckhoff, editor-in-chief of the journal *Die Tat*, and received a prison sentence in 1933 for his associations with the Communist Party. He and his wife Sophie both became key figures in several groups. The Red Orchestra group met regularly in two rooms on the fifth floor of the Hasenheide apartment that was sublet from a relative of the writer Stefan Heym.

In 1941 and into 1942, Harro played a major role in many tangible political resistance activities, creating pamphlets as well as leaflets, all of which advised against the war and predicted its dangerous consequences for Germany. Hundreds of printed handbills were pasted onto walls, notice boards and trees, the primary intention being to ridicule the 'Soviet Paradise' exhibition in Berlin that was calling for support for the war against the Soviet Union.

On 10 May 1942, the exhibition was opened by Goebbels. Organised by the Nazi Party's propaganda office, it was designed to show the German public by means of a number of simple-looking displays that the Russians were a backward people with little culture. Additionally, military equipment, uniforms, automatic weapons, guns, tanks, planes and such like were shown to evidence the big difference between the poverty of the people and the excellent equipment of the Bolshevist army. Displays of prison cells, torture equipment, torture cells, and death chambers were intended to show how the Russian people were being suppressed. After the exhibition had closed its doors in Berlin it was rather ambitiously transported to other cities throughout the Reich.

The high-profile action against the exhibition by the Red Orchestra group was inevitably going to attract intense investigations by the Gestapo who at that time were actively attempting to locate the radio transmitter used by the group. The Germans had apparently known of the existence of a Soviet spy ring operating at fairly high levels of the Reich government administration as early as 1941, and unbeknown to Harro, the Russians had transmitted information to one of their agents in Germany that included his address. The ineluctable consequences of the group's poster campaign and the Abwehr's intelligence gathering occurred on 8 September 1942, when the Gestapo arrested both Harro and Libertas. Under interrogation, Harro admitted what he had done, without revealing information about his fellow conspirators—a brave action, as he would have known that this would induce further interrogation and a probable death sentence. He devised a plan, pretending to have delivered incriminating documents about the German government to Sweden, in the hope that this would delay the case against him and other members of the Red Orchestra.

The Gestapo officers elected to regard Luftwaffe officer Harro as the leader of the Berlin resistance group and continued to focus their investigations on alleged espionage with the Communists. At the same time an indictment for treason was compiled against him. The case was passed to the prosecuting counsel, Manfred Roeder, a man truly devoted to and empowered by the Nazi regime. Roeder did not indict all the members of the resistance group, but had smaller groups brought before the court in turn, an act calculated to minimise public awareness of the known organisation around Arvid and Harro and to avoid the impression of a large resistance organisation having been in operation. Roeder had become a feared man and took delight in brutality, displaying a total coldness towards the defendants brought before him in court.

The trial of those who were perceived to have been the most important members of the Red Orchestra, including Arvid and Mildred Harnack, and Harro and Libertas Schulze-Boysen, began on 15 December 1942. That said, the Germans had by this time infiltrated the Russian network and captured radio operators, including their grand master Trepper, on or around 16 November 1942. The publicly managed trials were undertaken before the Reich Court Martial at Berlin-Charlottenburg. The accused knew that they were likely to be sentenced to death, as a gallows with several hooks was erected in Plötzensee Prison not long before the trial.

Many members of the Red Orchestra were denied the quick death of the Fallbeil, and were to die hanging from a short rope in what Hitler conceived to be the most dishonourable way. The sequence of events would have been imposed upon the executioner: the condemned prisoner was placed on a stool and a thin noose slipped around his neck; the noose was then tightened and hung from the hook on the gallows bar and the stool was pulled away from them; strung from the meat hook, the prisoner slowly strangled to death. As a serving Luftwaffe officer, Harro should have been shot in accordance with normal Military Court sentencing practice, but Hitler denied him this method of execution and would have had the satisfaction of knowing that his life ended by strangulation, hanging from the butcher's hook on the evening of 22 December 1942.

Four other men were executed alongside Harro, and three women and three men from the group were decapitated by the Fallbeil. All had been convicted of high treason. Harro's wife Libertas was amongst those who suffered the indignity of exposing her neck to the Fallbeil's blade, which swiftly and effectively decapitated her. Arvid Harnack was also executed that evening. His wife Mildred was initially spared the death penalty, instead being sentenced to six years in prison. However, Hitler refused to accept the sentence and ordered a new trial, which unsurprisingly ended with a sentence of death on 16 January 1943. Mildred was beheaded on 16 February, and the court officials with their normal efficiency later posted to her family the fees to be paid for the death sentence, the room and boarding charges whilst imprisoned, the executioner's fees, and court costs including postage.

Adam Kuckhoff was arrested in Prague on 12 September 1942, sentenced to death on 3 February 1943, and executed on 5 August in Plötzensee Prison. His wife Greta was sentenced to ten years' imprisonment but was liberated from Waldheim Prison by the Red Army in May 1945.

John Graudenz, who had supported Harro in obtaining information that was used to further their cause, was arrested on 12 September 1942, sentenced to death on 19 December, and executed three days later in Plötzensee Prison.

Sophie and John Sieg were arrested on 11 October 1942. John hanged himself in his cell on 15 October; he was determined to commit suicide to avoid betraying anybody. Sophie was imprisoned in Ravensbrück concentration camp in June 1943, and fortunately survived until her liberation by the Red Army on 30 April 1945.

Maria Terwiel, a 32-year-old secretary who had assisted in flyposting against the 'Soviet Paradise' exhibition and had secreted the group's radio transmitter, was arrested on 17 September 1942, tried on 26 January 1943, and executed at Plötzensee on 5 August. Similarly, nineteen-year-old Liane Berkowitz, the daughter of a Russian conductor who had fled from the Soviet Union, also took part in the flyposting and was arrested in September 1942. She was pregnant when sentenced to death on 18 January 1943. On 12 April, she gave birth in prison to a daughter who was later taken into the care of her grandmother. Just four months later, on 5 August 1943, Liane was executed in Plötzensee. Her baby daughter Irene is suspected to have lost her life, swept up during one of the many Nazis purges against mentally ill people. Liane's mother was half-Jewish, a factor that may well have contributed to Irene's death.

Hans Coppi and his wife Hilde were both active members of the Red Orchestra. Hans had been responsible for attempting to create a radio link with Moscow. Both were arrested by the Gestapo on 12 September 1942, Hilde giving birth to their son in a filthy prison cell on 27 November. Hans was sentenced to death on 19 December and was executed three days later in Plötzensee Prison. On 20 January 1943, his wife was also sentenced to death but was not taken to Plötzensee until 5 August, having handed her 9-month-old baby into the care of her mother three days earlier. Hilde was executed as directed by her court sentence. On 13 May 1943, the executioners had carried out thirteen further death sentences, and on the evening of 8 August 1943, nineteen more men and women from the group were executed in Plötzensee.

The case of Mildred Elizabeth Harnack is deserving of further explanation. She was an American citizen, and appears to have been the only American woman to be executed on Hitler's orders. Her execution was correlated and interwoven with the German defeat at Stalingrad. Hitler was aware that she was an active member of the Red Orchestra and his retribution upon her would no doubt have also been influenced by his dislike of American citizens. He gave no consideration to the original court sentence imposed upon Mildred; her initial sentence was for being an accessory to espionage and not a conspirator. Her defence lawyer had succeeded in convincing the judges that she had been occupied with her literary activities and that having translated important German books into English, she had served Germany well, only ever wishing to help her husband.

With Hitler's refusal to accept the first trial sentence, the Wehrmacht legal department was faced with a dilemma in finding grounds for a new trial. It cited paragraph 4 of the Regulation on Violent Criminals, which read: 'A punishable attempted crime or offence or abetting of the same is generally punishable by the penalty permitted for the crime itself.' This allowed the lesser crime of 'aiding in the preparation of espionage' to be made punishable by the death sentence. In addition, material was sought to portray Mildred as an adulteress, the Gestapo's intention being to show that members of the Red Orchestra, all of whom were professionals, were sexually intimate within their group. Little imagination is required to understand the level of manipulation that took place. Mildred was degraded and had been reduced to a frail form as a result of her harsh treatment in prison, the Plötzensee chaplain Harald Poelchau later providing evidence that her torture and ill treatment had turned her hair ashen white and that she was unable to walk unaided. Mildred never divulged any information against any member of the Red Orchestra group, and the chaplain reported that despite her ailments she went to her death courageously. It is difficult to understand how the legal system gained any satisfaction in sentencing and executing Mildred in such circumstances. Despite being an American citizen, born in Milwaukee, she had openly loved Germany.

In nineteen individual trials that took place between 15 December 1942 and July 1943, the Military Courts of Nazi Germany convicted seventy-six members of the Red Orchestra. Forty-five of them were sentenced to death, whilst twenty-nine received various jail sentences. Just two defendants were acquitted on the grounds of insufficient evidence. As we have seen, under German law the bodies of those who had been executed for high treason were taken to university anatomy departments, primarily the University of Berlin. The anatomist Hermann Stieve who worked there had developed a research programme on the effects of stress on human reproductive systems, and the lawful supply of human corpses allowed him to develop that work by means of female dissections. Stieve had known Mildred from the circle of professional people in which they had both circulated and recognised her corpse when it arrived at the university. In normal circumstances the bodies sent to the various universities simply became lost in the mire of dissection, but Stieve saw to it that Mildred's remains were cremated and her ashes preserved. This act of humanity, undertaken in an environment far removed from such events, enabled the Harnack family the rare privilege of being able to bury the remains of a victim who had been condemned to death by Hitler's courts.

Intelligence professionals and post-war historians have mooted that the Red Orchestra was one of the most successful spy rings that operated during the Second World War. German investigations into this one organisation led to more than 600 people being arrested in Germany, France and Belgium. Leopold Trepper, arrested in November 1942, had been immediately recognised as a significant agent by the Gestapo and German intelligence services. He was managed and coerced into becoming a double agent but took advantage of a compromised message back to Moscow, escaping from custody in 1943 and joining the French resistance. Wolfgang Havemann, the nephew of Arvid Harnack, was captured by the Russians whilst on the Eastern Front in March 1944, and through interrogation the Russian intelligence service became aware of the purge of the Red Orchestra members in Berlin. After the war, Trepper provided valuable information on the Red Orchestra's operations, calculating that some 143 'musicians' had been executed following their arrest and brutal torture, which extracted sufficient information to completely destroy the Communist-based organisation.

Didry-Fillerin Escape Line

During the early period of the Second World War, Allied forces attempted at all odds to escape and avoid capture during the invasion of the Lowlands and France by Hitler's army. Nazi tyranny was in full flow, and persecution by the regime was tangible for all to see. Inevitably, Allied pilots and air crew would attempt to evade capture throughout occupied Europe if they were fortunate enough to avoid immediate arrest. The Third Reich was well aware that these airmen represented a significant financial investment by the Allies in training over several years, and in the early stages of the war were greater prizes for the Reich than the aircraft they had shot down. There were 2,803 air crew of the RAF and Commonwealth air forces shot down during the Second World War who managed in the majority of cases to evade capture, or to escape from captivity. In many instances they eventually return to Allied territory by clandestine means with the help of resistance groups, and by so doing forced the enemy to devote scarce resources in attempting to try and stop them. Those who succeeded also gave encouragement to the Allied forces operating over enemy territory.

Escapers and evaders were almost always reliant on the goodwill of ordinary people—peasants, businessmen, priests, nurses, housewives, bakers, young girls and boys—all of whom were extraordinarily brave people rebelling against Nazi rule. Across the occupied countries they risked their lives to assist these vulnerable soldiers and airmen, knowing that, if discovered, they faced the ultimate penalty, death, and the possibility that their families would be sent to concentration camps. German posters and other notifications confirming the imposition of such sentences on civilians sympathetic to the Allies were prominently displayed in towns and mayoral offices, and many hundreds of citizens paid the price for helping Allied air crew. For example, in Brittany, the young son of Madame Guiho was detained for being engaged in such work and was shot before her eyes. Other families saw their sons, husbands or elders snatched away by the Gestapo or other German units, never to see them again. It did not matter where they were, whether in the fatherland or in occupied territories, the same heinous penalty applied.

By June 1940, one gallant Frenchman, Norbert Fillerin, had formed a local network of trusted friends in villages near Renty, his home in the Pas-de-Calais. In due course an alliance was formed with a similar group organised by Désiré Didry in St Omer some 20 km to the north-east. It was undoubtedly one of the earliest French resistance groups, having been formed in May 1940. For the Didry and Fillerin groups there was at first little trade in Allied air crew, with the Battle of Britain being fought across the English Channel and RAF Bomber Command making very few raids on Germany. Apart from a couple of instances, it was not until March 1941 that Norbert took any further evaders to Marseille in unoccupied Vichy France, 1,000 km to the south of Renty. The two small resistance groups had established contact with a group in Marseille that was run by British officers. Rather than try to get home themselves these officers had remained in Marseille, doing what they could to help other British servicemen who had escaped from occupied France to get back to England. That they were able to do so was largely thanks to the tolerant attitude of the French police in Marseille and to the financial assistance that came from generous local residents and from the British government via the American consulate in Marseille. Without these large sums of money they could not have paid for necessities such as railway tickets, food and official or fake passes. Travelling long distances, either from the Pas-de-Calais to Marseille or from Marseille over the Pyrenees, adding a further 370 km to the journey, was an expensive business and well beyond the pockets of men such as Norbert and Désiré.

With an organisation that was growing stronger as each month passed, all went well for the Fillerin and Didry groups for over a year. Several RAF airmen shot down in the Pas-de-Calais were successfully sent home via Marseille in 1941. The Gestapo, however, were developing an effective means of dealing with this form of resistance. They infiltrated people into the known or suspected escape routes that were so bravely conceived; once ensconced in the group, the spy was able to secure sufficient information to capture as many operatives as possible. One particularly hideous character was Harold 'Paul' Cole, who became the organisation's contact in Lille and from late 1940 had been collecting escapers and evaders and holding them in secure safe houses. Cole had been a petty criminal and con-man in Britain before the war, later enlisting in the Royal Engineers. He had become an early prisoner of war but escaped in the chaos that ensued after the fall of France and forged a life for himself in occupied France. Technically he was a deserter, but it must be said he became a valued asset to the resistance group by becoming an audacious and successful courier and was later trusted to act as an escort taking Allied evaders to Marseille until the day he was exposed. The Fillerin and Didry resistance groups suffered a serious setback on 8 December 1941, when as a result of the treachery of Harold 'Paul' Cole, Désiré himself and Alfred Lanselle, another key member of the group, were arrested by the Abwehr at St Omer station. The Abwehr dealt exclusively with human intelligence, especially reports from field agents and other sources. On that same day, in a co-ordinated drive against the resisters, Désiré's wife and daughter were also arrested and several other operatives in the area were rounded up for interrogation. Fortunately for the Fillerin group they were saved, as it appears that Cole had little first-hand information on the individuals in that group and, surprisingly, other persons known to Cole were not arrested during this purge on the resistance. Amongst others arrested as a result of Cole's treachery were Protais Dubois, Marcel Duhaye and Pierre Carpentier.

Born in 1912 at Libercourt, Pierre Carpentier later entered into the priesthood and was ordained on 29 June 1938. During this time he was required to undertake military service and gained a place at the famous Special Military Academy of Saint-Cyr where he was granted the rank of *sous-lieutenant* (2 Lt). In September 1939, he was called up to serve but was demobilised following the fall of France to Hitler's crushing army in May 1940. Returning to his previous calling, he became the vicar of Abbeville and joined the resistance, where he was an expert at forging documents to help Allied airmen escape from France into Spain.

The last member arrested as a result of Cole's betrayal was Bruce Dowding. Born in Melbourne, Australia, in May 1914, at school he studied French and British history, becoming a student teacher in 1933, studying for a degree at the University of Melbourne. He later enrolled at the University of Paris, but frequently travelled to England where he later gained employment as an English tutor. In late 1939, following the outbreak of war, he enlisted in the Royal Army Service Corps and found himself sent to France ,where he was taken at Dunkirk on 22 May 1940. The Germans captured a significant number of Allied soldiers at Dunkirk, and Bruce was one of several men who managed to escape by taking advantage of the massive numbers being moved to prisoner-of-war camps, making his way south to Marseille. During his escape he made contact with the embryonic resistance movements and was given the code-name Andre Mason. By early 1941, Bruce had become actively engaged in assisting others along the escape route that he had himself had sought, his excellent command of the French language being a primary reason for his involvement. He became responsible for the dangerous task of taking escapees towards the Spanish border by train via Toulouse and Perpignan, and was present when suspicions against

Cole were aroused. He had been guarding Cole, who managed to escape from the confrontation that was about to take place, an event that eventually led to the arrests of those brave resistance operatives.

The Abwehr took the detained suspects to Loos Prison in Lille. Presumably at some time the Gestapo would have become involved, but after eight months in Loos prison, Désiré and his fellow resisters also betrayed by Cole were eventually taken to Bochum in Germany. Although Bruce was a serving Commonwealth soldier, it appears he was dealt with as a political prisoner. However, some confusion exists on this issue, as the Germans allowed him to write a 'captured prisoner of war' postcard to his parents, the type of communication normally issued to all prisoners of war and sent very swiftly after their initial arrest. Sometime later the decision was made to try the resistance operatives in central Germany, and on 29 June 1943 they were all sentenced to death by decapitation. At 19.15 hours on the following day, at Dortmund Prison in Lübeckerstrasse, Pierre Carpentier, Bruce Dowding, Marcel Duhaye, Protais Dubois, Désiré Didry and five others were executed on the Fallbeil and their remains cremated and placed in an unmarked grave in a cemetery in Dortmund.

After the arrests in France, Cole went to ground in Paris, marrying Suzanne Warenghem on 10 April 1942, but things soon went wrong for them. The couple were arrested in Lyon by the Vichy police in June and charged with espionage. On 21 July, they were brought to trial in the French courts and Cole was sentenced to death; Suzanne was acquitted. In November 1942, Cole was saved from execution and his sentence commuted to life imprisonment. When the Germans took over Vichy France, Cole was released and recruited to work with the SS major Hans Kieffer, a senior German intelligence officer in Paris, at his infamous headquarters at 84 Avenue Foch. Kieffer was later executed following the post-war Nuremberg Trials, having been found guilty of committing heinous offences. Cole was eventually arrested in June 1945 in Saulgau by MI5 investigators and sent to a prison in Paris. Incredibly, he escaped once more in November, only to be shot dead in January 1946 when resisting arrest by two gendarmes looking for deserters.

Following the end of the war, a British parliamentary committee, known as the Committee on the Grant of Honours, Decorations and Medals produced a document, Command Paper 6833, setting out the conditions for the award of war medals and campaign stars. Amongst their considerations was the fact that, in November 1943, the Imperial Prisoners of War Committee decided that prisoners of war belonging to the Royal Navy, Army and RAF who were killed while trying to escape should be regarded as eligible for consideration for the award of a posthumous Mention in Despatches (MID). For the most part, Germany complied with the provisions of the Geneva Convention, which protected prisoners of war, and escaped prisoners were not shot as a matter of course. The exception to this was the 'great escape' from Stalag Luft III where direct orders from Hitler resulted in executions by shooting and the award of the MID was applied *en masse* to the escapers because of the extraordinary circumstances of that case. Individual cases were additionally evidenced and Cpl

Bruce Dowding was posthumously awarded a mention in despatches for 'gallant and distinguished services in the field' on 13 September 1946. He was additionally posthumously issued with a Certificate of Appreciation by the *Bureau de Recherches sur l'Aide Apportée aux Evadés Alliés*. His remains were secured and moved to the Reichswald Forest Commonwealth War Graves Cemetery where an official headstone commemorates his life. Corporal S/131722 Kenneth Bruce Dowding was a member of the British Army who was tried as a civilian in Germany and executed on the orders of a Third Reich judge by decapitation on a Fallbeil.

SOE Agents

The Special Operations Executive (SOE) was a British organisation officially formed on 22 July 1940 by Hugh Dalton, the Minister of Economic Warfare, in order to conduct espionage, sabotage and reconnaissance within occupied Europe and to aid local established resistance movements based within the occupied territories. SOE candidates were all volunteers who undertook rigorous training for operations behind enemy lines. This included instruction in paramilitary skills at Inverailort House, near Mallaig in Scotland, parachute training at RAF Ringway (now Manchester International Airport), and several months at the SOE radio school at Thame Park in Oxfordshire.

Alphonse Delmeire was a Belgian 'gypsy' who was called to serve in his home army at just 19 years of age. He fought with his regiment and experienced the fall of Belgium to German control but managed to escape to England, demonstrating resilience that belied his age and demeanour. Despite his young age, Alphonse had experienced a great deal, having previously participated in smuggling activities across the Franco-Belgian border and gaining skills that no doubt assisted him in reaching England. He was recruited into the SOE because he had shown himself to be ideal for the role of escorting agents from France into Belgium and proved to be a worthy individual who, after training, was selected to operate in the field as part of a mission codenamed 'Canticle', under the control of SOE 'T' Section in Belgium.

Valère Passelecq was another recruited SOE agent who had passed through the organisation's training school in Scotland. He was selected to be dropped into occupied Europe by the RAF alongside Alphonse, although he was scheduled to work within another sector, so they knew little about each other's activities. Valère was to engage in political warfare and sabotage activities, a role very different from that of Alphonse. Unbeknown to the British, one of their agents who had been sent into the Low Countries by parachute with a secret wireless transmitter, Armand Campion, had been arrested whilst transmitting. He had immediately denounced all of his contacts and family whilst under interrogation. Armand's treachery was not disclosed for a long time, and many agents were therefore dropped into prearranged areas unaware that the Germans were waiting for them.

On 1 March 1942, Valère and Alphonse climbed aboard the large Whitley aircraft operated by No. 138 (Special Duties) Squadron from one of its secret airfields. The pilot of the Whitley, Sgt Wilde, took off at 18.18 hours to head towards the French coast, north of the River Somme. At Douai he descended to an estimated 400 feet over the prearranged drop zone but no resistance support was seen on the ground. They circled the area for fifty minutes before moving to another dropping area where the two agents safely parachuted down. In addition, some messenger pigeons for use by the 'Canticle' group were also dropped and, to disguise the operation, propaganda leaflets were dropped from the air all across Douai. Wilde safely returned to his airfield at 01.50 hours and reported to the SOE unit based there.

It was only good fortune that prevented Alphonse from dropping into the lap of the waiting Germans. Once on the ground, however, he followed procedures and eventually made contact at the appointed location, where he was immediately arrested. The fate of any captured agent was likely to be traumatic. They would inevitably be exposed to torture in order to extract information. At the time of Alphonse's arrest the Germans had been regularly capturing agents as a result of Campion's treachery, so on the assumption that Alphonse would provide little if any additional information of any value to them, he was interrogated and moved into St-Gilles Prison in Brussels, a historic location that held many men and women suspected of being engaged in anti-Nazi resistance.

Valère had slightly better fortune than Alphonse, in that he experienced around sixteen weeks of freedom in the field of SOE resistance operations. However, he was eventually captured by the Germans in company with a fellow Belgian, Raymonde Thonon, whom he had known from his youth. Valère and Alphonse were reunited once again in the political prison camp in Esterwegen, which also housed many Germans arrested under Hitler's 'Nacht und Nebel' orders. In many instances these people had simply disappeared during the night, their families having no knowledge of where they had been taken. Esterwegen was considered to be a *Strafgefangenenlager* or punishment camp for selected prisoners. The living conditions were the same as in the concentration camps, with an emphasis on torture, executions and forced work. Valère and Alphonse were imprisoned as resistance members, but unlike the vast majority of prisoners they had been trained in specific skills under the control of the British. Over a period of time and with great ingenuity they managed to scrounge sufficient material to build a basic crystal set on which they were able to receive news broadcast from Britain, a network of people passing the information around the extensive camp. The radio device was eventually found by the Germans, and that may well have induced Valère and Alphonse to join together in a plan to escape. However, before any plans could be put in place, both men were subsequently tried by the German judiciary and found guilty of a capital offence for which they were sentenced to death.

On 7 June 1944, the day following the Allied invasion of occupied Europe, the Belgian military agents Alphonse Delmeire and Valère Passelecq were beheaded at

Wolfenbüttel Prison. Alongside them was the civilian Raymonde Thonon, who also suffered the same fate.

Another member of the 'Canticle' resistance group to be parachuted into the Lowlands of occupied Europe was 22-year-old wireless operator Gaston Aarens. Once again it was to be Sgt Wilde of No. 138 Squadron who was to fly the agents from England, this time on the night of the 28 January 1942. He was carrying three agents in what proved to be very bad weather conditions and, to make matters worse, snow was falling heavily across the dropping area. However, the agents safely left the Whitley aircraft and parachuted to the ground. The dangers of being a wireless operator were once again illustrated by Gaston's arrest on 27 March 1942. It would appear that he was subjected to brutal interrogation and torture, sufficient for him to disclose vital information which the Abwehr used to good effect against the British operations managed by the SOE. By the close of October 1942, out of forty-five agents who had been dropped into Belgium, an estimated thirty-two had fallen immediately into the hands of the Germans.

London communicated with the resistance groups operating under Nazi occupation by coded communication over the BBC radio broadcasts via Pierre Holmes who was an announcer on the BBC. Between 1942 and 1944, a nightly programme called *The French Speak to the French* broadcast instructions and coded messages to resistance fighters on supply drops. Famously, the Allied invasion of France on 6 June 1944 was announced by Holmes quoting a verse from the poet Paul Verlaine: 'Long violin sobs rock my heart in monotonous languish.'

One of the other agents who dropped from the Whitley that January night in 1942 was Achille Hottia, a twenty-year-old Belgian trained by the SOE in industrial sabotage at Brickendonbury Manor near Hertford. Following his landing in the drop zone he was astute enough to realise that the organisation had been compromised, so he tried to escape towards Spain but was forced to return to Belgium. He made contact with the Belgium-based Comet escape line, which assisted Allied airmen to return to England by escorting them across Belgium, through France and over the mountains into Spain and thence to Gibraltar. Achille joined company with several British airmen: Sgt William Cole and WO Frank Hugo, both from the same crew within No. 7 Squadron, and Sgts Arthur William Edgley and Sidney Maxted, crew members of RAF Stirling serial number BK611 from No. 15 Squadron that had crashed in the vicinity of Venlo in the Netherlands in the early hours of 26 May 1943.

The Comet line couriers took the group into Paris for an exchange, following which the group would be taken further south. Gertrude Moors was a young Comet line courier member who played a significant part in the escape of twenty-five Allied airmen. She escorted the evaders from Belgium into France where an exchange would take place, leaving her free to return to her home in Dilsen. However, as a result of German infiltration of the Comet line, Gertrude was captured by the secret *Feldpolizei* in Paris on 18 June 1943. Severely tortured in the prison of St-Gilles and in the Begynestraat in Antwerp, Gertrude was condemned to death on 2 July 1944.

Despite brutal interrogation, she never betrayed her country or her fellow partisans, tragically dying in Ravensbrück in March 1945.

Prosper Dezitter was one of the traitors who operated within the Comet line. He was on the payroll of the Germans and operated from a fake safe house in Brussels where he arranged German interceptions in Paris. The SOE agent Achille Hottia and his accompanying RAF evaders, unbeknown to them, were being set up to be arrested. In Paris, on 9 July 1943, they were forcibly detained and taken to the infamous Gestapo headquarters in Avenue Foch where they were segregated and interrogated. The group were all in civilian clothing and therefore treated as spies, which meant that the Gestapo could threaten them with being shot—a normal interrogation method used to extract information swiftly. The British airmen struggled to establish their credibility as members of the RAF, which meant they would be regarded as British prisoners of war, whilst the SOE agent needed to distance himself from any military connection. The men were beaten and suffered various facial wounds, and all appeared unkempt, dirty and demoralised when they were later taken to the prison at Fresnes, Val-de-Marne, just south of Paris. They were placed before an examining justice, who was thought to have military powers as opposed to civilian. Having been condemned to death, they were taken back to Fresnes as criminals awaiting execution. Achille was sent back to Brussels, where he was separately tried and sentenced to death on 1 September 1943. On the last day of that month he was taken to the Tir national shooting range in Schaerbeek and executed. It was there that the famous British nurse Edith Cavell was executed by a German army firing squad in 1915. The British airmen's lives were thankfully saved as a result of the Luftwaffe intervening and establishing that they were aviator prisoners of war and as such fell under its jurisdiction and control. Many instances are recorded whereby the Luftwaffe engaged with the Gestapo and secured the release of captured evading Allied airmen, who then spent the rest of the war within the Luftwaffe's Stalag camps.

Returning to the SOE agents who dropped from the Whitley aircraft on 28 January 1942, the last individual was a Belgian, Oscar Catherine. He had been wounded in 1940 during the German invasion of the Low Countries and was extremely fortunate to have been evacuated to England. He was recruited by the SOE and received trained at its sabotage school. Oscar was effectively still in the Belgian army and gained a commission as an officer before returning by clandestine means to occupied Europe. He landed by parachute in the snow and made brief contact with his radio operator, Gaston Aarens, before parting some time later. Oscar moved between several locations and was made aware that his radio operator had been captured. Making use of personal friends, he established contacts that were secure and successfully engaged in resistance work by sabotaging the railways. However, Oscar's luck ran out when he was arrested after having been operational for nearly one year. On 17 January 1943, he had been visiting a Jesuit priest when he was seized and imprisoned. It would appear that the arrest was not connected to any resistance investigation by the Germans and so Oscar was able to provide a plausible explanation. He was sent to the concentration camp at Dachau where he survived until being released by the Allies in 1945. Four female SOE agents who had been arrested and brutally interrogated—Yolande Beekman, Madeleine Damerment, Noor Inayat Khan and Eliane Plewman—also ended up at Dachau, but early on the morning of 12 September 1944, they were forced to kneel down in pairs and each one was shot in the back of the head. Their bodies were burned in Dachau's infamous crematorium.

The bravery of these SOE resistance operatives has in many cases been recognised. In the case of Inayat Khan, the announcement of the award of the George Cross was made in *The London Gazette* of 5 April 1949. The full citation reads:

The KING has been graciously pleased to approve the posthumous award of the GEORGE CROSS to: Assistant Section Officer Nora INAYAT-KHAN (9901), Women's Auxiliary Air Force.

Assistant Section Officer Nora INAYAT-KHAN was the first woman operator to be infiltrated into enemy occupied France, and was landed by Lysander aircraft on 16th June, 1943. During the weeks immediately following her arrival, the Gestapo made mass arrests in the Paris Resistance groups to which she had been detailed. She refused however to abandon what had become the principal and most dangerous post in France, although given the opportunity to return to England, because she did not wish to leave her French comrades without communications and she hoped also to rebuild her group. She remained at her post therefore and did the excellent work which earned her a posthumous Mention in Despatches.

The Gestapo had a full description of her, but knew only her code name 'Madeleine'. They deployed considerable forces in their effort to catch her and so break the last remaining link with London. After 3½ months she was betrayed to the Gestapo and taken to their H.Q. in the Avenue Foch. The Gestapo had found her codes and messages and were now in a position to work back to London. They asked her to co-operate, but she refused and gave them no information of any kind. She was imprisoned in one of the cells on the 5th floor of the Gestapo H.Q. and remained there for several weeks during which time she made two unsuccessful attempts at escape. She was asked to sign a declaration that she would make no further attempts but she refused and the Chief of the Gestapo obtained permission from Berlin to send her to Germany for 'safe custody'. She was the first agent to be sent to Germany.

Assistant Section Officer INAYAT-KHAN was sent to Karlsruhe in November, 1943, and then to Pforsheim where her cell was apart from the main prison. She was considered to be a particularly dangerous and unco-operative prisoner. The Director of the prison has also been interrogated and has confirmed that Assistant Section Officer INAYAT-KHAN, when interrogated by the Karlsruhe Gestapo, refused to give any information whatsoever, either as to her work or her colleagues. She was taken with three others to Dachau Camp on the 12th September, 1944. On arrival, she was taken to the crematorium and shot.

Assistant Section Officer INAYAT-KHAN displayed the most conspicuous courage, both moral and physical, over a period of more than 12 months.

In 2003, the National Archives released the file on Noor Inayat Khan to the public. Within the extensive documentation is the statement of an unidentified Dutch prisoner imprisoned at Dachau, known only by the initials A. F., who claimed to be an eyewitness to her execution.

The White Rose

In 1942, Hans Scholl, a medical student at the University of Munich, his sister Sophie, Christoph Probst, Willi Graf, and Alexander Schmorell founded the White Rose movement, one of the few German groups that spoke out against Nazi genocidal policies. All of the male individuals from this group had previously been called into service with the Hitler Youth, which later provided moments to witness the horrors of the Nazi regime. Hans was called to the Eastern Front, where he and the other students alongside him would experience the inhumanity of war for a period of three months. It was their later decision to study medicine that fatalistically threw them together at the university in Munich. Sophie was required, as a prerequisite to her university studies, to serve in the *Reichsarbeitsdienst*, the National Labour Service, and this military-like regime had caused her to change her personal views of National Socialism.

Any form of organised resistance was practically impossible in Germany, so speaking openly even with close friends was fraught with danger as individuals never knew whether they might or might not be a Nazi Party member or a collaborator. So well organised was the control and surveillance of the populace by the Nazi Party that city apartment blocks had individuals assigned to spy and report on their neighbours. Ostensibly these individuals were responsible for the well-being of the residents of the block, but in reality they were monitoring, recording and reporting on activities and conversations.

Hans and Sophie's father, Robert Scholl, had served in the First World War as an infantry soldier and as a medic. In the 1930s, Robert was successfully employed as a tax adviser, but openly told his children that Hitler and the Nazis were, in his opinion, leading Germany down a road of destruction, and attempted to dissuade them from any party activity. When, in 1942, Robert made a comment to his secretary that he felt the war was lost and that the Russians would soon be sitting in Berlin, his comments were reported and led him to a term of imprisonment.

The Nazi Party controlled the news, the police, the armed forces, the judicial system, communications, travel and all levels of education from nursery to university, and a high level of control was imposed upon all cultural and religious institutions. Political indoctrination of the German population started at a very early age and continued by means of the Hitler Youth, with the ultimate goal of complete control. Children were exhorted in school to denounce even their own parents for derogatory remarks about Hitler, and evidence exists to show such levels of indoctrination were worryingly achieved.

Remarkably, the medical students who had grown up under the influence of this regime resolved to take a stand against Nazi tyranny. Many suggestions have been made concerning the significance of the title of their movement; however speculative, it may be that the colour white is synonymous with peace, and that alone highlights the group's ideology. They were all medical students, with the exception of Sophie who was studying biology and philosophy, and it was nothing other than fate that had brought them all together. Jointly they had seen Jewish friends and scholars driven from Germany. To maintain secrecy, membership of the White Rose movement was extremely small, and their main activity was to produce anti-war leaflets. This was obviously very dangerous to engage in, and capture would mean facing the inevitable charges of treason with inescapable consequences. Everyone knew each other in the movement and was convinced of the loyalty of the others.

The members of the White Rose were active between June 1942 and February 1943, and during that time they created several graffiti campaigns and studiously created six anti-war/anti-Nazi leaflets. This represented significant dedication, as paper was scarce and the creation and distribution of the leaflets was fraught with danger. A sufficient number were produced for them to be distributed in public, others being posted to specific individuals. Some students at the University of Hamburg began copying and distributing the leaflets themselves, which increased the distribution significantly. Leaflet No. 3 contained within its text the subject of sabotage:

Everyone must find his own way to realize resistance.

Sabotage in armaments factories and other businesses vital to the war effort. Sabotage in all assemblies, rallies, festivities, organizations that were breathed into life by the National Socialist Party, prevention of the smooth operation of the war machine (a machine that operates only for one war, one that focuses on the preservation and maintenance of the National Socialist Party and its dictatorship). Sabotage in all scholarly and intellectual realms that exist for the continuance of the current war—this whether it be in universities, colleges, laboratories, research facilities, or technical offices. Sabotage at all cultural events that could possibly exalt the 'prestige' of Fascists among the people. Sabotage in all branches of the fine arts that have the least connection to National Socialism and serve its goals. Sabotage in all areas of literature, all newspapers that are on the payroll of the 'government', and that fight for their ideas, for the dissemination of the brown lie. Do not put even one penny in the collection plate, even if it is disguised as a charity … Many, perhaps most, of the readers of these leaflets do not see clearly how they can practise an effective opposition. They do not see any avenues open to them. We want to try to show them that everyone is in a position to contribute to the overthrow of the system.

A further leaflet was headed 'To the fellow fighters in the resistance' and was written in early 1943, after the German defeat at Stalingrad. Prof. Kurt Huber, a philosophy teacher at the university, provided advice to Hans and Alexander and assisted in editing the text for the leaflets. Having obtained a duplicating machine, the White Rose issued its fifth leaflet in January 1943, and ultimately created several thousand copies.

> The day of reckoning has come—the reckoning of German youth with the most abominable tyrant our people have ever been forced to endure. We grew up in a state in which all free expression of opinion is ruthlessly suppressed. The Hitler Youth, the SA, the SS have all tried to drug us, to regiment us in the most promising years of our lives. For us there is but one slogan: Fight against the party. The name of Germany is dishonoured for all time if German youth does not finally rise, take revenge, smash its tormentors. Students! The German people look to us.

On 18 February 1943, Hans and Sophie arrived on the university campus with a suitcase full of printed leaflets. They left large stacks outside fully occupied lecture halls, knowing that they would be collected by the large numbers of students as they moved about the campus. Deciding that they would ensure that the rest were also distributed, from the top floor they tossed the remaining leaflets in the air and let them float down to the ground below. This rather reckless action was seen by the caretaker, Jakob Schmid, who promptly sought to restrain the culprits and saw to it that the police were called. Upon their arrest for the possession and distribution of the leaflets, all the evidence needed by the Gestapo, both Hans and Sophie admitted their full responsibility in an attempt to end any form of interrogation that might result in them revealing the names of other members of the movement. Hans had with him a draft of another leaflet that had been written by Christoph Probst, but despite Hans's intention to avoid the Gestapo finding the draft and implicating Christoph, it was recovered and the pieces revealed all of its content and Christoph's fatal connection with it. The leaflet in its entirety read:

Stalingrad!

200,000 German brothers were sacrificed for the prestige of a militaristic imposter. The human conditions of surrender set down by the Russians were hidden from the soldiers who were sacrificed. For this mass murder, General Paulus received the Oak Leaves [decoration]. High-ranking officers escaped from the slaughter in Stalingrad by aeroplane. Hitler refused to allow those who were entrapped and surrounded to retreat to the troops behind the line. Now the blood of 200,000 soldiers who were doomed to death accuses the murderer named Hitler.

Tripoli! They surrendered unconditionally to the 8th English Army. And what did the English do? They allowed the citizens to continue living their lives as usual. They even let police and bureaucrats remain in office. Only one thing did they undertake to do thoroughly: They cleansed the great Italian colonial city of every false ringleader and subhuman. The annihilating, overwhelming super-power is approaching on every side with dead certainty. Hitler is less likely than Paulus to capitulate. There would be no escape for him. And will you be deceived as were the 200,000 who defended Stalingrad in a losing cause, so that you will be massacred, sterilized, or robbed of your children?

Roosevelt, the most powerful man in the world, said in Casablanca on January 26, 1943: Our war of extermination is not against the people, but against the political systems. We will fight for an unconditional surrender. More contemplation may be needed before a decision can be made. This is about the lives of millions of people. Should Germany meet the same fate as Tripoli?

Today, all of Germany is encircled just as Stalingrad was. All Germans shall be sacrificed to the emissaries of hate and extermination. Sacrificed to him who tormented the Jews, eradicated half of the Poles, and who wishes to destroy Russia. Sacrificed to him who took from you freedom, peace, domestic happiness, hope, and gaiety, and gave you inflationary money.

That shall not, that may not, come to pass! Hitler and his regime must fall so that Germany may live. Make up your minds: Stalingrad and destruction, or Tripoli and a future of hope. And when you have decided, act.

This dangerous material obviously led to Christoph's immediate arrest. The Gestapo refused to believe that only three people were involved in what appeared to be a significant and well-organised group engaged in the distribution of illegal material. After further interrogation and the searching of addresses of individuals connected to those arrested, they gathered details of several other suspects. These suspects, some of whom were not involved, were arrested, resulting in an estimated eighty people being seized by the Gestapo over the ensuing few days. The majority were taken to Stadelheim Prison and Nazi officials convened the People's Court to try the three primary defendants within just three days.

It was to be one of Roland Freisler's first major cases, attracting attention from across Germany and further afield. The Gestapo in Munich, well aware that they had been the focus of attention in catching the White Rose perpetrators, drafted a circular in Himmler's name and distributed it to all university teachers and students, calling for the leaders to come forward. They were strongly of the belief that more senior figures were implicated than those they had detained. In fact, it was only the sole figure of Prof. Huber who was subsequently arrested.

Freisler presided over the trial of Hans, Sophie and Christoph on 22 February 1943. In retrospect, it appears that he conducted himself with greater control than in many of his later trials; it is possible that this high-profile case induced him to control his temperament so as not to intrude into the proceedings. Exceptionally, the accused were given the right to speak at the end of the trial, something that Freisler generally saw no reason to grant. The official court transcript of the sentence explains:

Transcript I H 47/43

In the Name of the German People
In the action against

1.   Hans Fritz Scholl, Munich. Born at Ingersheim, 22 September 1918.
2.   Sophia Magdalena Scholl, Munich. Born at Forchtenberg, 9 May 1921.
3.   Christoph Hermann Probst, Innsbruck. Born at Murnau, 6 November 1919.

Now in investigative custody regarding treasonous assistance to the enemy, preparing to commit high treason, and weakening of the nation's armed security, the People's Court, first Senate, pursuant to the trial held on February 22, 1943, in which the officers were:

President of the People's Court Dr. Freisler, Presiding,
Director of the Regional [Bavarian] Judiciary Stier,
SS Group Leader Breithaupt,
SA Group Leader Bunge,
State Secretary and SA Group Leader Koglmaier, and representing the Attorney-General to the Supreme Court of the Reich, Reich Attorney Weyersberg,
find:

That the accused have in time of war by means of leaflets called for the sabotage of the war effort and armaments and for the overthrow of the National Socialist way of life of our people, have propagated defeatist ideas, and have most vulgarly defamed the Führer, thereby giving aid to the enemy of the Reich and weakening the armed security of the nation.

On this account they are to be punished by Death.
Their honour and rights as citizens are forfeited for all time.

Grounds
The accused Hans Scholl has been a student of medicine since the spring of 1939 and, thanks to the solicitude of the National Socialist government, has begun his eighth semester in those studies. He has served meanwhile on temporary duty in a field hospital in the campaign in France and again from July to November 1942 on the Eastern Front as a medical aide. As a student he is bound by duty to give exemplary service to the common cause. In his capacity as a soldier—on assignment to medical study—he has a special duty of loyalty to the Führer. This and the assistance which he was expressly granted by the Reich did not deter him in the first half of the summer of 1942 from writing, duplicating, and distributing leaflets of the 'White Rose'. These defeatist leaflets predict the defeat of Germany and call

for passive resistance in the form of sabotage in war industries and for sabotage in general, to the end that the German people would be deprived of the National Socialist way of life and thus also of their government.

Returning from Russia in November 1942, Hans had requested his friend, the accused Christoph, to provide him with a manuscript that would open the eyes of the German people, and a draft of a leaflet was delivered at the end of January 1943. Hans and his sister Sophie decided to carry on leaflet propaganda in the form of a campaign against the war and in favour of collaboration with the plutocratic enemies of National Socialism. Brother and sister, who had quarters in the same rooming house, collaborated in the writing of a leaflet, 'To All Germans'. In it they predicted Germany's defeat, urged a war of liberation against 'National Socialist gangsterism', and demanded the establishment of a liberal democracy. In addition, they drafted a leaflet, 'German Students!' (in later versions, 'Fellow Fighters!'), wherein they called for a struggle against the Nazi Party. They wrote that the day of reckoning was at hand, and were bold enough to compare their call to battle against the Führer and the National Socialist way of life with the War of Liberation against Napoleon in 1813. In reference to their project, they used the military song, 'Up, up, my people, let smoke and flame be our sign!'

Hans and Sophie, partly with the help of Alexander Schmorell, duplicated the leaflets and by common agreement distributed them as follows, as reported at the trial:

1. Schmorell travelled to Salzburg, Linz, and Vienna and put 200, 200, and 1,200 leaflets addressed to places in those cities in the post; and in Vienna an additional 400 were directed to Frankfurt am Main.
2. Sophia Scholl posted 200 in Augsburg and on another occasion 600 in Stuttgart.
3. Hans Scholl, with the aid of Schmorell, scattered thousands of leaflets in the streets of Munich at night.
4. On February 18 the Scholls deposited 1500-1800 copies in bundles in the University of Munich, and Sophia Scholl let drop a large number from the third floor down the lightwell of the building.

Hans Scholl and Schmorell also, on the nights of August 8, 1942, and February 14, 1943, defaced walls in many places in Munich, and particularly the university, with the words 'Down With Hitler', 'Hitler the Mass Murderer', and 'Freedom.' After the first incident Sophia Scholl learned of this action, was in agreement with it, and requested—though without success—to be allowed to help in the future!

Expenses were covered by the accused themselves—in all, about 1,000 marks.

Probst likewise began his medical studies in the spring of 1939 and is now in his eighth semester, a soldier on student duty. He is married and has three children aged two and a half, one and a quarter years, and four weeks. He is a 'non-political man'—hence no man at all! Neither the solicitude of the National Socialist Reich for his professional training nor the fact that it was only the National Socialist demographic policy which made it possible for him to have a family prevented him from writing at the behest of Scholl—in cowardly defeatism—a 'manuscript' which takes the heroic struggle in Stalingrad as the occasion for defaming the Führer as a military swindler and which then progressing to a hortatory tone, calls for opposition to National Socialism and for action which would lead, as he pretends, to an honourable capitulation. He supports the promises in this leaflet by citing— Roosevelt! And his knowledge about these matters he derived from listening to British broadcasts!

All the accused have admitted the facts stated above. Probst offers as excuse his 'psychotic depression' at the time he drafted the leaflet, a depression which he claims arises from Stalingrad and the childbed illness of his wife. But such explanations do not excuse a reaction of this scope.

Whoever has, like the three accused, committed acts of high treason, weakening the home front and thereby in time of war the security of the nation, and by the same token has aided the enemy (Par. 5 of Special War Decree and Par. 91 b of the Criminal Code), raises the dagger for a stab in the back of the Front! That applies also to Probst, though he claims that his manuscript was not intended for use as a leaflet—since the tone and style of the manuscript proves the opposite. Whoever acts in this way—and particularly at this time, when we must close our ranks— is attempting to cause the first rift in the unity of the battle front. And German students, whose traditional honour has always called for self-sacrifice for Volk and fatherland, were the ones who acted thus!

If a deed of this sort were to be punished otherwise than by death, we would be forging the first links of a chain whose end—in an earlier time—was 1918. Therefore, for the protection of the Volk and the Reich at war, the People's Court has found but one just punishment: death. The People's Court knows that it is at one with our soldiers in this decision.

Through their treason to our Volk, the accused have forever forfeited their citizenship.

As criminals who have been found guilty, the accused will pay the court costs. Stier.

(*signed*) Dr. Freisler

Sentenced to death by beheading, they were taken to the guillotine that afternoon. At 17.00 hours, Sophie Scholl was taken first, followed by Hans, who just before he was beheaded cried out, 'Long live freedom.' Christoph Probst was the last to lay his neck upon the Fallbeil in what must have been the most horrendous circumstances for him, the device thick with fluids and the floor visibly evidencing the previous events before his eyes. Confirmation of the executions was sent by telex to Berlin at 18.50 hours.

The death of Christoph Probst and the Scholls was followed on 19 April 1943 by the trial of Willi Graf, Helmut Bauer, Susanne Hirzel, Alexander Schmorell, Prof. Kurt Huber, Eugen Grimminger, Gisela Schertling, Heinrich Guter, Falk Harnack and Katharina Schüddekopf, all of whom had been rounded up by the Gestapo, several of them having tenuous links to the White Rose group. Like those before them, Karl Huber, Alexander Schmorell and Willi Graf were sentenced to death by the infamous Freisler. All but one of the other defendants received jail terms ranging from ten years to six months; Susanne Hirzel was acquitted by Freisler, apparently in thanks for the Führer's birthday.

On 3 May 1943, the portable Erika typewriter No. 507 540/6 confiscated by the Gestapo and presented as evidence of the White Rose activities was claimed by the People's Court for use by the Attorney-General's office. Likewise, the Remington typewriter No. NL 82 533M, which was also seized and presented to the People's Court, was made available to the Reich's special operation for locating typewriters. It was ironic that these machines that had once been used to produce anti-Nazi communications were to be used forthwith within the regime's judicial processes.

The execution sentences imposed on 19 April for Alexander Schmorell and Kurt Huber were not carried out until 13 July. On that day, at 17.00 hours in Stadelheim Prison, Alexander was taken to the execution room where the Fallbeil severed his head from his body. The most experienced executioner, Johann Reichhart, then swiftly accepted the professor and once again the blade of the Fallbeil did its work. In keeping with the standard practice of charging for the services of the Fallbeil, letters were typed and sent to the families of the individuals who had been executed. Earlier that same day, the third trial for associated White Rose members had begun. However, Freisler was not required to hear the case against Wilhelm Geyer, Harald Dohrn, Josef Soehngen, and Manfred Eickemeyer. Within just an hour of the White Rose executions conducted that day, three of the accused were remarkably acquitted in the courtroom, whilst Josef Soehngen received just six months' imprisonment.

It is likely that Willi Graf was supposed to have been executed on 13 July alongside his fellow White Rose defendants. However, his name was removed from the execution list for that day, probably due to an administrative error. But his fate was finally sealed on 12 October 1943, when he was taken to the Fallbeil and beheaded.

Unbeknown to those White Rose members who had lain on the bench of the Fallbeil, their legacy of resistance continued to speak out to the German people. Their organisation's sixth leaflet, composed by Kurt Huber, was successfully smuggled out of Germany and passed on to the Allies, subsequently ending up in the hands of the British government's Political Warfare Executive. Having established the authenticity of the leaflet, and realising its importance, the PWE reproduced it in significant numbers:

German Students!

Our nation stands shaken before the demise of the heroes of Stalingrad. The brilliant strategy of a Lance Corporal from the World War has senselessly and irresponsibly driven three hundred and thirty thousand German men to death and destruction. Führer, we thank you!

Unrest ferments among the German people: Shall we continue to entrust the fate of our armies to a dilettante? Do we wish to sacrifice the remainder of our German youth to the vile instinct for power of a Party clique? On no account!

The day of reckoning has come, the reckoning of our German youth with the most abominable tyranny that our nation has ever endured. In the name of all the German youth, we demand that Adolf Hitler's government return to us our personal freedom, the most valuable possession a German owns. He has cheated us of it in a most contemptible manner.

We have grown up in a nation where every open expression of opinion is callously bludgeoned. Hitler Youth, the SA and SS have tried to conform, revolutionize, and anaesthetize us in the most fruitful years of our educational lives. The despicable methodology was called 'ideological education'; it attempted to suffocate budding independent thought and values in a fog of empty phrases. 'The Führer's pick'– something more simultaneously devilish and stupid could not be imagined.

This 'Führer's pick' raises its future Party bosses in Ordensburgen so they will be godless, brazen, and conscienceless users and assassins, blind, stupid disciples of the Führer. We 'Workers of the Spirit' would do well if we bludgeoned this new class of men. An intellectual and moral elite of student leaders and Gauleiter hopefuls distracts us systematically from every disciplined, deep course of study. They seek to fritter away our time with roll-calls, Party gatherings, and trade association conferences. Soldiers who have fought on the front lines are reprimanded like schoolboys by these gentlemen. The Gauleiter and student leaders insult the honour of female students with lascivious jokes.

German female students at the college in Munich have given a dignified answer to the besmirching of their honour. German male students have gone into action on behalf of their female comrades and stood firm. This is a beginning in the fight for our free self-determination; without this, intellectual values can never be created. Thank you to all the brave comrades who have led the way with such an illuminating example!

For us now there is but one watchword: Fight against the Party! Get out of the Party organizations in which they wish to keep us politically muzzled! Get out of the lecture halls of the SS-Noncom-or-Major-Generals and the Party sycophants! This has to do with genuine scholarship and true freedom of thought! No threats can dismay us, not even the closing of our colleges.

This is a battle that we all must fight for our future, our freedom and honour in a political system that is conscious of its moral responsibility.

Freedom and honour! For ten long years, Hitler and his associates have abused, stomped, and twisted these two glorious German words till they are loathsome. Only dilettantes are capable of doing this, dilettantes who cast the highest values of a nation before swine. Over the last ten years, they have more than shown us what freedom and honour means to them—they have destroyed all material and intellectual freedom and all moral substance in the German people. The terrible blood-bath that they have caused in all of Europe in the name of the freedom and honour of the German people—a blood-bath that they cause anew every day—has opened the eyes of even the stupidest German.

The German name will be forever defamed if German youth does not finally arise, avenge, and atone, if he does not shatter his tormentor and raise up a new intellectual Europe. Students! The German nation looks to us! In 1943, they expect from us the breaking of the National Socialist terror through the power of the spirit, just as in 1813 the Napoleonic terror was broken. Beresina and Stalingrad are going up in flames in the East, and the dead of Stalingrad beseech us: 'Courage, my people! The beacons are burning!' Our nation is awakening against the enslavement of Europe by National Socialism, in a new pious revival of freedom and honour!

The White Rose leaflets reproduced by the PWE were transported across England and delivered to the airfields of RAF Bomber Command stations. Avro Lancaster and Halifax bombers supported by other small aircraft carried the leaflets on bombing operations and distributed them by dropping them across Germany to ensure the words of the White Rose group were read by the widest possible audience.

The value of these 'nickelling' operations had been previously well established by the PWE. These leaflets ('nickels') were often created specifically to lower the morale of enemy troops. In addition, pseudo-currency and ration books were printed and dropped to create financial instability over occupied countries, whilst the publication *Le Courrier de l'Air*, a miniature French language newspaper, was intended to boost morale and give positive Allied information to inhabitants across France. The German authorities were strict in enforcing the rule that it was illegal to possess or simply read Allied dropped material.

The RAF was well aware of the value and responsibility of delivering the propaganda material. Bundles of leaflets, several inches deep, were banded together and thrown out of the aircraft at dedicated and precise locations. It was estimated that at around 12,000 feet, these bundles of printed pages or booklets took up to an hour to gently flutter to the ground. Thousands of leaflets would cover a huge built-up area and prove almost impossible for the German authorities to collect and destroy.

Today the main square at the University of Munich, Geschwister-Scholl-Platz, is named after the Scholl siblings. On the anniversary of Hans and Sophie's execution, a public ceremony is held to commemorate their lives. Fittingly, throughout Germany there are many streets and schools in particular that are named after the Scholls, and the members of the White Rose resistance group who were once considered traitors by the Nazi judiciary are now respectfully regarded as heroes. The White Rose memorial museum and archive department was established in 1997 and is appropriately housed in the University of Munich.

Baum Group

In central Berlin, Herbert and Marianne Baum became the nucleus for a Jewish resistance group that had originated from various youth groups with a Communist background and consolidated itself with young Jewish members. The leader, Herbert Baum, was born at Poznań in 1912, but grew up in Berlin. As a Jew, he was removed from further education by the Nazis, and he joined the Communist Youth League in 1931. The persecution of the Jews in Berlin was obviously significant to Herbert, but his involvement in the Communist circle of friends became his priority and within his group, which included many Zionists, he held court with a small but intimate group of just fourteen members, seven of whom were women. The youngest was Hildegard Löwy, born in 1922, who was disabled with one arm; Charlotte Päch, aged 32, was by far the oldest member.

In 1934, Herbert organised the CYL in the south-western district of Berlin. It was at this time that he associated with Marianne Cohen, whom he would later marry. Realising that his group needed to become more resilient, Herbert actively recruited members from within similar organisations. Although members of the group were not active in resistance against the Nazi dictatorship, they passively communicated such resolve in their meetings about Communist activists, but things changed in 1939 when membership of anything other than the Hitler Youth movement became illegal. The Baum Group were forced to change tactics, as they were all only too well aware that the combination of being Jewish and sympathising with Communism created a recipe for Nazi attention. Herbert and Marianne's best friend Felix Heymann was nearly always by their side, and a married couple, Sala and Martin Kochmann, allowed the group to meet in their apartment. The majority of the Baum Group members were employed as forced labour performing war work in various factories, and Herbert in particular saw this as an opportunity to recruit into his group. The yellow star that they wore at all times announcing their Jewish status served as a constant reminder of the Nazi oppression imposed upon them.

Following Germany's invasion of the Soviet Union in the summer of 1941, the Baum Group began the prolific writing and distributing of leaflets outlining the injustices and dangerous consequences of the war. This set in motion other diverse leaflet distribution, even encouraging housewives to protest at the serious food shortages. Other independent resistance groups were also creating this form of resistance, which was particularly despised by the German police and the Gestapo.

On 15 April 1942, Hildegard Löwy was arrested and imprisoned. Despite her physical disability, she tried to escape a week before her trial but her attempt at freedom was thwarted. Hildegard, aged twenty, appeared before the People's Court in Berlin and received the death sentence. Rarely had an executioner been tasked to decapitate a disabled young woman like Hildegard. She was decapitated on 4 March 1943, just five days short of her birthday. The delivery of her torso, devoid of limb and head, to Berlin University for Hermann Stieve's dissection is difficult to comprehend.

Being comprised primarily of Jewish Communist sympathisers, the Baum Group were prompted to be even more proactive in their resistance to the deportation of Jews and the Nazi Ministry of Public Enlightenment and Propaganda's focus of attention on the life of Russian peasants. The anti-Bolshevik 'Soviet Paradise' exhibition in Berlin was what prompted Herbert to instigate an attack. Combining with another resistance group, they planted an incendiary device inside one of the exhibits on 18 May 1942, in the hope that the entire exhibition would be destroyed. The device did detonate and a small fire caused minor damage, but it was far from the desired effect. Herbert was arrested on 22 May, and subjected to such horrific and sustained torture that his life ended in Moabit Prison on 11 June 1942. His wife Marianne had also been arrested with him, and on 16 July 1942, she was tried by a Special Court in Berlin and sentenced to death. Her execution took place in Plötzensee Prison on 18 August 1942. Some conjecture exists that Herbert may have committed suicide, but whatever the true circumstances surrounding his death, the Baum Group was destined for many more of its operatives to be arrested and imprisoned. The initial trials took place in the People's Court on 10 December 1942, the accused being charged with 'organised Communist treason'. Needless to say, all of the initial defendants were found guilty and sentenced to death. Heinz Rotholz, Heinz Birnbaum, Hanni Meyer, Marianne Joachim, Lothar Salinger, Helmut Neumann and Siegbert Rotholz were all beheaded in Plötzensee on 4 March 1943.

Baum Group members Harry and Edith Fraenkel suffered the loss of their baby son just six months after his birth in 1941. Edith was arrested on 18 July 1942, and on 10 December was sentenced to five years' imprisonment at Cottbus. There was very little evidence against her in relation to any involvement with the group, other than merely attending social meetings. In October 1943, the Gestapo transferred her to the Theresienstadt transit camp for Jews from which the Germans deported individuals in large numbers to killing centres, concentration camps and forced-labour camps. An estimated 10,000 people had passed through this camp, and after the war, in 1946, the Association of Jewish Refugees began its attempt to compile a register of these people. In Edith's case, records indicate that she was eventually sent to Auschwitz and murdered in circumstances that remain unknown.

Charlotte, the oldest member of the Baum Group, was born in Berlin in 1909. She had trained as a nurse and joined the Communist youth group that was founded in the Jewish hospital where she was working. She joined the Baum Group after meeting Herbert in the hospital. It was here that she met Gustav Päch and they married in 1932, their daughter Eva being born in August the following year. Shortly after Eva's birth, Gustav was arrested by the Gestapo for suspected Communist sympathies and imprisoned for sixteen months. Although Gustav was eventually released from prison, the couple never reunited as a family, as Charlotte had forged new friendships in the Baum Group and had met Richard Holzer in 1941. She was eventually arrested on 8 October 1942 for distributing illegal ration coupons as opposed to any connection with her membership of the Baum Group. The fake ration coupons may well have been those printed in Britain and distributed by the RAF in an effort to destabilise food rationing across Germany. Charlotte was convicted of 'violating the war economic order of Germany' and sentenced to eighteen months' imprisonment at Leipzig.

The Gestapo were later able to connect her to the Baum Group and Charlotte was once again to be tried, this time alongside other group members in the People's Court in early 1943. However, she never appeared with her fellow Baum defendants as she had contracted scarlet fever whilst imprisoned at Leipzig, a factor that clearly saved her life. She was moved to several different prisons and labour camps, eventually ending up in the Jewish transit camp at Schulstrasse. In June 1944, she managed to escape from her pitiful existence in the camp and successfully made contact with Dorothea Schneider in Potsdam. Dorothea was a pastor's widow who lived with her daughter and risked everything to help Jews like Charlotte. Dorothea survived the war, dying in August 1946, and the Jewish community later awarded her the status of 'Righteous Among the Nations' for the rescue of German Jews such as Charlotte. After the war, Charlotte married Richard Holzer in Germany—two rare survivors of the Baum Group able to testify about their activity—and the couple had a baby son, who sadly died shortly after birth. Richard predeceased Charlotte, who died in Berlin on 29 September 1980. Richard, Charlotte and their son now lie together in the Jewish cemetery at Weissensee.

Two sisters, Alice and Hella Hirsch, were both members of Herbert's group and both were arrested on 8 July 1942. The younger sister, nineteen-year-old Alice, appeared in court on 10 December and was sentenced to three years' imprisonment. The Gestapo moved her to two different prisons, but on 14 October 1943 she was sent to Auschwitz where her life was taken in unknown circumstances. Hella, aged 21, was sentenced to death at the same court appearance and was executed in Plötzensee Prison on 4 March 1943. Her beheaded body added to those supplied to Berlin University's Institute of Anatomy, as did the body of Marianne Joachim, sentenced and executed on the same day as Hella.

Suzanne Wesse was not a Jew; she originated from France and had moved to Germany. Whilst employed in Berlin she met her husband Richard who, although half-Jewish, possessed the German certification of the Nuremberg Race Laws that gave him the status of a *mischling* (half-breed) of the first degree. As such, and despite his deferred Jewish blood-line, he was allowed to keep his German citizenship. In April 1937, their daughter Katherina was born. Suzanne joined the Baum Group, involving herself in poster and leaflet design, but on 23 May 1942, Suzanne and her husband were both arrested. Richard was later released after just three weeks' detention, but Suzanne was sentenced to death on 16 July 1942 and swiftly executed in Plötzensee Prison on 18 August.

Sala Kochmann, a Polish Jew, and her husband Martin, a close friend of Herbert Baum's, were amongst the first members of the group. They were participants in the failed arson attack and both were arrested on 23 May 1942. Following her arrest, Sala tried to take her own life by jumping from a window at the police headquarters in order to avoid being tortured by the Gestapo. She suffered critical injuries and was taken to the hospital where Charlotte Päch was working. Fortunately, Charlotte was able to warn other members of the group. Sala was presented at trial on 16 July 1942, strapped on a stretcher, and was sentenced to death, the Fallbeil at Plötzensee removing the head from her broken body on 18 August. Her reproductive organs were immediately removed when her body arrived in Hermann Stieve's mortuary.

Several others received death sentences for their involvement in the rather small and isolated resistance group that surrounded Herbert Baum. Thirty-one members of the group died during the war: twenty-two were executed by decapitation, while nine died in death camps. The German press was forbidden to publish any stories about the attack, so the German people were never informed that a small but well-organised resistance circle of Jewish Communists had partially destroyed a major Nazi propaganda exhibition, one which the regime needed in order to maintain the morale of the German people, despite the true situation being played out in the battles against the Russians in which the Third Reich was suffering monumental losses. The winter of 1941–42 was one of the harshest in Russian history, and the German army was unprepared. There was no winter clothing for the troops, priority having been given to the production of ammunition and arms in an effort to destroy the Red Army. The German public experienced a startling appeal for the collection of winter clothing for the soldiers on the Russian front, which in itself must have raised serious doubts in their minds about what was actually happening in Hitler's war.

The Dutch Council of Resistance

On 10 May 1940, Hitler ordered his troops into the Netherlands without any declaration of war between the two countries, even though the country had adopted a policy of strict neutrality. However, this had afforded them no protection from the Nazi onslaught across their country and the purge towards France.

Following the invasion, the persecution of the Jewish population in the Netherlands progressed, with the Nazis greatly assisted in their efforts once the Dutch Church Tax registration documents came under their control. These registration forms had been compiled before the war by the Dutch authorities, who required each individual to register their religion in order to enable the distribution of the respective finances amongst the various religious organisations. The Nazi government sought to demand from the Dutch populace employed in public office the statutory submission of an 'Aryan Attestation' document on which their religious and ethnic ancestry was stated. This so-called *Ariërverklaring* process was rebuffed by many, but German SS enforcement was widespread and the combined documentation process enabled the Nazis gradually to implement the removal of Jews from within the Netherlands. There were Dutch civilians who resisted the enforced *Ariërverklaring*, and many of those gradually formed into resistance groups. It has to be said that primarily the initial resistance simply involved assisting the persecuted groups sought by the Nazis. However, this developed into groups secreting those same people in hiding. The case of Anne Frank is a classic example of how a Jewish family was hidden by underground operatives in the Netherlands. The same applied to the protection afforded to young conscription-age Dutchmen and Allied pilots and crew members. Collectively these people were known as *Onderduikers*, literally under-divers, who were engaged in resistance activities.

One man, Gerrit van der Veen, an artist and sculptor, tried to help Jews in a very practical way. Together with Jan van Gilse, a musician, and an openly homosexual artist named Willem Arondeus, he established the underground organisation 'De Vrije Kunstenaar' (The Free Artist) that sat within what was to become one of the most active Dutch resistance groups amongst the 'Raad van Verzet', the Dutch Council of Resistance. Together van der Veen, van Gilse and Arondeus incited their fellow artists to resist the Nazi occupation by publicising the fact that Jews registering with the local authorities were being deported to concentration camps and from there to the death camps. The artists published a newsletter calling for resistance against the occupation and strove to help the Jewish people by better means than simply hiding them. When the Germans introduced personal identity documents, which additionally distinguished between Jews and non-Jews, the Free Artists sought the help of a printer, Frans Duwaer, as they planned to design and produce some 80,000 false identity papers. They had little problem in producing fake documents of superb quality, which were printed in secret at the weekends at Duwaer's printing works. The group worked together to accumulate the paper and card required for this monumental task, such resources being very difficult to acquire without arousing suspicion.

The false documents passed initial Nazi scrutiny with ease, but when they were compared to the Church Tax registrations in the Amsterdam Registry Office, minor errors in them soon became obvious. The Registry was housed in what had been a large concert hall and contained the names of an estimated 70,000 Amsterdam Jews. The Free Artists conceived a plan to try and destroy the official records, based on their previous exploits in breaking into official buildings at night, setting fires and using whatever explosive material they had to destroy the records and documents being used to assist Nazi control. On 10 February 1943, the group attacked the Regional Employment Board, followed on 27 March by a similar attack on the Population Registry. For that attack, several members of the Free Artists donned police uniforms created by Sjoerd Bakker, a master tailor and resistance member. The group forced their way into the Registry and ignited their arsenal of pyrotechnics, setting fire to the identity papers. It proved difficult to destroy them because of their confined storage, but the flames eventually took hold and the fire brigade's hoses themselves did untold damage to many thousands of the cards. This attack was deemed a success and no doubt added to the protection of those Jews in possession of fake identity documents. Unfortunately, it did nothing for the significant numbers of men, women and children who had already been deported to predictable fates.

On 29 April 1943, a further type of deportation was announced when the Germans directed that all former members of the Dutch armed forces were required to report for work in Germany. The Council of Resistance, seeing an opportunity to cause unrest, encouraged workers to withhold their labour throughout the Dutch factories. This unexpectedly created more volunteers coming into the proactive resistance movements, and in particular into the groups within the Council of Resistance. Their activities were progressively becoming more effective, as power stations and other strategic targets were sabotaged. Rudolf Bloemgarten, a medical student in Amsterdam, was a member of van der Veen's resistance group and took part in a failed attack on Amsterdam's Procurator-General Jan Feitsma in 1943. Feitsma was also adviser to Anton Mussert, one of the founders of the National Socialist Movement in the Netherlands. The attack failed to kill Feitsma but injured his son. In retribution, fifty randomly selected civilian men were sent to Camp Vught as a reprisal for the attack. The Gestapo had been actively engaged in fighting Dutch resistance, which included Communist activists, but the activities of the Free Artists were now a priority for investigation as a result of their heightened level of activity. It was not an uncommon practice in the Netherlands for resistance suspects, once captured, to be immediately imprisoned with no judicial process undertaken.

Van der Veen and his loyal group of artists had played a vital part in thwarting the Nazi expulsion of Jews from the Netherlands, particularly Amsterdam, through their attempts to destroy the registration documents. However, despite the security imposed around their small group, it appears that they were betrayed to the Gestapo and within two weeks of the final arson attack the majority of them had been arrested. Amongst those captured was one of the founders of the group, the well-known writer and painter Willem Arondeus, the Jewish medical student Rudolf Bloemgarten, the writer Johan Brouwer, and the architect Koen Limperg, who had been a vitally important member of the group, having been in a position to provide plans of many of the buildings attacked by the group. Van der Veen, together with Willem Sandberg, the then curator of Amsterdam's Stedelijk Museum, managed to escape the Gestapo's efforts to capture the entire group and mounted a predictable but unsuccessful attempt to get his friends out of the Amsterdam detention centre. During the attempt, van der Veen was shot in the back but once again managed to escape. He was finally captured around 12 May 1944. The increasing attacks against Dutch Fascists and Nazi rule led to widespread reprisals against the Dutch people, and evidence confirms that large groups of civilians were swept up and deported.

The fate of the resistance members in the Free Artists group arrested in April and May of 1943 was decided at a trial on 18 June 1943. They were detained in Weteringschans Prison, used as the Gestapo's headquarters during the Nazi occupation of the Netherlands, and were later presented to the SS and Police Court in Amsterdam. All thirteen defendants were found guilty of sabotage and treason and condemned to death, following which they were executed or 'fusilladed' in the dunes near Bloemendaal, just beyond Haarlem, on 1 July 1943. At the time of his execution, 48-year-old Willem Arondeus was the oldest resistance fighter in the group. His dying wish was to let it be known that homosexuals were not cowards and that they could be as brave as anyone else. Gerrit van der Veen had created a unique group of individuals who had bravely fought the Nazi dictatorship in the Netherlands, and the lasting memory of his heroic actions and those that died alongside him ensures that the brave Free Artists will not be forgotten.

In the summer of 1944, Hitler issued the *Niedermachungsbefehl* orders, which stated that resistance fighters arrested in the Netherlands no longer had the right to a trial and that those who were armed when they were arrested could be executed on the spot. In addition, if handed over to the SS, that organisation could decide which detainees would be executed by shooting. The frequently used term 'fusillade' was indicative of the many deaths of resistance operatives by the Nazis, and in the Netherlands these were initially undertaken at remote locations. However, from the autumn of 1944 onwards, fusillades generally did not take place in such places but in public next to roads and on squares, with the bodies often remaining *in situ* for several days as an intentional and macabre deterrent. From the end of August 1944 until September 1944, 450 people were executed under the authority of the *Niedermachungsbefehl*.

After the war, in late 1945, attempts were made to locate those who had paid with their lives for the freedom of others and whose bodies had been placed in shallow graves in the Bloemendaal dunes. The last person to perish at that location, on 17 April 1945, was executed on the express orders of Willy Lages, the commander of the Amsterdam office of the Sipo, the Nazi security police. Lages denied the Dutch resistance operative Hannie Schaft any form of trial for her activities within the Council of Resistance and she became the only female to be added to the many resistance operatives buried in the shallow graves at Bloemendaal. Just seventeen days after her unlawful execution, the Allied forces completed the liberation of the Netherlands. Hannie's remains were reinterred at the Cemetery of Honour in Bloemendaal on 27 November 1945, when the enormity of the executions by the Germans upon the Dutch resistance was recognised by the presence at the ceremony of Queen Wilhelmina of the Netherlands and other members of the Dutch royal family. Significant efforts were undertaken to locate and recover all of the victims, the final interment taking place ten years later. A total of 422 persons were found in the dunes and adjacent areas and laid to rest alongside Hannie Schaft.

One of the surviving members of Gerrit van der Veen's resistance group, Willem Sandberg, designed a plaque to commemorate the brave raid on the Registry in

Amsterdam that had taken place to help the Jewish people. To this day, the plaque can be seen on the building.

Witaszek Resistance Group

On 4 October 1943, Heinrich Himmler delivered a speech to a secret meeting of high-ranking SS officers in Poznań. As head of the SS, he had immense power and responsibility for internal security in Nazi Germany, and spoke frankly about the extermination of the Jews. The Gestapo headquarters at Poznań was located in a relatively new Polish military garrison building that accommodated an estimated 200 officers and included a basement used as a detention unit and for interrogations. It quickly gained a reputation for the torture and despicable treatment meted out to anyone unfortunate enough to be detained there. Prisoners that passed through it frequently ended up in either the prison in Młyńska Street or the nineteenth-century penal camp Fort VII where vast numbers of prisoners were shot by regular firing squads.

The University of Poznań, in keeping with Nazi education policy, was managed and staffed as much as possible by Germans. However, a minority of posts had been retained by Polish academics provided they were considered 'desirable'. Amongst them was Helena Siekierska, a young medical student who worked in the microbiology laboratory. Unbeknown to the Germans, Helena was a member of the Polish resistance within a group organised by Dr Franciszek Witaszek. This small group of around thirty well-motivated men and women came from various backgrounds and included railway workers, engineers, waiters and scientists. In the university's laboratories they were able to produce toxic chemical weapons and explosive-based materials, all of which were for deployment against the Nazis. As well as Helena, the Witaszek group included Magdalena Cegłowska, Maria Gaussowa, Dr Henryk Gunther, Dr Franciszek Pokora, Dr Güntram Rolbiecki, Sonia Górzna, Jarogniew Gucki, Tadeusz Janowski, Paweł Bronikowski, Roman Kamerduła, Stanisław Karolczak, Teodor Konarski, Henryk Kulesza, Józef Kunert, Czesława Milian, Henryk Nickel, Edward Norbecki, Lucjan Nowicki, Florian Przygodziński, Jerzy Przystanowski, Henryk Rakowski, Hieronim Schöpke, Tadeusz Skrzypek, Marian Spychała, Franciszek Stefaniak, Sylwester Ulmański, Czesław Wachowiak, Władysława Kwintkiewicz, Bolesław Wojtczak and Zenon Pluciński.

Inevitably, on 25 April 1942, Dr Witaszek was arrested, most probably having been betrayed to the Gestapo by an unknown informant, and was brutally interrogated about who the other members of his group were and what they were manufacturing in the laboratory Even so, this was a most unexpected event, as Helena in particular had been very guarded about her work in the university. Having been engaged in stealing vials of cultured medicine and other materials, she was well aware of the penalty should she have been found doing so. Dr Gunther and laboratory assistant

Sonia Górzna were also arrested and subjected to the same barbaric treatment in the basement of the Poznań Gestapo headquarters.

During a purge of suspects connected to the resistance group, 22-year-old Helena was arrested on 15 May 1942. She was held for two weeks in the Gestapo headquarters and subjected to daily interrogation and torture in an attempt to force her to disclose the identity of the chemists engaged in making what the Gestapo assumed to be serums and bacterial products. She survived her initial interrogation and, following a swift court appearance, was sentenced to death and imprisoned in Fort VII. On 8 January 1943, after nine months in prison, a heavily tortured Dr Witaszek and Helena Siekierska were executed along with other members of their organisation, all of whom had refused to co-operate with the Nazis in exchange for their life and the protection of their families, many members of which were by then also imprisoned. In all probability, specific orders were issued for the Witaszek group members to be hanged, as this method was regarded as an appropriate death for such anti-Nazi resistance.

Conversely, a most unusual set of events seems to have additionally occurred. Following these executions, their heads were later guillotined at the Młyńska Street prison. It would appear that their severed heads were destined for the University of Poznań, where the Dean of the medical department was the infamous German anatomist and professor, Dr Hermann Voss. It was known that he had used the bodies of executed prisoners for the preparation of skeletal displays. Voss worked with Dr Josef Wastel from the anthropology department of the Vienna Museum of Natural History and supplied him with skulls for his personal research. The museum currently retains extensive documentation on the role it played in the Nazi regime's racial programmes. The Poznań execution room was illustrated in a short Russian newsreel clip taken when the area was liberated in 1945 by Soviet troops.

The Fallbeil guillotine was situated in a tile-lined room with an antiquated and primitive stove in the corner. It appears that there was a hosepipe wound on a reel next to the stove and also a porcelain sink, and situated in close proximity to the Fallbeil were some very thick industrial rubber gloves on a table. Hanging on the wall were similar thick rubber aprons, presumably worn by the operatives of the Fallbeil.

It can be assumed that the People's Court heard the cases against the Witaszek group and their family members. Dr Witaszek's wife was sentenced and sent to Auschwitz. From there she was moved to Ravensbrück, but at no time did she have any knowledge of the whereabouts of her husband, who was already dead, or their five children. Her brother-in-law died whilst imprisoned in Fort VII, and several other family members of those who were executed never returned from Auschwitz or from other camps. Dr Witaszek's wife survived the terror of two formidable Nazi extermination camps and, following the liberation of Ravensbrück by the Allies, she returned to Poznań in May 1945. Her expectations of re-forming her family were shattered when she was told of her husband's execution and that her children had also suffered. Two of her daughters had been taken away for the purpose of

'Germanisation', an annual selection made from children within the six to ten year age bracket who met German racial standards. The selected children were taken to Germany, where they would have their names changed and, after racial schooling, be placed into German families.

The decapitated heads of Franciszek Witaszek, Henryk Gunther, Sonia Górzna and Helena Siekierska were preserved in formalin, but this was by no means an isolated act. Dozens of examples were known to have been preserved in this way, ostensibly for medical purposes and most probably in accordance with Wastel's wishes. After the war, their heads were identified and recovered for a full military burial at the Poznań Citadel of Heroes. Helena Siekierska was posthumously awarded the 'Virtuti Militari', one of the highest Polish awards available, in recognition of her unique bravery, whilst Dr Witaszek was posthumously awarded the Polish Cross of Valour.

The Kreisau Circle

Two of the leading figures in the Kreisau Circle were Helmuth James Graf von Moltke, a great-grandnephew of the Prussian field marshal Helmuth von Moltke, and Peter Graf Yorck von Wartenburg, the descendant of a Prussian noble family. Both men were highly academic and employed in legal capacities. Von Wartenburg served on the Reich Price Commission in Berlin from 1936 to 1941, but refused to join the Nazi Party and was disillusioned about its policies. He had first become involved in the German resistance in 1938, working in close collaboration with von Moltke, who as a rising lawyer had many high-level contacts with politicians and intellectuals. Von Moltke had also refused to join the NSDAP, with the result that he was barred from a promising career as a judge. Together they secured several close friendships, one of which was with Fritz-Dietlof Graf von der Schulenburg, the Deputy Regional Commissioner of Breslau (now Wrołcaw); another was with Ulrich-Wilhelm Graf Schwerin von Schwanenfeld, a landowner who served as an officer in the Wehrmacht in Berlin. These men founded what was fundamentally an intellectual group of individuals opposed to the Nazi Party who harboured a desire to remove Hitler from power whilst at the same time envisaging the establishment of a European democratic order in Germany. The Kreisau Circle over time became embroiled in a planned assassination of Hitler, an act that would eventually cost the lives of many of its members and those of many other resistance organisations. They would later appear in the People's Court to be sentenced to death, in many instances simply for being suspected of involvement in the planned assassination.

The members of the Kreisau Circle infrequently travelled to von Moltke's estate at Kreisau (now Krzyżowa) in Silesia, but in addition to the large meetings held there, smaller and more frequent meetings took place across Germany in order to avoid arousing the suspicion of the authorities. Von Moltke was already known for his pre-war activities as a lawyer in assisting Jewish families to use legal means to recover property and possessions confiscated by the Nazi Party, and with the outbreak of war he was drafted into the Abwehr, the German military intelligence organisation, to work for the foreign division of the counter-intelligence service. The Abwehr had been created in 1921 when the German government was allowed to form the Reichswehr, the military organisation of the Weimar Republic. Von Moltke's knowledge of international law was seen as an asset to the Abwehr and so he was mainly involved in collating information from abroad, through foreign newspapers and military attachés. The Kreisau Circle had contacts with various resistance groups in the occupied countries of France, Belgium, the Netherlands and Norway, so von Moltke was well placed to engage in direct communication with some of those selected groups. Members of the Kreisau Circle were driven only by their desire to remove Hitler and were free of any religious allegiance; indeed, many of the members were of differing beliefs and political leanings.

Adam von Trott zu Solz, a well-travelled diplomat, was another member of the group with a legal background. He had visited both Britain and the US prior to the war, advising on the Nazi Party and Hitler's apparent intentions. Unsuccessful in achieving meaningful communications, he returned to Germany and ingratiated himself with the Nazi Party, with the intention of gaining intelligence. Another member of the group was Adolf Reichwein, who had spent his life in education and at the time that Hitler came to power held a professorship at the newly founded Higher Education Academy in Halle. Having been removed from his post by the Nazis as an 'undesirable', he sought various positions of employment. In Berlin he was introduced to the Kreisau Circle and brought with him a high level of cultural and educational expertise. It should be acknowledged that the group consisted of an estimated twenty individuals who fulfilled key positions in the new German government.

There were three large meetings at the Kreisau estate where a significant number of the group were in attendance. Two were held in the spring and autumn of 1942, the remaining meeting taking place in the spring of the following year. These were vital strategy meetings in which discussions took place on what a future democracy in Germany would look like and how it would function in detail.

In March 1942, von Moltke asked Augustin Rösch, the Jesuit superior of the Upper German Province, for assistance as the Kreisau Circle sought the presence of a learned sociologist, a member capable of managing the Christian social order in Germany. Rösch nominated Alfred Delp, a promising intellectual and philosopher, to be his representative at the meetings, and he became one of the younger members of the group. He had been ordained into the priesthood of Jesuits by Cardinal Michael Faulhaber at Munich in 1937, but Nazi restrictions imposed on the Jesuits severely restricted his development in the Church. Jesuits were member of the Society of Jesus, which the Gestapo treated with great suspicion.

Another man of the cloth, Harald Poelchau, also joined the Kreisau Circle. He had been the appointed chaplain at Berlin's Tegel Prison from 1933, and during the Nazi era of persecution he counselled hundreds of inmates who had been sentenced to death, accompanying them to their execution by beheading. Harald joined the group in 1941, and in addition to his work within the group also continued in his own personal resistance to the Nazi regime by offering Jews secure hiding places across Berlin and further afield.

The Kreisau Circle had very few opportunities to know the extent of the full membership or the additional supporters that surrounded them. Most members tended to know of two or three main associates. Draft working papers submitted to the co-ordinated controllers, von Moltke and von Wartenburg, consisted of in-depth plans for a functioning democracy once the Nazi regime had been overthrown and its leaders held to account in the German courts. The military resistance from several quarters of the Kreisnau Circle was crucial if they were to achieve their aims, and it was only after several failed attempts on the Führer's life that the group themselves actively planned to assassinate him.

In early 1943, the Gestapo arrested several people, predominantly Germans, allegedly involved in various resistance activities that included a plot to overthrow Hitler. Several groups had such intentions but few had credibility. The SS and Gestapo suspected others of having been involved, including Hans Oster, an Abwehr officer who was also a member of the Kreisau Circle. As a result of their suspicions, he was dismissed from his post in January 1944 and rearrested soon afterwards. A German officer, Maj. Claus Schenk Graf von Stauffenberg, subsequently became the leader of a military-based group that was interwoven with the Kreisau Circle leadership. These members of the German military, including members of the Kreisau Circle, had planned on an announcement of Hitler's assassination to initiate the seizure by German troops stationed in Berlin of a small number of key government buildings and the shutting down of communication centres and radio stations. That key responsibility fell to Gen. Fritz Thiele, a communications specialist at the Bendlerblock military headquarters in the German capital. It was ultimately decided that Hitler's death was essential if they were to make peace with the Allies, and after establishing control of Germany that would be their primary objective. In April 1944, with the consent of von Stauffenberg, Adolf Reichwein and Julius Leber got in touch with the Operative Leadership of the Communist Party in Germany, which was to be the largest Communist resistance group in Germany. The two leaders of that group, Anton Saefkow and Franz Jacob, talked about bringing their organisation into the conspiracy to assassinate Hitler. There were further meetings on 22 June and 4 July 1944 to consolidate the agreement but they were denounced by an informer and when Jacob and Saefkow arrived at the meeting place the Gestapo arrested them. The Communist group members would later be sentenced to death by the People's Court on 5 September 1944, and were executed on 18 September at Brandenburg-Görden Prison.

Despite the events surrounding the conspirators, German military officers continued to engage in their attempt to assassinate Hitler in his Wolf's Lair headquarters at Rastenburg on 20 July 1944. Claus Schenk Graf von Stauffenberg carried two small explosive devices in his briefcase as he attended a meeting with military leaders at Hitler's Eastern Front headquarters. Fate saw von Stauffenberg struggle to arm the devices due to a physical handicap, the result of injuries sustained in the First World War. However, the device was eventually planted under the planning table in close proximity to Hitler, but a staff officer unsuspectingly moved the briefcase away from Hitler, von Stauffenberg excusing himself from the room shortly before the device detonated. This assassination attempt should have been the start of a sequence of events to bring the war to a conclusion, but Hitler had been shielded from the main blast and received only minor injuries even though the explosion claimed the lives of four officers. The audacious plan to rescue Germany crumbled, with drastic consequences for those involved, the majority of whom were disaffected senior military officers. The SS immediately began their manhunt for those responsible. That night, Stauffenberg and three senior co-conspirators were executed by firing squad in the courtyard of the Bendlerblock in Berlin. Over the following weeks the SS arrested several hundred military and civilian personnel, the number of arrests rising to several thousand by mid-August 1944.

Many members of the Kreisau Circle and those who sympathised with its aims were arrested, tortured and executed after having appeared in the People's Court. The judges and prosecutors were again instructed to ensure that the death sentences imposed were carried out by hanging, which in effect was slow strangulation. Roland Freisler presided over the trials of those immediately implicated in the plot, and the first to suffer an undignified death was Peter Graf Yorck von Wartenburg. He was hanged from a short length of corded wire material suspended from a meat-hook on 8 August 1944, others following him to the gallows the very next day. Alfred Delp was arrested after morning Mass in his parish church on 28 July and for the ensuing five months was held in custody, interrogated and tortured during the Gestapo's frenzied quest for information on resistance operatives involved in the July plot.

Although the People's Court hearing tried to implicate Father Delp in the assassination attempt, its efforts failed as no evidence was presented. Despite this, on 11 January 1945, together with Helmuth James Graf von Moltke, Father Delp was found guilty of high treason. He was hanged in Plötzensee Prison on 2 February 1945. He left behind many thought-provoking quotes from notes smuggled out of the prison, none more profound than the last words uttered by him to the prison chaplain, Peter Buchholz, who accompanied him to his execution. He said, 'In half an hour, I'll know more than you do.'

Von Moltke was sent to his death on 23 January 1945. The ramifications of the plot in July to kill Hitler had seen significant numbers of people executed by hangings and beheadings, many of whom had little if any connection to the actual plot itself.

CHAPTER 10

Central Execution Sites by Order of Hitler

Plötzensee Prison

Berlin's Plötzensee Prison, built between 1869 and 1879, was part of a secure complex that covered an area of over 60 acres with a twenty-foot wall along its entire boundary. It could accommodate 1,200 prisoners within buildings constructed in a panoptic design with cell blocks in a cruciform construction, the accommodation wings leading off the central building. This facilitated prison staff being able to view each floor of the cell blocks, a design seen in many prisons, with netting present between the open floors to prevent suicides.

Within its high walls Plötzensee comprised a self-contained environment, living quarters for prison staff being provided outside the walled area. Inmates were worked hard in the solitude of their cells, many sitting for twelve hours each day picking oakum. This involved unpicking small quantities of old rope into many thousands of individual short strands which had to be unrolled, usually on their knees, using their hands until they became loose and fibrous. Picking oakum was painful because significant amounts were required from each prisoner, and those who failed to match the quantities achieved by the fastest workers were penalised with reduced food rations.

Many executions were carried out at Plötzensee. From 1890 to 1932, a total of thirty-six prisoners convicted of murder were put to death with an executioner's axe in the prison courtyard. In stark contrast, 2,891 inmates were executed at the hands of the judiciary in Plötzensee during the twelve years of National Socialist terror from 1933 to 1945. With the judicial changes taking place in Germany during the period between 1933 and 1936, a total of forty-five people were put to death by the executioner's axe. However, these were to be the last people to be beheaded by the axeman; on 14 October 1936, Hitler approved Reich Minister of Justice Franz Gürtner's proposal that the guillotine be used for carrying out capital punishment in the future. The Treachery Act of December 1934, responsible for the creation of the Special Courts, enabled the Fallbeil to become one of the deadliest weapons deployed in the National Socialism's judicial system. At this time, the Executioners Ordinance was enacted with the purpose of regulating every aspect of the duties imposed upon

Germany's professional executioners. The three executioners Johann Reichhart (Munich), Ernst Reindel (Magdeburg) and Wilhelm Röttger (Berlin) were reputedly responsible for having conducted over 11,800 sentences during their service.

In 1937, a workshed was designated as the site of future executions in the prison, and on 17 February that year a Fallbeil guillotine was transported from Bruchsal Prison and erected in what was to be the prison's execution chamber, an area also referred to as the execution cell despite it being far removed from the cell blocks. The execution building was an imposing two-roomed, single-storey brick structure with a low gabled roof. The first room was simply where documentation was compiled, the furthest room being where the Fallbeil was positioned. Thirty-seven persons were decapitated with the new machine during the remainder of 1937, followed by fifty-six people in 1938, and ninety-five in 1939.

The executions carried out were recorded in a ledger and evidenced the efficiency of the Plötzensee executioner: by March 1940, the accumulative total registered 277. The condemned prisoners were kept in the large cell block known as 'House III' (or the 'house of the dead' as the inmates called it) directly adjacent to the execution chamber. They spent their final hours restricted by shackles in special cells on the ground floor. From here they would then take their final steps through a small courtyard to the execution chamber. Executions were normally carried out in the early evenings, but clearly this was by no means statutory as executions at Plötzensee had also previously been carried out early in the morning. Each prisoner would be informed of the impending execution that morning in the presence of a public prosecutor. The prisoner would later be bound with their hands tied behind their backs, and a visit by the prison chaplain was permitted. The two chaplains known to have worked at Plötzensee were Peter Buchholz and Harald Poelchau. Poelchau, an opponent of the Nazi regime, counselled hundreds of inmates and accompanied them to their executions. Prison guards, some of whom had reputations for being sadistic and brutal, would lead the prisoner across the yard to the execution chamber at the prescribed hour. Standing alongside the prisoner would be the chaplain as the court verdict was read out, followed by the executioner's assistants taking hold of the prisoner and presenting them to the executioner, who carried out the sentence in a matter of seconds.

The following account of the sentence imposed upon the Czech prisoner Karel Koncel, beheaded in Plötzensee on 19 March 1943, provides that evidence. The official report gives the name of the executioner as Röttger, accompanied by three assistants.

Carrying out the death sentence verdict against Karel Koncel
Present:
As the person in charge of carrying out the sentence: Dr Pilz.
As a justice department official: Karpe
At 18.34 hours the prisoner was brought in with his hands cuffed behind his back by two prison officials. The executioner Röttger from Berlin stood ready with three assistants. Also present was the chief inspector of the prison Nowack.

After confirming the identity of the prisoner, the prisoner was turned over to the executioner for carrying out the sentence. The condemned was calm and with his hands cuffed he let himself be placed on the guillotine without resistance. Then the executioner used the guillotine to separate the head from the body and announced that the verdict had been carried out. The execution took 17 seconds from the time the prisoner was brought in to the announcement that the verdict had been carried out.

It was common for the state prosecutor to sit in the ante-room at a table covered with a black cloth on which two burning candles were placed. The condemned inmate was turned over to the executioner with the words 'Scharfrichter, Walten Sie Ihres Amtes' (Executioner, do your duty). A black curtain was opened to reveal the Fallbeil, and the unfortunate prisoner was seized by the executioner's assistants and placed on the bench with the restraint lunette lowered onto his neck and the blade immediately released by the executioner. Immediately after the fall of the blade the executioner stepped to the open curtain and spoke these words to the state representative: 'Herr Staatsanwalt, das Urteil ist Vollstreckt' (Mr Prosecutor, the verdict is enforced). The curtain would then be closed and, about two minutes later, another prisoner entered the chamber and the whole process was repeated again. The Plötzensee executioner came to the prison twice a week, guillotining individuals at three-minute intervals, which included compiling the report and releasing the bodies to the Berlin Institute of Anatomy.

There was a regular supply of severed heads and torsos to the institute, so many in fact that it requested that the Reich Judicial Administration should bear the cost of providing cadaver cases for all corpses, otherwise the institute would be forced to restrict the cadavers to those that it actually needed. Clearly, this request was complied with, enabling the institute to store the body parts in a more efficient manner.

In late 1942, at the request of Otto Georg Thierack, the newly appointed Reich Minister of Justice, the Plötzensee execution chamber was fitted with a steel beam to which initially five and subsequently eight iron hooks were fastened. This most basic form of gallows was then used for hangings, as sentences administered in the courts were specific in stating the means of execution to be deployed. Members of the Red Orchestra resistance movement were the first to die from these gallows. Meanwhile, the desire to speed up efficiencies in executions saw Thierack issue a circular the provisions of which shortened and simplified the execution process, one element being the prohibition of the presence of the prison chaplain. The courts were by now handing down a significant number of death sentences, as evidenced by the 300 prisoners awaiting execution in Plötzensee in mid-1943, when Allied attacks inadvertently accelerated their executions.

On the night of 3 September 1943, RAF Bomber Command sent 316 Lancaster bombers to attack Berlin. The frequency of raids on the German capital had seen Plötzensee develop a well-rehearsed procedure ensuring a total blackout, and although the prison was most unlikely to be deliberately targeted by the RAF, there was always a possibility that it would be damaged from the intense bombing of Berlin. On this particular night, as the raid approached Berlin from the north-east, the bombers dropped bombs in Charlottenburg and Moabit, a number of stray bombs landing within the walled area of Plötzensee and causing damage to the holding wing for condemned prisoners, 'House III'. During the raid, the RAF lost twenty-two Lancasters and over 150 British and Allied air crew failed to return to their aerodromes in England. Miraculously, three prisoners owed their freedom to the RAF that night—a bomb blast blew open their cell doors enabling them to escape. The execution chamber suffered damage along with the Fallbeil, rendering it unserviceable. The timing of this incident was remarkably close to the Reich Minister of Justice's circular of 27 August 1943, which provided for accelerated executions due to the increased risk of air raids. Four days after the raid by the RAF, Thierack, acting at Hitler's request, shortened clemency proceedings and instigated the execution of all condemned prisoners in Plötzensee in rapid succession. Sadly, this included the three prisoners who had escaped in the bombing, who had since been recaptured. It would be several weeks before the Fallbeil could be returned to service, and on 6 September the Ministry of Justice was further advised:

> The roof of the execution chamber was stripped; the tile floor was partially destroyed; and the guillotine was damaged by fire, torn out of its underpinnings, and lay on the floor. The extent to which it remains serviceable must be determined by closer inspection, which has already been delegated to Tegel Prison.

Following orders to expedite executions, the Plötzensee executioner and his assistants prepared to hang the prisoners. During the evening of 7 September, a regional court director representing the senior Reich prosecutor of the People's Court together with a public prosecutor from the regional court in Berlin arrived as enforcement supervisors. Hangings commenced with mass executions in which eight prisoners at a time were strung up by candlelight, the executioners repeatedly using the gallows throughout the night. A further raid by the RAF caused the only interruption to this frenzy of extermination of human life after 186 people had died hanging from the gallows. After pausing for only twelve hours, the executioners hanged a further sixty victims during the following nights. More than 250 prisoners were murdered between 7 and 12 September 1943; the Nazi judicial system having exterminated the lives of Czech, Polish, French and fellow Germans. The convicted Poles included members of the 'Armia Krajowa' (Home Army) who had been accused of sabotage and high treason, and the Serbian based 'Narodna Odbrana' (People's Defence) who also engaged operatives of the disbanded Czech army. German penal institutions together recorded 12,656 Czech 'political prisoners' detained in late March 1943—11,823 men and 833 women. The heavily persecuted Poles also suffered terribly within the Nazi prison system, and during the same period in March that year 36,148 Polish 'political prisoners' were detained—25,746 men and 10,402 women. A large number of these Polish convicts ended up in SS concentration camps.

The Reich Ministry of Justice required legal officials to report upon prisoners with sentences of one year or more, or indeed any prisoner who offered no prospect of good behaviour, who were to be rearrested on the day of release. Later the system was adjusted to allow these Polish prisoners to be routinely transferred from the penal institution to a concentration camp by the SS. This general transfer escalated during the war, many thousands of Jews being sent to concentration camps where they were worked to death or simply murdered in the plethora of ways developed by the SS.

Amongst the French and Belgians in Plötzensee were several young men convicted of criminal burglary; in effect they were slave labourers who had been working in Berlin and had been reduced to stealing food to survive. Another inmate was Karlrobert Kreiten, one of the most talented young pianists in Germany, who was to lose his life hanging from the gallows alongside seven people he did not know. He had been arrested by the Gestapo after his neighbour reported him for expressing doubts about Hitler's conduct in the war. Sentenced to death in the People's Court on 3 September 1943 by the vindictive judge Roland Freisler, he was hanged at Plötzensee during the purge that took place on the night of the 7 September. The orders to reduce the period of clemency denied his parents any opportunity to try and save his life, and he was murdered even before his death warrant had been issued. Karlrobert was an example of the many Germans who were betrayed by friends, neighbours and even family.

As a result of the RAF bombing, Brandenburg-Görden replaced Plötzensee as the main central execution site for Berlin. Repairs were, however, undertaken to the damaged Fallbeil, and it was restored to operational effectiveness at Plötzensee as it was anticipated that the prison would still function and take its share of prisoners sentenced to death by the People's Court. The predicted respite was but short-lived, the assassination attempt on Hitler's life seeing the People's Courts in Berlin thrust into sequential hearings against the many suspects. The infamous Freisler was again to sit in judgment over those swept up in the Gestapo's investigations undertaken by Ernst Kaltenbrunner, the Reich security chief. Between 8 August 1944 and 9 April 1945, ninety death sentences were implemented, but many other suspects had been subjected to severe torture, which drove several to commit suicide whilst confined in the many squalid detention facilities across Berlin. The conspirators found guilty of being involved in the unsuccessful July plot were executed in Plötzensee and are respectfully recorded alongside the date of their execution below:

> Robert Bernardis, 8 August 1944
> Hans-Jürgen Graf von Blumenthal, 13 October 1944
> Hasso von Boehmer, 5 March 1945
> Eugen Bolz, 23 January 1945
> Eduard Brücklmeier, 20 October 1944

Walter Cramer, 14 November 1944

Alfred Delp, 2 February 1945

Heinrich Graf zu Dohna-Schlobitten, 14 September 1944

Max Ulrich Graf von Drechsel, 4 September 1944

Hans Otto Erdmann, 4 September 1944

Erich Fellgiebel, 4 September 1944

Eberhard Finckh, 30 August 1944

Reinhold Frank, 23 January 1945

Elisabeth Gloeden, 30 November 1944

Erich Gloeden, 30 November 1944

Carl Friedrich Goerdeler, 2 February 1945

Fritz Goerdeler, 1 March 1945

Nikolaus Grob, 23 January 1945

Hans Bernd von Haeften, 15 August 1944

Albrecht von Hagen, 8 August 1944

Kurt Hahn, 4 September 1944

Georg Hansen, 8 September 1944

Ernst von Harnack, 5 March 1945

Paul von Hase, 8 August 1944

Ulrich von Hassell, 8 September 1944

Theodor Haubach, 23 January 1945

Egbert Hayessen, 15 August 1944

Wolf-Heinrich Graf von Helldorf, 15 August 1944

Otto Herfurth, 29 September 1944

Roland von Hoblin, 13 October 1944

Erich Hoepner, 8 August 1944

Caesar von Hofacker, 20 December 1944

Friedrich Jaeger, 21 August 1944

Jens Jessen, 30 November 1944

Hermann Kaiser, 23 January 1945

Franz Kempner, 5 March 1945

Bernhard Klamroth, 15 August 1944

Johannes Georg Klamroth, 26 August 1944

Friedrich Karl Klausing, 8 August 1944

Ewald von Kleist-Schmenzin, 9 April 1945

Gerhard Knaak, 4 September 1944

Alfred Kranzfelder, 10 August 1944

Elisabeth Kuznitzky, 30 November 1944

Fritz von der Lancken, 29 September 1944

Carl Langbehn, 12 October 1944

Julius Leber, 5 January 1945

Heinrich Graf von Lehndorff-Steinort, 4 September 1944

Paul Lejeune-Jung, 8 September 1944

Ludwig Freiherr von Leonrod, 26 August 1944

Bernhard Letterhaus, 14 November 1944

Franz Leuninger, 1 March 1945

Wilhelm Leuschner, 29 September 1944

Hans Otfried von Linstow, 30 August 1944

Ferdinand Freiherr von Lüninck, 14 November 1944

Wilhelm Friedrich Graf zu Lynar, 29 September 1944

Hermann Maass, 20 October 1944

Rudolf Graf von Marogna-Redwitz, 12 October 1944

Michael Graf von Matuschka, 14 September 1944

Joachim Meichssner, 29 September 1944

Helmuth James Graf von Moltke, 23 January 1945

Arthur Nebe, 2 March 1945

Erwin Planck, 23 January 1945

Johannes Popitz, 2 February 1945

Karl Ernst Rahtgens, 30 August 1944

Adolf Reichwein, 20 October 1944

Alexis Freiherr von Roenne, 12 October 1944

Joachim Sadrozinski, 29 September 1944

Friedrich Scholz-Babisch, 13 October 1944

Friedrich-Werner Graf von der Schulenburg, 10 November 1944

Fritz-Dietlof Graf von der Schulenburg, 10 August 1944

Georg Schulze-Büttger, 13 October 1944

Ludwig Schwamb, 23 January 1945

Ulrich-Wilhelm Graf Schwerin von Schwanenfeld, 8 September 1944

Günther Smend, 8 September 1944

Franz Sperr, 23 January 1945

Berthold Schenk Graf von Stauffenberg, 10 August 1944

Helmuth Stieff, 8 August 1944

Carl-Heinrich von Stülpnagel, 30 August 1944

Fritz Thiele, 4 September 1944

Busso Thoma, 23 January 1945

Adam von Trott zu Solz, 26 August 1944

Nikolaus Graf von Üxküll-Gyllenband, 14 September 1944

Fritz Voigt, 1 March 1945

Peter Graf Yorck von Wartenburg, 8 August 1944

Hermann Wehrle, 14 September 1944

Carl Wentzel, 20 December 1944

Oswald Wiersich, 1 March 1945

Josef Wirmer, 8 September 1944

Erwin von Witzleben, 8 August 1944

One rather touching account of a victim of the Gestapo's reaction to the plot against Hitler's life concerns the Catholic clergyman Hermann Wehrle, his name appearing towards the end of the alphabetical list of victims provided by the Plötzensee Memorial Centre. In his confessional box he heard of the rumoured assassination plan, which he left as a matter of conscience with the individual, who happened to be a German officer. The confession was subsequently divulged in the People's Court during the hearing against the officer in question, Maj. Ludwig Freiherr von Leonrod. Having been called to the court as a witness, Father Wehrle was subsequently charged as an accessory to the crime and sentenced to death by Freisler on 14 September 1944. He was hanged the same day in Plötzensee, alongside three of the significant July plotters: Heinrich Graf zu Dohna-Schlobitten, a German officer and resistance fighter; Nikolaus Graf von Üxküll-Gyllenband, who under interrogation outlined the atrocities in the concentration camps as the reason for his involvement in the coup attempt; and Michael Graf von Matuschka, a man who had fought bravely in the First World War but was politically opposed to Hitler. In early 1944, the Reich Ministry of Justice Information Service published the following:

> Pursuant to the Führer's directive to the judiciary to resort to the most drastic measures in combating traitors of the people, saboteurs, social pests, violent criminals and antisocial habitual criminals during the war, the number of death sentences has steadily risen since war broke out. This period of time has produced the following totals.

1939—99
1940—926
1941—1292
1942—3660
1943—5334

These official statistics were presumably secured from what became known as the 'Murder Register', which recorded in detail the executions at Plötzensee and elsewhere. Only parts of this register were found after Germany's surrender in 1945, and the basis for post-war research is the thousands of small individual file cards that were recovered. The true statistics will never be known, but Plötzensee Prison was without doubt one of the most significant venues used by the National Socialist judiciary to inflict its ultimate sentences in order to uphold Nazi laws. Plötzensee became overcrowded, and chronically poor living conditions were experienced by the inmates in the second half of the war. They were provided with little nutrition, in many cases insufficient to maintain heath in all respects. One of the likely resting places for the remains of those executed at Plötzensee is a mass grave at the cemetery of Altglienicke in Berlin. Many prisoners were released in the spring of 1945, and by the time the Soviet army took control of the prison on 25 April that year, very few inmates remained. Following the takeover by the Russians, the execution chambers were subject to extensive press coverage and numerous images were published of the Fallbeil, an instrument of death that had created fear amongst the prisoners and had ultimately decapitated so many courageous men and women.

In 1951, the Berlin Senate decided to erect a memorial in Plötzensee. Portions of the execution chamber were removed and a memorial wall was erected to the front of the building. The cornerstone was laid on 9 September 1951, the memorial being officially inaugurated the following year. Since that time it has become a place of remembrance and reverence for all the victims who lost their lives under the National Socialist dictatorship led by Hitler and his henchmen. Remarkably, the Plötzensee chaplain Harald Poelchau, who together with his wife had been responsible for the survival of a number of Jewish children, survived the war. His position in the prison had uniquely allowed him to pass the last messages of the many victims he accompanied to the execution chambers to their families, no doubt bringing unimaginable grief but also a final understanding that would otherwise not have been available to them. In 1972, Harald and his wife were recognised in Jerusalem as 'Righteous Among the Nations' an acknowledgement that they had risked their own lives to protect Jewish individuals during the German persecutions. Their names are on the Wall of Honour in the Garden of the Righteous at Yad Vashem in Jerusalem.

Stadelheim Prison

The large prison at Stadelheim had been founded in 1894 within the Giesing district of Munich. It famously became associated with Hitler when he served the first of two periods of imprisonment there in 1922. The large and comfortable cell occupied by him, cell 70, would subsequently be occupied by other notorious figures connected with the Nazi regime, including the SA leader Ernst Röhm, whose death, engineered by Hitler, took place in that same cell in 1934. The prison was built to hold over 1,500 inmates, but during the war years held significantly more than had ever been envisaged at the time of its construction.

Many defendants sentenced to death in Hitler's courts were executed by Johann Reichhart in Stadelheim. Amongst the many cases that were tried under the indictment of 'helping the enemy and being prepared to commit high treason' was that of Walter Klingenbeck. Born in Munich, Walter became a member of the Catholic Youth Congregation until it was forced to disband by order of Hitler in 1936. He was interested in modern radio, listening regularly to foreign news broadcasts, and was employed as an apprentice at the Rohde and Schwarz radio communications works in Munich. Together with fellow apprentices Daniel von Recklinghausen, Hans Haberl and Erwin Eidel he formed a group of young Catholics opposed to National Socialism and wrote leaflets calling for the overthrow of the regime. In the summer of 1941, the 16-year-old electronics apprentices built a small radio station to broadcast news secured from BBC broadcasts. They possessed enough technical ability to build a radio transmitter that could rebroadcast forbidden foreign programmes on a varying frequency in order to avoid detection by the Nazi detector vans.

Having heard an appeal by the BBC to spread the 'V for Victory' sign, a propaganda symbol adopted for an Allied victory over Germany, Walter encouraged the group to continue their protests by painting the sign on many buildings across Munich. However, his luck ran out when on one such occasion, on 26 January 1942, he was detained and arrested. It has to be presumed that under interrogation Walter disclosed the names of his associates, as they too were arrested. Fortunately, sufficient time had been available after Walter's arrest for the transmitter to be disabled and disposed of, an action that would lead to the saving of the lives of his fellow apprentices. At the age of nineteen, Walter was sentenced to death by the People's Court on 24 September 1942 and decapitated at Stadelheim on 5 August 1943. Daniel and Hans had also been sentenced to death for their actions in creating leaflets and painting victory signs, but their sentences were reduced a few days later to eight years' imprisonment, the same sentence that had been handed down to Erwin. Immediately before he was executed, Walter was made aware of his friends' reduced sentences and was able to write to them. He told them that he had received the sacrament and was quite composed but if they wanted to do anything for him then they should say the Lord's Prayer a few times.

After the war, Daniel von Recklinghausen was freed by the Allies from a satellite camp at Dachau and succeeded in finding his family who had been forcibly relocated to a refugee camp. In 1947, they moved back to the US, where Daniel had been born in 1925, and he was able to return to his love of radio communications. During his career, he patented over twenty devices associated with circuits and high-quality sound reproduction, and deservedly received a gold medal in recognition of his work in FM receiver technology in 1978—a remarkable accolade for a brave man who so nearly lost his life alongside his friend in 1943. Daniel carried the memories with him until his death in 2011.

Stadelheim is estimated to have undertaken at least 1,035 executions between 1933 and 1945, and during that time the University of Munich's Institute of Anatomy benefited by receiving and using the bodies of a large number of executed corpses for scientific purposes. Such institutes also received bodies of euthanasia victims from nearby nursing homes and mental institutions, victims of other Nazi directives designed to improve the Reich. From 1939, in accordance with a Reich Department of Justice decree, the distribution process for dead bodies was changed; article No. 39 of the Reich's ordinance of 19 February 1939 required the Institute of Anatomy to confirm the arrangements to recover the corpses. Details of the actual delivery of bodies can be found in a number of execution reports written by execution overseers and in body registers of the respective institutes.

Roter Ochse Prison

Halle (Saale) in central Germany saw the Nazi penal system incorporate Roter Ochse (Red Ox) Prison within its official execution sites. In 1934, this relatively small prison was extended to hold 600 prisoners and was converted to accommodate those serving longer, hard labour sentences. By the end of the war, it held approximately 1,200 prisoners, including German men and women and a mixture of prisoners from the invaded countries of Europe, all deemed to be political opponents or persons considered to be resisters of the National Socialist regime. From 1942 until 1945, part of the building was adapted and used as a courtroom for the Wehrmacht and the People's Court. Roter Ochse saw 549 men and women condemned to death, their sentences being carried out by the resident executioner who beheaded them with the Fallbeil.

Krystyna Wituska, a Polish teenager, had returned to her home country from finishing school in Switzerland. At the age of twenty, she joined the Polish underground movement and due to her ability to speak fluent German was assigned the dangerous task of collecting information on German troop movements at the airport in Warsaw. In 1942, she was arrested by the Gestapo and interrogated before appearing at the People's Court on 19 April 1943. Krystyna was sentenced to death by beheading 'for spying and participation in the crime of high treason'. After a request for clemency was rejected by Hitler she was taken to Roter Ochse where, on 26 June 1944, the death sentence was finally carried out. She had left behind many letters written during her long incarceration, and these would eventually be found and published many years later.

The Jehovah's Witness community suffered intense persecution at Roter Ochse. Fifty-seven youths were beheaded because they refused to be conscripted into the German army on religious grounds. One incredibly fortunate survivor was Lothar Hörnig, who had been born near Leipzig on 22 April 1928 into a family of Jehovah's Witnesses with a small bakery business. However, after Hitler's rise to power they refused to give the Nazi salute and that saw them ostracised by those around them. They were banned from public places and their business began to collapse through lack of trade. Lothar's father Otto was arrested in 1936 as a resister of the National Socialist Regime and for not acknowledging the Nazi salute. He was imprisoned in Roter Ochse but even though he served his sentence, he was sent to Buchenwald concentration camp, a victim of the SS system of feeding 'undesirables' into concentration camps from the German judiciary in order to remove them from society.

On 11 August 1944, a close family friend and fellow Jehovah's Witness, Otto Guse, was beheaded at Roter Ochse because he had refused to serve in the German army. In December 1944, sixteen-year-old Lothar inevitably received orders to report for army service and attended the Gestapo offices in Halle, where he bravely stated that for religious reasons he was unable to serve. The pressures applied by the Gestapo to this young boy would have been immense, but he steadfastly refused to be intimidated. Too young to be judged in a Military Court, Lothar was detained by the Gestapo and taken via Leipzig, Dresden and Prague to the Hungarian border. This journey may well have been taken with others, but no reasonable explanation can be found to rationalise the events, particularly as other cases exist where 16 year olds were denied the protection they deserved and were presented in various German courts throughout the occupied lands. It was, however, a fortunate set of events for Lothar, because the advancing Allied troops then forced the Wehrmacht into retreat and Lothar suddenly gained his unexpected release.

His father was also fortunate to survive in the horrific conditions of Buchenwald. Built in a vast forest clearing and surrounded by high electrified fences and guard towers, the camp held more than 25,000 shaven-headed, underfed and abused prisoners from across Europe. It was a truly terrible place, and the sickly stench from the belching crematorium chimney never ceased. Otto would have worn the purple triangle to denote his faith, alongside the thousands of Jews wearing the yellow star. At the point of freedom, he witnessed the immediate Buchenwald memorial constructed by the Allies in the main courtyard acknowledging the conservative estimate of 50,000 deaths that had occurred in the camp.

Roter Ochse Prison was liberated on 17 April 1945 by the US army and handed over to the Soviet occupying forces on 1 July. The prison was used from 1950 until December 1989, during which time it is estimated that more than 9,000 people were incarcerated and subjected to interrogation by the Stasi, the secret police agency of the former German Democratic Republic (East Germany). The agency was one of the most feared institutions of the East German Communist government and, tragically, after years of internment in the Nazi concentration camps, Jehovah's Witnesses had again been pursued and imprisoned.

Brandenburg-Görden Prison

Constructed over a nine-year period and completed in 1935, Brandenburg-Görden became one of Germany's largest prison establishments and was designed to accommodate up to 1,800 prisoners. Although all the cells were fitted with electric lights and the design created well-ventilated conditions, there was no doubt that it was a maximum security prison. All the roofs and open areas were floodlit to prevent escapes, and watchtowers with armed guards were positioned to cover extended lines of sight. The first Nazi killings took place in January 1940, when Brandenburg experienced the shocking killing of supposedly insane persons by carbon monoxide gas. In effect, these were experiments carried out to establish facts on such methods of mass murder that were subsequently adopted and deployed in the prison from January to October 1940. The last experimental deaths took place on 29 October, when children from the asylum in Brandenburg-Görden were murdered. It is estimated that several thousand men, women and children were killed in the Brandenburg euthanasia centre within those ten months in 1940. Tuberculosis was also a prevalent killer within the prison, and hundreds of prisoners died from the rampant disease that spread amongst those who were confined in the prison workshops for twelve hours a day sewing military uniforms.

Brandenburg-Görden was to become one of the Nazi-selected central execution sites. The then Reich Minister of Justice, Franz Gürtner, had been made aware that a Fallbeil guillotine and gallows had been installed in the execution chamber, rendering the prison capable of conducting executions ordered by the Nazi judiciary. The prison was extensively used to hold male prisoners of particular interest to the regime, primarily political prisoners with Communist roots from the Berlin district. The Nazis also utilised the high-security status of the prison to hold an entire wing of men categorised as 'dangerous habitual criminals', employing militant Nazis as prison wardens to enhance the strict rules of military discipline within the prison system. Prison wardens were induced to join the Nazi Party and failure to do so might well have led to attacks by Nazi activists.

The Law on Habitual Criminals of 1933 had allowed the courts to imprison people for committing simple offences of theft for indeterminate periods, with their cases being reviewed by the courts at least every three years. Roland Freisler had advised state prosecutors that in general he could not accept the release of such prisoners—a prime example of the overbearing legal terror inflicted by the German courts. The National Socialist justice system is estimated to have executed more than 2,000 people at Brandenburg-Görden from the time of the commissioning of its execution facility until the Allied forces liberated the prison on 27 April 1945.

Brandenburg-Görden appears to have been the only penal institution that engaged in the recovery of blood from those executed. In 1944, Dr Rudolf Bimler of the Brandenburg-Havel Hospital gained permission to collect blood from the deceased at the point of decapitation. He selected prisoners of desired blood types based upon previously obtained blood samples, and at the execution he and his assistant were on hand to immediately collect the blood being expelled under pressure. Bimler later divulged to the Allies that he attended approximately twenty-five executions in order to use the blood in transfusions at his hospital. His claims are evidenced in documents held in the National Archives, WO309/199. Many have subsequently speculated why the blood was collected in this barbaric manner.

A total of 1,722 people were sentenced for political reasons and subsequently executed at the prison, the final thirty-three being executed on 20 April 1945, Hitler's birthday. Although in previous years across the Third Reich this was a day when no executions would be scheduled, legal officials in 1945 insisted that no time should be lost and so the executions were duly authorised and carried out.

Amongst the sordid facts of misery and death by decapitation is the case of one man who was held in Brandenburg-Görden by the Nazis with a very special purpose. The physicist Robert Havemann had been condemned to death in the People's

Court, but his cell within the prison was converted into a laboratory and he was forced to conduct research for the Wehrmacht. Havemann studied chemistry in Munich and Berlin from 1929 to 1933, receiving his doctorate in physical chemistry with a thesis elaborated at the Kaiser Wilhelm Institute of Physical Chemistry and Electrochemistry in Berlin. He was removed from his position by the Nazi regime because of his membership of the German Communist Party, which he had joined in 1932. Unbeknown to them, at that time Havemann had also harboured motives to help persecuted Jews and later formed the European Union resistance group. This group, including the physician Georg Groscurth and several other like-minded individuals who worked in privileged positions, not only helped victims of political persecution including Jews and forced labourers to survive in the illegal underground but also used their connections and the information at their disposal to support other resistance activities.

Groscurth studied medicine and completed his PhD at the University of Berlin. He met Havemann at the Kaiser Wilhelm Institute and was the personal doctor of several prominent National Socialists at the Robert Koch Hospital in the German capital, which placed him in an ideal position to gather information. In 1943, he met the Ukrainian doctor Galina Romanova, who had been brought to Germany as a forced labourer. Groscurth provided her with medicines and supported her in organising resistance to the Nazis among her compatriots who were being forced to work for the Wehrmacht. By this time a number of other significant members of the European Union group, such as Paul Rentsch and Herbert Richter, were also engaging in dangerous activities in close proximity to prominent Nazi Party members. Richter managed to gain commissions as a freelance architect from several National Socialist institutions and these provided access into restricted areas that would otherwise have been impossible to penetrate. However, their luck ran out when Havemann, Groscurth, Rentsch and Richter were all arrested by the Gestapo on 5 September 1943. They were interrogated about their Communist sympathies and were eventually sentenced to death, along with several other members of their group, by the People's Court on 16 December 1943.

Following these arrests of the core members of the European Union, Galina Romanova and her friends continued their resistance activities until they too were arrested. Galina's associate Alexei Kalinitchenko died during his brutal interrogation, and Galina, who had been arrested on 6 October 1943, was sentenced to death on 27 April 1944. She was decapitated in Plötzensee Prison on 3 November 1944. On 8 May 1944, the Fallbeil in Brandenburg-Görden took the lives of Herbert Richter, Georg Groscurth and Paul Rentsch. Robert Havemann's sentence was deferred and instead he remained in the prison and was forced to work for the Wehrmacht.

Incredibly, Havemann survived the war. He was liberated from Brandenburg-Görden on 27 April 1945 by the Soviets. Whilst in prison, he built a radio receiver in his laboratory cell from parts smuggled in, and created a form of explosive material for use against the SS should the need have arisen. The experience of detention under the constant threat of death must have affected him deeply. After his release he went on to lead an academic life in the field of science, which continued to be controversially entwined with politics until his death in 1982.

Moabit Prison

Situated in Berlin and completed in 1849, Moabit was a historic star-shaped building used during the Third Reich to house a large population of Polish and Czech prisoners alongside Jews and German convicts serving lengthy custodial sentences. The prison had five wings projecting from a central section with several floors extending upwards, the cells being uniformly constructed and accessible from a walkway. Each cell enabled a prisoner to pace seven steps lengthways and four paces widthways. A metal cot bed frame with a thin straw mattress guaranteed to be crawling with bedbugs was fixed to the wall during the daytime, and each cell had a simple wooden chair and table. The capacity of the building was approximately 3,000 prisoners, of whom a relatively low proportion were females. Daily life was regulated by loud bells, each one initiating the requirement to comply with routine events during the day. The Gestapo used Moabit as a holding centre and conducted interrogations in specific rooms. A functioning Fallbeil was installed in the prison's execution chamber, and a tunnel connected the prison directly to the central criminal court buildings.

Poland had endured an extremely brutal occupation by Nazi Germany. Having initially annexed western Poland, the regime established a government whose objectives were to erase Polish nationhood and force the Poles to become subservient to the new German empire. Approximately one million Polish citizens were initially removed from German-occupied areas and replaced by Germans, whilst over two million Poles went into forced labour camps in Germany. Within the numerous Polish resistance elements that arose, the Patriotic Polish National Forces (PPNF) created intelligence-gathering cells to assist in the fight against the Nazi occupation and its blatant persecution. It was very early in the war when the Gestapo realised that the Polish resistance's capabilities of sabotage needed to be crushed, but the Polish problem was significant and a dedicated unit known as the *SS-Sonderkommando* was charged with suppressing and eliminating such resistance. Unbeknown to them at that time, the PPNF deployed well-established intelligence-gathering units in Germany that operated in secrecy as self-contained groups.

These units operated in various locations, including central Berlin. The leader of the Berlin PPNF unit was Boguslaw Wojciechowski. One of his couriers, Miroslawa Kocowa, carried intelligence between Warsaw and Berlin, and her work exposed her to other members of similar units including Witold Dyczynski, who was head of the Berlin intelligence-gathering unit. Security and the protection of identities were paramount within the resistance network, but as a courier this was difficult to achieve. Another female Pole who acted as a courier was Wanda Wegierska. She operated in Luckenwalde, south of Berlin, an area that had a high concentration of Polish slave labourers employed in factories that extended into the industrial Ruhr valley. The PPNF were very proficient at evidence gathering, which included providing the Allies with the initial indications of Germany's V1 flying bomb development, having established that a factory in Bydgoszcz, Poland, was manufacturing vital components for the secret weapon. Additionally, the PPNF had agents in the German dockyards at Gdynia, on the south coast of the Baltic Sea, and were able to monitor the movements and battle damage of several important vessels. Acknowledging their work, the British Intelligence Service secured a formal agreement with them, ensuring a line of communication was established and requesting specific information from the Polish allies in Berlin. However, unbeknown to them, the SS had managed to infiltrate the Polish network in Germany and had gained intelligence of their infrastructure, presumably achieved through the services of an unknown collaborator or collaborators. On 18 February 1942, the SS finally struck and arrested individuals at various addresses, amongst them the majority of operatives in Berlin, along with the head of the Hamburg-Bremen unit, Edward Konieczny. The German counter-intelligence operation was a significant success, resulting in the decimation of the Polish operation codenamed 'Stragan' and the Gestapo having many subjects to imprison and interrogate in Moabit Prison.

The interrogation and torture of those detained provided further information on which the Gestapo acted, other Polish operatives being arrested in March 1942, including another key member, Antoni Ingielewicz. At the end of the following month, the intelligence units operating in the Ruhr valley had also been arrested and Wanda Wegierska was by great misfortune also captured. Moabit was destined to hold many Polish resistance operatives who had been engaged in covert intelligence gathering across Germany.

In July 1942, the British paid tribute to the Polish Home Army, a term used to encapsulate the Polish resistance and intelligence-gathering operations, reporting that:

> The Polish Intelligence Service is our best source of information on the 'Order of Battle' on the Eastern Front. Identifications in Poland have been of great value and an outstanding feature has been the hospital lists giving depot units of German wounded. Generally speaking, the reports are of a very high standard and very much appreciated [...] We cannot over-emphasise the importance and value attached to the very excellent services which have been rendered by this magnificent organisation, whose difficulties we can well imagine and to whom we offer our very sincere thanks and wishes for their past, present and future work which we know will be of signal service to our common cause.

Miroslawa Kocowa, a trained accountant, and Wanda Wegierska, a clerical worker, were both based in Warsaw but frequently carried intelligence to and from Berlin.

Both were tortured after their arrests, and Wanda's father and brother were sent to concentration camps from which they never returned. Additionally, Henryka Veith, a 28-year-old actress, and 21-year-old Halina Konieczna, another accountant, also suffered brutal treatment before being tried for 'high treason'. All were sentenced to death and beheaded amongst two groups on 16 February and 25 June 1943. The bodies of these four women were subsequently subjected to anatomical examination and dissection by Hermann Stieve at Berlin University.

Amongst the brave Polish subjects who were brutally tortured by the Gestapo, and subsequently tried, sentenced to death and then beheaded on the Moabit Fallbeil were the following:

Jozef Baranski, age 31
Stanislaw Czerwik, age 21
Ryszard Dobryniecki, age 21
Antoni Dominiak, age 31
Jan Duszynski, age 22
Witold Wilhem Dyczynski, age 17
Marceli Jan Gonia, age 19
Helena Hensel, age 51
Stefan Hensel, age 22
Bernard Hofmanski, age 17
Antoni Ingielewicz, age 24
Stanislaw Jagodzki, age 20
Stanislaw Ludwik Jeute, age 32
Czeslaw Kalek, age 22
Franciszek Kawecki, age 31
Miroslawa Kocowa, age 34
Halina Marion Konieczna, age 21
Janusz Zbigniew Konieczny, age 20
Tomasz Koperski, age 29
Czeslaw Marciniak, age 23
Jan Mieczyslaw Meisner, age 32
Zbigniew Mizera, age 22
Leon Mucha, age 22
Kazimierz Napieralski, age 24
Leon Norojek, age 22
Jerzy Padlewski, age 29
Czeslaw Pieczynski, age 38
Jan Pieczynski, age 34
Ignacy Przybylski, age 36
Andrzej Reksinski, age 21
Marian Sauer, age 47

Wlodzimierz Stepczynski, age 22
Leon Szultz, age 21
Jan Tomanek, age 23
Witold Trabski, age 23
Henryka Veith, age 28
Boguslaw Wojciechowski, age 20
Andrzej Wojcik, age 50
Wiktor Wrzesinski, age 24
Zygmunt Wyzuj, age 21
Jerzy Zarembski, age 20

The final mention in relation to the executed Polish inmates at Moabit should be that of a Catholic priest, Father Bruno Binnebesel, an opponent of the Nazis who served his parish in Gdańsk on the Baltic coast. The reason for his arrest was not for any involvement with the Polish resistance but purely on suspicion of listening to foreign radio transmissions and advising others of such broadcasts. Roland Freisler judged his case in Berlin, finding him guilty of 'undermining the spirit of the defence of the German people', for which he was sentenced to death and beheaded on 13 November 1944. The Roman Catholic Church was suppressed and its priests were persecuted throughout Poland because historically they had led nationalist forces fighting for Poland's independence. The Germans systematically closed churches in Poland and most priests were murdered, imprisoned or deported. Between 1939 and 1945, an estimated 3,000 members of the Polish clergy were killed; of these, nearly 2,000 died in concentration camps.

Wolfenbüttel Prison

In 1937, the prison at Wolfenbüttel became one of the central execution sites for northern Germany, a Fallbeil being moved from Hanover Prison and delivered to the site. Several hundred prisoners condemned by the Nazi judicial system were executed by Friedrich Hehr in both Hamburg and Wolfenbüttel during the Third Reich. Between 1935 and 1945, Göttingen University alone received more than 600 corpses for medical dissection from Wolfenbüttel.

The execution chamber in the prison courtyard at Wolfenbüttel was a two-storey brick construction with an unusual clocktower at one end of the steeply slanting roofline. Executions would normally take place at 18.00 hours, with Hehr receiving 65 Reichsmarks per execution in addition to his annual salary of 3,000 Reichsmarks. These sums were significant, as in 1943 alone, his work in Hamburg netted him 4,320 Reichsmarks.

During late 1943, Wolfenbüttel housed many resistance fighters from Belgium. Marguerite Bervoets, a school teacher in Tournai at the time of the German invasion in 1940, joined the Belgian resistance and helped publish the underground newspaper *La Délivrance*. Following her capture while taking photos of a German air force base in 1942, she was eventually sent to Wolfenbüttel and was beheaded there on 7 August 1944. Unusually, the cemeteries within the local district hold records relating to many of those who were executed at Wolfenbüttel and were buried in several unmarked graves.

Amongst the many executions at Wolfenbüttel, the story of Erna Wazinski deserves to be told. Erna was a young German girl who experienced the tragedy of losing her father before she had reached the age of thirteen. She lived with her widowed mother in Braunschweig (Brunswick) and worked night shifts as a labourer in a munitions factory. On the night of 14 October 1944, RAF Bomber Command mounted a large raid in which over 200 Avro Lancasters bombed the city. Erna was working that night and at 04.00 hours the following day she tried to make her way home through the devastation of the burning and rubble-strewn streets. Her home and many others had sustained serious damage in the bombing, but her mother had escaped to the air-raid shelter and so she and Erna tried to recover what they could from the rubble of what had once been their home. Amongst the items Erna retrieved were two small cases in which she placed whatever she could salvage, including clothing and a few pieces of jewellery that would later be valued at 240 Reichsmarks. A complaint by a neighbour was investigated and Erna was immediately arrested. Treated very roughly, she confessed and appeared in court on 21 October, charged with 'looting and being a public enemy'. The Special Court judge Walter Lark and the court prosecutor Horst Magnus swiftly found nineteen-year-old Erna guilty of a 'reprehensible and vile offence against the people' for which the death penalty was decreed. She was taken to Wolfenbüttel to be executed and at midday on 23 November, her head was severed from her body. Roland Freisler had only recently called for greater harshness in the courts, so this was by no means an exceptional case.

After the war Friedrich Hehr acted as executioner for the Allied occupation forces, dispatching a further eighty-five individuals. The *Montreal Gazette* dated 11 June 1945 published a notice confirming that the beheading of three German soldiers had taken place by Hehr the previous day for failure to surrender their weapons. During the immediate post-war period the illegal possession of military weapons by defeated Germans was punishable by death, and Allied occupation forces enforced this punishment in several cases. Field Marshal Montgomery signed the execution warrants of the three Germans who had concealed pistols after having been disarmed under the terms of the surrender, the 21st Army Group HQ publicly announcing that they had been decapitated. Montgomery had frequently said, 'We have won the German war, let us now win the peace', but with no immediate German government in existence and the British-occupied sector of Germany holding an estimated population of over 20 million people, Allied control was of utmost importance. Records indicate that by 7 July 1947, the British Military Courts had issued sixty-seven death sentences, which had been lawfully carried out.

Breslau and Kattowitz Prisons

The historic city of Breslau (now Wrocław) became part of the German Empire in 1871 and was of some significance to the Third Reich, firstly because its citizens resoundingly voted for Hitler's NSDAP party in the 1933 elections, and secondly because the city suffered horrendous casualties in an epic siege in 1945, which left it in ruins. The struggle against the Soviet forces, called 'Fortress Breslau' by Hitler, was a brutal siege which lasted for fourteen weeks and cost the lives of 170,000 civilians, 6,000 German troops and 7,000 Russian troops. During the war, Breslau had been an important communication and industrial hub for the German war machine, containing numerous heavy industrial plants operated by forced labour housed in various camps. The broken city was forced to capitulate on 6 May 1945.

During the period of Nazi rule, the executioner's Fallbeil in the large and imposing prisons at Breslau and Kattowitz (now Katowice) had been utilised with ruthless efficiency in support of Hitler's judicial terror. Breslau was an area that had previously developed with a high concentration of Czech and Polish immigrants, and Nazi persecution of both them and the Jews was ruthless. Many of the city's estimated 10,000 Jews were deported to the pre-war concentration camps, and during the war significant numbers of Czech and Polish prisoners, as well as resistance members from Western Europe, were executed in both prisons.

Breslau was the execution site for the south-eastern part of Germany and occupied Poland. Executions in Breslau and Kattowitz were carried out by the appointed executioners, Bordt and Henschke from Poznań and Hehr from Hanover. However, in 1943, Hehr's former assistant August Koestner was appointed as a result of the ever-increasing numbers of death sentences handed down in the courts. One of those concerned Maruška Kudeříková, a Czech Catholic who joined a Communist-based Youth Union. She had graduated in 1940, just prior to the Nazi movement closing the Czech universities. The Youth Union initially began to produce anti-Nazi posters and leaflets, following which they escalated their actions to sabotage before Gestapo activity in 1941 resulted in several arrests. Maruška was arrested on 5 December in Brno, south-east of Prague, where the university's law faculty had been transformed into the Gestapo headquarters. The university dormitory was used as a prison and would become renowned as a place of illegal detention and torture for many thousands of Czech subjects during the war. Following interrogation, Maruška was sent for trial at the People's Court in Breslau and, on 16 November 1942, was sentenced to death by beheading. While imprisoned in Breslau Prison awaiting sentence, the 22-year-old managed to get several letters smuggled out by friends and sympathetic guards. However, on 26 March 1943, she was decapitated in the execution chamber at Breslau.

The execution toll at Breslau from April 1942 until March 1943 was 264, whilst at Kattowitz there were 214 executions between January and December 1942. The 'Red Widow' Fallbeil reputedly claimed 552 decapitations during its deployment, predominantly those convicted of resisting the German Reich. Inevitably, their remains were taken to the Auschwitz crematorium ovens, 50 km from Kattowitz.

Ernst Kaltenbrunner, Germany's most senior member of the SS to be captured alive at the end of the war, had been the Gestapo leader at Kattowitz. He had contacts with the Political Department at Auschwitz and frequently sent prisoners direct to the concentration camp there for imprisonment or execution. Kaltenbrunner was subsequently tried at Nuremberg and sentenced to death for his crimes against humanity. One of the many victims who became embroiled in the intimacy between Auschwitz and Kattowitz was the Polish scout leader and teacher Józef Pukowiec. He co-ordinated a secret anti-German resistance movement in Upper Silesia and worked in the armed forces of the Polish underground. In December 1940, as a result of collaboration, Nazi intelligence infiltrated the Polish unit resulting in several arrests, including Józef. He was tortured for information but divulged nothing and was later imprisoned in several locations before ending up at Auschwitz. Having experienced the horror of the extermination camp, 38-year-old Józef was taken to Kattowitz, most probably for further interrogation, and on 14 August 1942, he was decapitated by the Fallbeil and his body returned to the ovens in Auschwitz for disposal.

Koestner is estimated to have carried out 579 executions during his career. Some speculation exists that the Fallbeil employed by him is quite possibly the machine now currently stored and displayed in the Auschwitz-Birkenau museum.

Münchner Platz Prison

The prison complex at Münchner Platz in Dresden was situated adjacent to the resident Nazi courts, providing a convenient six-storey building in which hundreds of suspects could be detained. Within the complex was a courtyard containing the Fallbeil, which was securely bolted to the ground. Individuals sentenced by the courts were swiftly executed due to the close proximity of the execution courtyard, thus enabling National Socialist justice to be administered with ease. In addition, until mid-1943, death sentences handed down by the Prague Special Court, several other Special Courts, and the People's Court were also carried out at Münchner Platz Prison, and it is estimated that in excess of 1,300 people were decapitated within its execution facilities during the Second World War.

Amongst those statistics were five young Catholic men who attended the St John Bosco Salesian Oratory School in Poznań. They were members of the Salesian Youth Association, one of the many innocuous gatherings that had been banned by the Nazi regime. However, solely for religious reasons they continued to meet and sing wherever possible, although it was to ultimately cost them their liberty. Arrested in September 1940, they were imprisoned in Poznań Fort where, despite lengthy questioning, they failed to convince the Gestapo of their innocence. The Gestapo failed to accept their accounts of the meetings, believing the young men to be part of a Polish resistance group. Almost two years after their arrest, on 1 August 1942, all five were condemned to death for high treason, indicted for belonging to a Catholic organisation suspected of giving rise to resistance. They were detained in several prisons before eventually ending up in Dresden's Münchner Platz. Although their precious rosary beads had long since been taken from them, they improvised as best as possible in order to continue in their prayers. On 24 August 1942, the inevitable occurred. Czesław Jóźwiak was the first to be beheaded in the prison courtyard. With him were his close friends, Edward Kazmierski, Edward Klinik, Franciszek Kesy and Jarogniew Wojciechowski, all of whom were beheaded in the same session of executions.

Other civilians subjected to the same judicial terror were husband and wife Karel and Jindra Jaklova, both Czech subjects who had chosen to resist Nazi rule by joining one of the many small resistance groups. They were captured by the Gestapo and were sentenced to death following their convictions on 17 April 1943 in one of the Dresden courts. On 15 September, the sentence was carried out in the courtyard at Münchner Platz Prison by beheading.

In Czechoslovakia, the tradition of puppetry was historically well established and extremely prevalent at that time. Travelling puppet theatres were common and one puppeteer in particular, Josef Skupa, had a reputation of excellence and commanded significant audiences. Initially the Germans did not grasp the avenue of rebellious propaganda that was played out by Josef in his shows, but it was not long before they realised that they needed to control the phenomenon of puppetry. Such performances were forcibly terminated, although Josef continued to find surreptitious ways to perform his anti-Nazi material even when being observed by the Gestapo. Such was Josef's following that the Nazis claimed openly albeit falsely that he was performing for them in Germany. Eventually, in January 1944, Josef was arrested by the Gestapo and later convicted of anti-Fascist resistance. It is unclear if he was sentenced to death, but he was imprisoned at Münchner Platz and would have been well aware of the regular executions that were taking place. An example was 50-year-old Anna Strunkova, who was decapitated on 17 November 1944 for having provided shelter to four escaped Russians.

Dresden by this time had become the seventh largest city in Germany and had escaped significant damage. However, this was to change in February 1945, when the Allies agreed to bomb the city, the Russians having formally requested strategic air attacks against Germany's eastern centres such as Leipzig and Dresden in order to progress their Eastern Front objectives. On the night of 13 February 1945, the RAF mounted a raid upon Dresden, an attack no different from any other major operation mounted by Bomber Command at this time. Münchner Platz Prison sat within the confines of the general target area, and unbeknown to Josef and the hundreds of other prisoners confined in their prison cells that night, Dresden was about to be consumed in a firestorm. Bomber Command sent 773 Avro Lancasters, and citizens barely had time to reach their shelters, partly as a result of a mass of refugees who had been swarming into Dresden to escape the Russian advance from the east. The first bombs fell at 22.09 hours in an attack that although of just twenty-four minutes' duration was to leave the inner city as a raging sea of fire. A few hours later, a further raid saw more bombs rain down onto the already glowing flames. Precision bombing had created a firestorm of immense proportions—one that claimed a horrific number of human casualties. During the two days that followed, the US sent over 527 heavy bombers to follow up on the RAF attack. Dresden was decimated and portions of the prison at Münchner Platz were seriously damaged, creating an opportunity for Josef Skupa to escape amongst the mayhem. He tried to make for home to reunite with his fellow puppeteers, but unbeknown to him, over a hundred of them had already been killed, whether by execution or in concentration camps. Those who survived had continued trying to entertain their fellow concentration camp inmates in an attempt to brighten their blighted lives, by making puppets from rags and improvising with the barest of items.

The execution victims of Münchner Platz Prison included several members of the National Committee for Free Germany. Within that group was Georg Schumann, a German Communist and long-term resister against the Nazi Party who had been persecuted and imprisoned in the early years of Hitler's rise to power. In particular, he had resisted against the National Socialist criminal justice system, and it was ironic that in July 1944, Georg was imprisoned at Münchner Platz and sentenced to death in that same building on 21 November, followed by his beheading on 11 January 1945 in the prison courtyard. Georg's resolute resistance against the Nazis was later recognised by the very courthouse that had sent him to his death, which was renamed the Georg Schumann Building. It now forms part of the Dresden University of Technology.

Dr Hermann Stieve

Born on 22 May 1886 in Munich, Hermann Stieve embarked on a life of medicine, becoming a professor of anatomy and one of Europe's most influential specialists in that field. From the 1920s, Stieve developed an interest in studying the influence of the nervous system on the reproductive system. His research was primarily undertaken on animals, but during the time of the Weimar Republic, rare opportunities existed for male persons sentenced to death to be examined in order to explore the consequences of chronic stress. It should be noted that women were not executed during the Weimar era. Stieve was employed as a lecturer at the Halle-Wittenberg University during Hitler's rise to power. Research suggests that he did not become a member of the Nazi Party, even though the Nazi regime removed 'undesirable' individuals from universities across Germany and this was therefore a great inducement to join the movement during those years. From 1935 to 1952, Stieve held the prestigious position of director of the Institute of Anatomy in Berlin, which trained hundreds of army and most probably SS medics. Stieve's histological research results placed him in opposition to Hermann Knaus, professor and director of the gynaecological and obstetric clinic at the German Karl-Ferdinand University in Prague, as he was critical of Knaus's assumptions regarding the predictability of ovulation and of 'safe' periods in the human menstrual cycle.

The events that took place during Hitler's ascendancy and the escalation of executions undertaken across Germany provided unexpected and unprecedented opportunities for Stieve. Driven by personal ambition and a desire to expand his theories, he co-operated with the Nazi judicial system for the sake of his research and came to practise on those condemned by the courts. From 1938 onwards, he became one of the most prolific anatomists in Europe, simply because of the abundance of corpses available to him. However, it must be remembered that regardless of Stieve's desires, the vast majority of corpses that came before him in his anatomy laboratory were headless—a stark and sobering fact evidencing the frenzied and widespread decapitations demanded by Hitler's courts. In Brandenburg-Görden, an estimated 2,000 executions took place, and in Plötzensee the figure was potentially closer to 3,000, many of them young women who represented unique opportunities in anatomical dissection for Stieve. The same opportunities, albeit to a lesser extent, occurred at Moabit where facilities were in place to secure and store the required bodies. This was a legal practice authorised by the administration of the People's Court and furthered in 1942 by legislation decreeing that universities were not to inform any family or others about the date of any execution or hand back any bodies to relatives.

The supply and delivery chain from Fallbeil decapitation to university mortuary or examination table became a very efficient process. Official correspondence from the People's Court to the director of the Institute of Anatomy advised of impending executions, giving the name, reason for execution, date and profession if known. The documents were pro-formas with available space for additional handwritten information, and this enabled specific selection or prioritisation of execution subjects for Stieve's anatomical work. A more than adequate evidence trail of documentation was present for each executed individual, but tragically much of that material was destroyed by Allied bombing during the closing years of the war. Sufficient documentation has, however, survived to establish the facts on many execution torsos and heads that were the subject of Stevie's research, some of whom were reportedly pregnant. Lucienne Tassin, aged twenty, was a French forced labourer who had been sentenced to death by the Berlin Special Court on 24 September 1943 for looting. Lucienne claimed to be several months' pregnant but was swiftly executed on 13 October, with no evidence existing to confirm her claim. In many instances, such individuals with an unborn child were deemed to be unlikely to contribute towards the Third Reich or likely to be in contravention of Nazi blood purity laws. The Office of Racial Purity frequently wrote about the 'honour of the German people' and how it could be diluted by 'unacceptable relationships', and the consequences of 'racial crimes' or 'blood treason'—an area that held no interest for Stieve but without doubt directly led to the supply of additional bodies to his establishment.

Russian-born Vera Obolensky would tragically and unknowingly provide her body for Stieve to extract her pelvic organs as part of his histological examinations. Vera had emigrated to France, where she worked as a model and secretary, becoming active in a resistance group that gathered intelligence and tried to assist in organising the escape of Allied prisoners of war. Arrested by the Gestapo on 17 December 1943, she was subjected to interrogation and torture to extract information on the people she worked with. Vera appeared in a military court in Arras in May 1944, charged with treason, and was found guilty and sentenced to death. The sentence was carried out on 4 August in Berlin, following which her body was almost instantly collected by the staff from the city's Institute of Anatomy. It is indeed salutary to consider what effect the sight of a headless torso that exhibited visible signs of torture would have had on the assistants and Stieve himself in the dissection rooms.

Wanda Kallenbach, the mother of an eleven-year-old girl, had lived in the Friedrichschain district of Berlin. Her body was to lie before Stieve, having been executed by the Fallbeil in Plötzensee Prison on 18 August 1944. Wanda had experienced the concentrated Allied bombing across Berlin and during August 1943 had sought refuge for herself and her daughter in their home village in East Prussia. It was a stark contrast to Berlin, and Wanda voiced her complaints about the bombing in Berlin to family and others known to her, criticising the false promises of safety issued by the likes of *Reichsmarschall* Hermann Goering, Commander of the Luftwaffe and Hitler's designated successor. Wanda returned to Berlin and continued working for the German war effort as a packer in a factory, but several months later, on 20 January 1944, she was arrested by the Gestapo and taken into custody, having been denounced by an undisclosed informant for her criticisms of the Third Reich. Wanda subsequently appeared in the People's Court in Berlin, where the infamous prosecutor Freisler presided over her short hearing. She had been charged with 'undermining the military and aiding the enemy' and was almost immediately found guilty. Following her execution, her headless body was supplied to further Stieve's work in Berlin University.

The July plot against Hitler in 1944 saw a significant number of executions as a result of some shameful People's Court deliberations. A 59-year-old nurse, Ehrengard Frank-Schultz, spoke to a Red Cross colleague and voiced an opinion that may have been induced by her widowhood, saying that she regretted the failure of the attempt on Hitler's life, adding that a few years under an Anglo-Saxon government would be better than under the violent Nazi regime. Those comments saw her tried in the People's Court on 6 November 1944, sentenced to death and subsequently executed by decapitation on 8 December. Ehrengard's body provided Stieve with the opportunity to undertake the removal of a mature set of pelvic organs, as the vast majority of his subjects had been of child-bearing age. Stieve wrote a number of papers on the changes in reproductive tissue on ageing women, and no doubt sought specific age groups of executed female subjects.

After the war, Stieve was investigated by the Allied forces, and there appears to have been no question of any prosecution, although the Soviet occupying forces took an interest in his activities during the period of the Third Reich. Stieve went on to undertake further research and published many papers on the subject. Some of those papers raised questions with regard to evidence relative to the migration of male sperm, which has led to post-war speculation that some females sentenced to death had been intentionally raped. The body registers at the university were never found, but Stieve constructed a list from his notes and from memory in 1946. This represented a very small number of the overall bodies that would have been delivered to his university—just 182 out of an estimated figure of 3,000. Interestingly, Stieve also recorded the receipt of eight men, disproving the theory that he used only female corpses. It appears that the male reproductive organs were also part of the overall studies, and it must be assumed that these men were specifically selected.

The world of academic medicine actively encouraged people like Stieve to secure the evidence needed to prove, disprove or merely hypothesise upon a theory. Hitler's various courts, empowered to take away someone's life on the basis of fragile evidence, created unique opportunities that were taken up by men like Dr Hermann Stieve. On the balance of probability, decisions made to advance medicine and their own careers undoubtedly influenced what took place during the Third Reich era, but the vision of a headless corpse displaying evidence of possible torture lying on a dissection table will always remain questionable.

The Ahnenerbe Institute

In 1935, Heinrich Himmler, head of the Gestapo and the SS, founded a Nazi research institute called the Ahnenerbe. Its official mission was to unearth new evidence of the accomplishments and deeds of Germanic ancestors using precise scientific methods. The Institute for Military Scientific Research, which became attached to the specialist Ahnenerbe research unit during the Second World War, conducted extensive medical experiments connected to survival from exposure and ballistic injuries, utilising human subjects primarily taken from concentration camps for experimentation.

An SS captain, Prof. August Hirt, commanded one of its divisions and served as a chairman at the Reich University in Strasbourg and was specifically engaged in the collection of human anatomical specimens, in particular Jewish skulls. The bodies of eighty-six Jewish men and women were specifically selected to create an exhibition and provide research on Jewish skull configuration. A process called maceration would eventually be required in order to remove all of the flesh and soft tissue to create the perfect examples, and it is understood that this process was undertaken at the university in Strasbourg. That work developed further into research on what is quoted as 'Jewish-Bolshevik skulls which represent the prototype of the repulsive but characteristic subhuman', a chilling statement relative to the work and objectives desired by Himmler and imposed upon the Ahnenerbe research institute. However, what is more disturbing is the fact that the best practical method for obtaining and collecting this material was by directing that all captured Jewish-Bolshevik commissars be turned over, alive, to the *Feldpolizei*. They were given special directives to pay the commissars close attention and take care of them until a special delegate arrived from the Ahnenerbe unit. The special delegates were required to take a series of photographs, make anthropological measurements and also determine as far as possible other personal data concerning the prisoners. The selected Jews were then taken from Auschwitz to Natzweiler, the closest German prison camp to the university, about 50 km south-west of Strasbourg and the only such camp to be situated in France. Natzweiler was a camp for the imprisonment of convicted German criminals and anti-Fascist resistance fighters. In 1943, Le Struthof, as the camp was known to the French, had a special gas chamber constructed by adapting a building formerly owned and used as a refrigerator room by the Struthof Hotel, which was located about a mile from the actual camp. Instructions were given for the head to be removed from the body of the murdered inmates and then forwarded to the university in a hermetically sealed tin can especially made for this purpose and filled with a conserving fluid. Having arrived at the laboratory, the head comparison tests and anatomical research on the skull would be carried out by Hirt.

The post-war medical trials conducted in August 1946 by the Allies saw the prosecution of Wolfram Sievers, the general secretary of the Ahnenerbe unit and later the director of the Institute for Military Scientific Research. During that trial it was established that 115 people were experimented upon in Strasbourg University. Seventy-nine were male Jews, thirty were female Jews, two were Poles and four were Asiatics, most probably Russian. Further evidence was exposed concerning other bodies stored at the university with an inconclusive history but from which Hirt had assembled a collection of eighty corpses that were being held in large vats filled with preservative. It was later established that several of those people were Greek Jews removed by the SS from the Baron Hirsch ghetto in Thessaloniki. Hirt had engaged in correspondence with Sievers over their remains and later requested what should be done with the collection stored in the vats of the Anatomical Institute in the event that Strasbourg should be endangered—presumably a reference to it being overrun by the Allies. That morbid evidence was read to the Allied trial judges:

The collection can be stripped of the flesh and thereby rendered unidentifiable. This, however, would mean that at least part of the whole work had been done for nothing and that this collection, the only one of its kind, would be lost to science, since it would be impossible to make plaster casts afterwards. The skeleton collection as such is inconspicuous. The flesh parts could be declared as having been left by the French at the time we took over the Anatomical Institute and would be turned over for cremating. Please advise me which of the following three proposals is to be carried out:

1. The collection as a whole is to be preserved.
2. The collection is to be dissolved in part.
3. The collection is to be completely dissolved.

Document No. 091, Exhibit GB 579, extracted from the trial, advises of the fate of these people. There are two notes from Himmler's file. The first note is signed by *SS-Hauptsturmführer* Berg:

> On 12th October, 1944, I had a telephone conversation with SS-Standartenführer Sievers and asked him if the Strassburg skeleton collection had been completely dissolved as directed by SS-Standartenführer Baumert. SS-Standartenführer Sievers could not advise me on that matter since he had not as yet heard anything further from Professor Hirt. I told him that in case the dissolution had not yet been carried out, a certain part of the collection should be preserved. However, guarantee should be given that a complete dissolution could be made in time in case Strassburg should be in danger. SS-Standartenführer Sievers promised me that he would find out about it and let me know.

And on 26 October 1944, a note for Dr Rudolf Brandt, Himmler's personal administrative officer, reads:

> During his visit at the Operational HQ on 21st October 1944, SS-Standartenführer Sievers told me that the collection in Strassburg had been completely dissolved in the meantime in conformance with the directive given him at the time. He is of the opinion that this arrangement is for the best in view of the whole situation.

Many instances exist where men and women sentenced to death for treason were sent to various concentration camps. The Ahnenerbe were very selective in their requirements of harvesting the heads required for their purposes. However, no doubt exists that decapitations took place by default from the Nazi courts as a result of the activities of Himmler's special unit, but at this time there is insufficient evidence to collate any evidential route from a People's Court to Hirt's collection of skulls. Part of the skull collection was reportedly moved to the Ancestral Heritage Archive at Mittersill Castle in late 1944, but little if any evidence can be found to substantiate this claim. Hirt was captured at Strasbourg by French troops, and French and American liberating troops later came across significant evidence at Strasbourg, much of which was used in the post-war trials. Research after the war revealed that a French assistant to Hirt, Henri Pierre, had secretly noted the numbers tattooed on the arms of the eighty-six torso victims, and it was this piece of vital evidence that was ultimately used to make their identification possible by cross-referencing with a surviving list of inmates vaccinated at Auschwitz. This painstaking work was undertaken many years after the war by Dr Hans-Joachim Lang, a professor at the University of Tübingen.

His research work was then corroborated by the surviving tattoo numbers from the remaining sixteen torsos and body parts that had been recovered from the vats of preservative at Strasbourg University in 1945. It should be noted that some efforts had been made to remove some sections of forearm tissue in an attempt to thwart any identification, and it is assumed that this was done at the time when many heads and body parts were most probably transported to the municipal crematorium in September 1944.

Hirt escaped trial by committing suicide in Schönenbach, in the Neustadt district of Austria, on 2 June 1945. Sievers stood trial at Nuremberg where, on 20 August 1947, he was found guilty of crimes against humanity, following which he was hanged for his crimes, on 2 June 1948. Brandt was found guilty of having taken part in a number of medical experiments including high-altitude and freezing experiments and was hanged in company with Sievers. Himmler, one of the most powerful and influential individuals next to Hitler, committed suicide after being captured by the Allies in 1945.

In 1951, the remains of the eighty-six victims were reinterred together in one location at the Cronenbourg-Strasbourg Jewish cemetery and, on 11 December 2005, memorials were unveiled at the Anatomy Institute of Strasbourg Hospital and at the Jewish cemetery in France. The ceremony was attended by a number of relatives of those victims who had been identified.

CHAPTER 11

The End of the Oppressive Judicial System and the Fall of Hitler

Following Germany's unconditional surrender, Allied military rule replaced the government of the defeated Nazi state and all German institutions came to a standstill. In order to prevent total collapse, the Allies ordered all civil servants to remain at their posts until dismissed. All German courts had ceased to function, creating an unprecedented judicial hiatus. The Allied Control Council and the Military Government promulgated laws and issued proclamations regulating the German judiciary—directives designed to exclude Nazi members and Nazi ideas from the reconstituted legal system. Law No. 4 of the Allied Control Council of 30 October 1945 stated:

> In order to reform the German legal system, all former members of the Nazi Party who gave their active support to the party, and all other persons who had a direct part in the penal methods of the Hitlerite regime must be removed from office as judges and public prosecutors, and may not be allowed to occupy such offices.

The Allies immediately repealed the most significant discriminatory laws, ordinances and decrees upon which the Nazi regime had rested and reopened the German ordinary courts: Magistrate Courts (*Amtsgerichte*), District Courts (*Landgerichte*), and Circuit Courts (*Oberlandesgerichte*). All special and party tribunals including the infamous People's Courts were dissolved, and the former Supreme Court, the *Reichsgericht*, closed permanently. It was estimated that over 90 per cent of all legal officials had belonged to the Nazi Party, many having been influential in upholding Hitler's judicial objectives, which had led to significant death sentencing over several years. The most notorious Nazis, including judges and prosecutors, were interned under the imposition of mandatory arrest. In as many instances as possible, these men were replaced. As far as possible, key positions were occupied by Chief Judges of the Circuit Courts and by those who were not implicated in the Nazi administration of justice—mostly older jurists who had retired upon Nazi assumption of power. Unfortunately, this system did not preclude a great many jurists from Hitler's Special Courts and People's Courts or military judges from being engaged in the new court system, as there were not enough untainted judges, prosecutors and court clerks available to staff the ordinary courts. In the Allied Soviet zone of Germany, Nazi jurists were absolutely excluded, so the occupation authorities appointed lay judges who were legally unqualified but politically reliable. In the western zones of Allied occupation, only qualified professional jurists were eligible for judicial office: in the American zone, and to a lesser degree in the French, this meant virtually no appointments. The courts were therefore seriously understaffed and slow to function effectively. In the British zone, the absence of unimplicated jurists led to a pragmatic compromise. A 50:50 rule was introduced whereby every unimplicated jurist was able to sit with an identified Nazi jurist, which proved to be effective in progressing cases that would otherwise not have been heard.

The Allied forces arbitrated in respect of how they should punish those responsible for war crimes, and foremost in the minds of many was the appalling evidence associated with the extermination camps and the horrors associated with the Nazi treatment of Russian prisoners of war. President Truman gave his full support for a judicial process in which those arrested for war crimes would stand trial in public for the allegations made against them, and in which the men on trial, regardless of the charges, would be given the opportunity to defend themselves. The legal basis for the trials was established by the London Charter issued on 8 August 1945, which restricted the first trials to major war criminals from the Axis nations only. The legal jurisdiction of the court came from the Instrument of Surrender of Germany, which had transferred political authority and sovereign power over Germany to the Allied Control Council. The four Allied occupation armies established tribunals to try Nazi criminals under Control Council Law No. 10, which had been issued in December 1945 to provide a 'uniform legal basis in Germany for the prosecution of war criminals and other similar offenders'.

The city of Nuremberg, situated in the American sector, had witnessed the infamous Nazi Party rallies, and its large Palace of Justice had been largely undamaged by Allied bombing. Alongside the Palace of Justice was a suitably large prison that was ideal for undertaking the predictably lengthy process of judicial hearings with multiple defendants. A walled and roofed boardwalk was constructed between the prison and the Palace of Justice to facilitate the constant movement of Nazi criminals between the two venues, and field marshals, generals, state secretaries, SS officers, Gestapo personnel, businessmen and judges were marched daily into the impressively large Palace of Justice.

The Nuremberg War Crime Trials conducted by the Allies between 1945 and 1949 were held in courtroom No. 600 in the eastern wing of the Palace of Justice. The most famous trials were those of the major war criminals that were held from 20 November 1945 to 1 October 1946, involving twenty-one senior Nazis. The International Military Tribunal had agreed and formulated four primary indictments, some of which were made against all twenty-one defendants. The trials were conducted by a joint United States-British-French and Soviet military tribunal, each nation supplying two judges. The four counts in the indictment were:

- Count 1—CONSPIRACY to commit crimes alleged in the next three counts.
- Count 2—CRIMES AGAINST PEACE including planning, preparing, starting, or waging aggressive war.
- Count 3—WAR CRIMES including violations of laws or customs of war.
- Count 4—CRIMES AGAINST HUMANITY including murder, extermination, enslavement, persecution on political or racial grounds, involuntary deportment, and inhumane acts against civilian populations.

Several of the initial twenty-one primary defendants were subsequently sentenced to death by hanging. On 16 October 1946, Joachim von Ribbentrop was the first to be taken into the execution chamber of Nuremberg Prison where he mounted the gallows and was hanged. He was followed in quick succession by Wilhelm Keitel, Ernst Kaltenbrunner, Alfred Rosenberg, Hans Frank, Wilhelm Frick, Julius Streicher, Arthur Seyss-Inquart, Fritz Sauckel and Alfred Jodl. Their bodies were then taken under guard from Nuremberg to the crematorium at Dachau concentration camp and their ashes were unceremoniously scattered into a small watercourse in Munich.

Twelve further trials of high-ranking German officials followed at Nuremberg and are often referred to collectively as the 'Subsequent Nuremberg Proceedings'. Between December 1946 and April 1949, Allied prosecutors tried 177 persons and secured the convictions of 97 defendants.

The overwhelming majority of post-war crimes trials involved lower-level officials and functionaries. However, many of their crimes were just as heinous and appalling. The four Allied powers occupying Germany (and Austria) additionally held trials in their zones of occupation in which a variety of perpetrators were tried for wartime offences. Many of these trials involved the murder of Allied military personnel who had been captured by German or Axis troops, and the four powers expanded their juridical mandate in order to try concentration camp guards, commandants and others who had committed crimes against Jews and other victims of persecution in the areas that the Allies occupied.

The first concentration camp war criminals to be brought to justice were members of the camp staff of Bergen-Belsen, who were prosecuted by a British military tribunal in November 1945. America soon followed a few days later, with proceedings against the camp staff at Dachau in a military tribunal held inside the camp complex.

The Soviet military tribunal proceedings against the Sachsenhausen concentration camp staff began on 23 October 1947 in Pankow town hall, Berlin. This was the first time that the Soviets had allowed the press and the public to attend one of their military tribunal proceedings, and this event soon became known in the press as 'The Berlin Trial'. Two defendants—Gustav Sorge, the record-keeper at Sachsenhausen, and Wilhelm Schubert, one of the block leaders—would later figure in an important additional trial connected to crimes against others in 1958. In addition to the concentration camp cases, the US military commissions tried large numbers of Nazi criminals at Wiesbaden, Ludwigshafen and Dachau. The British held trials in Germany and Italy; the French held them in Germany, France and North Africa.

Allied Control Council Law No. 10 authorised German courts of law to pass sentences for wartime crimes committed by German citizens against other German nationals or stateless persons. For this reason, occupation officials left crimes in which both victims and perpetrators were predominantly German nationals to be tried in the newly reconstructed German tribunals, which represented the first German national trials in the early post-war period. Both the German Federal Republic (West Germany) and the German Democratic Republic (East Germany) continued to hold trials against Nazi-era defendants in the decades following their establishment as independent states. However, Control Council Law No. 4 had specifically prevented the German courts from dealing with Nazi crimes, and before 1950, no German court was permitted to judge crimes committed against Allied nationals. This effectively and appropriately removed most wartime offences, including the mass murder of Jews, from German judicial jurisdiction.

As we have seen, the pragmatic approach to creating an immediate post-war functioning court system for the Allies was initially conceived to exclude judges from the Hitlerite Special Courts and the People's Courts, even though those judges who had supported Hitler's judicial system in those courts over many years claimed simply to be upholding the laws against defendants that were presented before them. On 19 October 1958, Dr Max Güde, the West German Federal Prosecutor-General, admitted that 'the mass of today's judges and public prosecutors were already active in legal office between 1933 and 1945 ... they were tools of illegality, and instruments of terror.' Dr Güde added that these persons had made themselves guilty—'because the rule of law perished, but they survived'.

During the mid-1950s the Committee for German Unity came up with proposals concerning measures to assist German reunification. The committee had voiced serious concerns over the evidence that the majority of Nazi judges had been returned to office and that 800 Special Court and Military Court judges, particularly implicated with the Nazi Party, were by then occupying responsible positions. As the Cold War commenced in 1948, the western Allies ended their restrictions on jurists with a Nazi past and slowly the implicated judges and prosecutors returned to office, in many instances occupying employment that their colleagues had kept open for them. In 1951, after the establishment of the Federal Republic, the law facilitated the return to their previous employment of all civil servants not actually convicted of a crime.

In 1956, the Committee for German Unity submitted evidence of their findings to the West German authorities. Many judges were ex-Nazi Party members responsible for sending significant numbers of defendants to their deaths, yet they were occupying the following positions within the current judicial system:

Employed in Provincial Courts, 222
Employed in District Courts, 213

Employed as Public Prosecutors, 126
Employed in Upper Provincial Court, 109
Employed as Senior Public Prosecutors, 55
Employed in other courts, 40
Employed in Federal Courts, 17
Employed in Ministries in the Federal Republic, 11
Employed in other judicial functions, 7

This publication confirmed that the West German government had reinstated 800 former active Nazi court operatives, who had been responsible for upholding the National Socialist judicial system and had been part of the instrument of terror used by the Nazi regime. According to statistics made public by Dr Thomas Dehler and Dr Max Güde, the regime's public prosecutors and judges had been responsible for the execution of 26,000 Germans and foreigners during the Second World War. Additionally, these judges had handed down significant 'hard labour' periods of punishment totalling hundreds of thousands of years, which in most cases equated to death sentences. In Nazi-occupied countries, they had upheld Fascist laws designed to decimate native populations, whilst in Germany itself they were charged with liquidating those who opposed the Nazi dictatorship and with implementing the laws that the dictatorship laid before its people. In 1959, the Committee for German Unity published *We Accuse: 800 Bloodstained Nazi Judges—Bastions of Adenauer's Militarist Regime* in which evidence from court extracts implicated the men who were currently employed in the German courts. Individuals included in these statistics are as follows:

- Dr Bruchhaus, formerly a public prosecutor in the People's Courts: On 26 June 1942, Bruchhaus demanded the death penalty for Otto Haeuslein and Adam Leis, both resident in Frankfurt and accused of being active on behalf of the Communist Party in Germany. Both men were sentenced to death.
- On 9 October 1942, on the application of Bruchhaus, the death penalty was imposed on Hanno Günther, Wolfgang Pander, Bernhard Sikorski, Emmerich Schaper, Alfred Schmidt-Sas and Dagmar Petersen, all Berlin residents. All were accused of being engaged in Communist activity. The wood-turner Sikorski and shorthand typist Petersen were additionally charged with listening to radio news broadcasts from London. All received the death penalty, with the exception of Petersen who was sentenced to seven years' hard labour.
- On 20 April 1943, Bruchhaus demanded the death penalty for plasterer Walter Richey. He was also charged with Communist connections and in fifteen cases had procured identity papers for Jewish citizens who were illegally living in areas occupied by the Wehrmacht. Richey was executed accordingly on an unknown date.
- On 23 July 1943, on the application of Bruchhaus, worker Kurt Gersing of Berlin was sentenced to death solely because he had worked with five German citizens who had been sentenced to death on 9 October 1942 for their anti-Fascist activities.

- On 8 September 1943 in the People's Court, Bruchhaus demanded the death penalty for general practitioner Dr Alois Geiger, for allegedly undermining the war effort and assisting the enemy. The infamous judge Freisler declared that the 'mental cruelty' he induced by comments alluding to the 'bravery in bringing another child into this world for if things should go wrong we should be in a sorry position' were summed up with a sentence to be punished by death for the sake of our victory.
- On 28 September 1943, Bruchhaus applied for the death sentence for storehouse worker August Beckmann, his wife Lina, railway worker Gustav Horstbrink, and his wife Frieda. They were all accused of being a Communist cell and listening to enemy radio programmes. Death sentences were imposed on the two couples. Carpenter Hugo Hillebrenner, who was charged with the same offence, received three years' hard labour.

Similar cases occurred during 1944, an additional five civilians being sentenced to death upon Bruchhaus's applications to the People's Court. All these case files provide irrefutable proof of the role Bruchhaus played in Hitler's courts, but in the post-war period he was engaged in the German courts as a public prosecutor at Wuppertal.

Another example concerns Dr Liebau, who had worked as an official for the Special Courts in the Reich Ministry of Justice, preparing and carrying out many cases that resulted in death sentences in association with Roland Freisler, Ernst Lautz and Otto Georg Thierack. Documentary evidence links Liebau with the cases of 62 people who were executed, including Englishman John Lennox on 10 November 1943. After the war, Liebau was employed as a senior district judge at Seesen after his promotion from the post of senior public prosecutor in Lüneburg.

Dr Ludwig was the senior public prosecutor in the Prague Special Court and the author of the bill of indictment against the Catholic clergyman and professor of religion Karel Kratina. Ludwig included accounts that Father Kratina had been responsible for spreading tales of horror about alleged maltreatment of prisoners by the Gestapo. He was subsequently sentenced to death on 6 December 1944.

Ludwig was also in charge of the executions imposed upon resistance fighters in Prague, handing down death sentences against twenty-two individuals. The following report is contained in the files of the case against a married couple named Limbursky, whose crime had been to provide shelter to a member of the Czech army:

Document No. 4 KLs 60/44 Prague, 12 January 1945.

The following attended in the execution room of the Pankrac prison in Prague during the infliction of the death penalty in the Limbursky-Wenzel criminal case: Chief public prosecutor Dr Ludwig ... executioner Weiss.

The condemned prisoner was led in by prison guards and three helpers. The executioner thereupon inflicted the death penalty with the guillotine [Fallbeil] at 15 hours 41 minutes.

Time taken:
1. From the arrival to the handing over of the prisoner, 5 seconds.
2. From the handing over to the executioner, 7 seconds.
This happened without incident; the body and head of the prisoner were handed to the prison guard for further disposal.

At 15.43 hours, just two minutes after her husband's head was severed from his body, his wife was executed upon the same Fallbeil. Her eyes and ears must have been witness to the terror of her husband's death for having done no more than offer shelter to another human being. Ludwig's signature on the document provides unquestionable evidence of his involvement. Despite this, he served as the public prosecutor in the post-war judiciary at Düsseldorf and would later receive a full pension for his services.

Jaager was a public prosecutor in the Vienna Special Court and he later became a prosecutor in the People's Court associated with Roland Freisler. His prosecution briefs were most welcome instruments for Freisler to endorse, allowing him to impose sentences against both German and Austrian anti-Fascists. Jaager's time in Vienna evidences cases of death sentences and hard labour, whilst his time in the People's Court saw prosecutions against a couple named Steinhorst who voiced an opinion, in their home, in 1943 that the war would soon be over. This defeatist utterance and other intimations were to see them lose their lives. Later in June 1944, Jaager prosecuted a truck driver, Oskar Billion, who was sentenced to death for listening to the radio and questioning the truth of German reports, especially of those from the Wehrmacht.

Several other similar cases exist in which Jaager prosecuted for the death sentence, one of the most thought-provoking of which concerned Ehrengard Frank-Schultz referred to in the previous chapter. Document No. 1 L 427/44—6 J 1906/44 confirms that on 6 November 1944, on the application of Jaager, the First Senate of the People's Court condemned Ehrengard to death for allegedly undermining the war effort. Jaager had little difficulty in proving his case, and Freisler once again ordered that the life of another 'supporter' of the July plot against Hitler be taken by means of decapitation. However, Jaager's actions and demeanour in the People's Court did not prevent him from serving in the immediate post-war period as a prosecutor. In fact, he was later promoted to the post of senior public prosecutor in the upper provincial court of Schleswig.

Many further examples exist of Hitler's prosecutors and judges being provided with positions within Germany's post-war judiciary, many of whom would subsequently be embroiled in cases involving high-profile Nazi members who had been tracked down and subsequently brought to trial. These events were taking place at a time when Nazi war criminals who had been sentenced to death by the Allies' courts but whose punishments were later commuted to prison sentences were being repatriated to their country. Many were openly welcomed with celebration and went on to lead a comfortable life on state pensions.

However, that was not the case for the two Sachsenhausen concentration camp staff, Gustav Sorge and Wilhelm Schubert. On 14 January 1956, the surviving SS men who had been convicted and sentenced to life in prison were released by the Russians and returned to the Federal Republic. After their return, most of the convicted war criminals from 'The Berlin Trial' were again tried in German courts for crimes against German nationals. Amongst them were Sorge and Schubert, who were put on trial on 18 October 1958 in a regional court at Bonn. On 6 February 1959, both were found guilty of murder, attempted murder, and complicity of murder and manslaughter. In view of the German government's previous reluctance to prosecute Nazi war criminals, this trial was particularly significant. It sent a resounding signal that those holders of high office who had given orders for mass executions, and those judges who had legalised terror, had played an integral part in the barbaric regime. Government and party officials as well as SS men were all accomplices in Nazi mass murder. The sadistic guards in the torture camps and the technicians in the death factories had worked at the end of an assembly line that had originated with the legal experts who drafted the text creating the racial laws. Without the help of these officials, Hitler could not have managed the war machine and ruled Germany and its occupied countries across Europe, least of all carried out the 'Final Solution'. The manipulation of the Third Reich's judicial system had been of immense importance, and two orders created by the Reich Minister for Justice in 1933 illustrate this most profoundly:

TRANSLATION OF DOCUMENT 2076-PS 1933 REICHSGESETZBLATT, PART I

Decree of the Reich Cabinet relating to the formation of special courts of March 21, 1933 On the basis of Chapter II, Part 6 of the third decree of the Reich President to safeguard economy and finances and to combat political excesses, of 6 October 1931 (Reichsgesetzblatt I pp. 537, 565) the following is decreed.

Section 1
(1) A special court will be created for the district of each court of appeals.
(2) The special courts are courts of the State [Land].
(3) The legal administration of the State [Land] determines the seats of the special courts.

Section 2
The special courts have jurisdiction over crimes and felonies enumerated in the decree of the President of the Reich for the defence of people and state, of 28 February 1933 (Reichsgesetzblatt I, p. 83) and in the decree relating to the defence against insidious attacks against the government of the national revolution provided that such offences are not within the jurisdiction of the Supreme Court or court of appeals.

Section 3

(1) The special courts also have jurisdiction when a crime or felony which is under their jurisdiction fulfils at the same time the specifications of another offence.

(2) If another offence is directly connected with the crime or felony which comes under the jurisdiction of the Special Courts, then the proceedings against the offenders and accessories of the other offence may be instituted in the Special Courts.

(3) The extended jurisdiction pursuant to Paragraphs 1 and 2 does not apply to offences for which the Supreme Court or courts of appeals have jurisdiction.

Section 7

Proceedings may be instituted also before the Special Court in the district of which the defendant was caught or where he is in custody. The release of the defendant does not affect this jurisdiction once it has been established.

Section 9

(1) No hearings relating to the warrant of arrest shall be held.

Section 11

A preliminary court investigation will not take place. If a preliminary investigation is pending at the time this decree becomes effective, the records are to be transferred at once to the prosecuting official with the Special Court.

Section 16

(1) No legal remedy is admissible against the decisions of the Special Courts.

Berlin, March 24, 1933

The Reich Chancellor
Adolf Hitler

For the Reich Minister of Justice
The Deputy of the Reich Chancellor
Von Papen.

TRANSLATION OF DOCUMENT 1401-PS 1933 REICHSGESETZBLATT, PART I

Law Regarding Admission to the Bar, 7 April 1933
The Reich Government has enacted the following law that is promulgated herewith:

Article 1. The admission of lawyers who, according to the Law for the Restoration of the Professional Civil Service, of April 7, 1933 (RGBI, I, p. 175), are of non-Aryan descent, may be cancelled till September 30, 1933.

The provision of clause 1 does not apply to lawyers already admitted before August 1, 1914, or, who, during the World War fought at the front for Germany, or its allies, or who lost their fathers or sons in the World War.

Article 2. Persons who, according to the Law for the Restoration of the Professional Civil Service of April 7, 1933 (RGBI, I, p. 175), are of non-Aryan descent, may be refused permission to practise law, even if there exists none of the reasons enumerated in the Regulations for Lawyers. The same rule applies in cases as where a lawyer described in Section 1, clause 2, wishes to be admitted to another court.

Article 3. Persons who were active in the Communistic sense are excluded from the admission to the Bar.
Admissions already given must be revoked.

Article 4. The Justice-Administration can issue an injunction against a lawyer until it is decided if use will be made of the right to revoke the admission in accordance with Article 1/1, or Article 3. The prescriptions of Article 9/b/2-4 of the Bar regulation (Reichs-Law-Publication 1933, I, p. 120) apply accordingly to the injunction against representation.
Against lawyers of that type as described in Article 1/2 the injunction against representation is only then permissible when the use of Article 3 is concerned.

Article 5. To revoke the admission to the Bar is considered an important reason for the cancelling of employment contracts which were concluded by the lawyer as employer.

Article 6. In case the admission of a lawyer is revoked in accordance with this law, then for the cancelling of leases of rooms which were rented by the lawyer for himself or his family, the regulations of the law about the cancelling right of persons concerned by the law for the renovation of professional bureaucracy, 7 April 1933, (RGBI, I, p. 187) will accordingly be used. The same will apply to employees of lawyers who lost their job owing to the fact that the admission of the lawyer was revoked or an injunction against representation against him was issued in conformity with Article 4.

Berlin, 7 April 1933

The Reich Chancellor
Adolf Hitler

The Reich Minister for Justice
Dr. Gürtner

The Nuremberg Judges' Trials

As we have seen, the Allied occupation forces in Germany were faced with ensuring that the administration of law was maintained in the immediate post-war period, whilst acknowledging the overwhelming evidence of malpractice and war crimes endemic in the German judicial system during the war. In October 1945, the Berlin Court of Appeals began functioning, to complete the legal hierarchy authorised by the Allies.

It is difficult to understand the ramifications for so many areas of the law that existed at that time and how they were managed. Reflecting many years later, some may choose to criticise the processes that were followed in order to prosecute and pass judgment on those who had 'judged' and sentenced to death many thousands of unfortunate men, women and young persons in Germany and the Nazi-occupied lands. In February 1947, the US Military Government for Germany created Military Tribunal III to try the case against those who had upheld the Nazi judicial system. This was the third of twelve such trials held at Nuremberg. The pre-trial evidence gathering and witness selection processes were obviously entwined with the all-consuming and ever-growing accumulation of documentation that had built up during the two years since hostilities had ceased. The challenge was daunting. The alleged perpetrators would need to be taken into custody and be in a sound mental and physical condition to stand trial; bilingual researchers, investigators and translators had to be hired, and qualified judges had to be recruited in the US.

On 4 January 1947, sixteen defendants were indicted on the evidence available: nine were officials in the Reich Ministry of Justice; the others were members of the People's Courts and Special Courts.

The indictment listed four individual counts, all the defendants being charged with the first three:

- Conspiracy to commit war crimes and crimes against humanity.
- War crimes against civilians of territories occupied by Germany and against soldiers of countries at war with Germany.
- Crimes against humanity against German civilians and nationals of occupied territories.

The fourth count of the indictment, with which seven of the defendants were additionally charged, was:

- Membership in the SS, SD, and/or the leadership corps of the Nazi Party.

Those had all been declared as criminal organisations by the preceding International Military Tribunal hearings, and the scene was set for the trial of those men who had sustained the oppressive Nazi legal regime.

The Allied prosecutors charged the defendants listed below with the preceding indictments and that of:

... judicial murder and other atrocities, which they committed by destroying law and justice in Germany, and then utilising the emptied forms of legal process for the persecution, enslavement and extermination on a large scale.

- Oswald Rothaug, senior public prosecutor of the People's Court; formerly Chief Justice of the Special Court in Nuremberg; member of the Leadership Corps of the Nazi Party at district executive level;
- Franz Schlegelberger, state secretary; acting Reich Minister of Justice;
- Rudolf Oeschey, judge in the Nuremberg Special Court and successor to Rothaug as Chief Justice of the same court; member of the Leadership Corps of the Nazi Party at district executive level (*Gauhauptstellenleiter*); and executive (*Kommissarischerleiter*) of the National Socialist Lawyers League;
- Herbert Klemm, state secretary of the Reich Ministry of Justice; director of the Legal Education and Training Division (Abteilung II) in the Ministry of Justice; deputy director of the National Socialist Lawyers League; *SA-Obergruppenführer*;
- Ernst Lautz, chief public prosecutor of the People's Court;
- Günther Joel, legal adviser to the Reich Minister of Justice on criminal prosecutions; chief public prosecutor of Westphalia at Hamm; *SS-Obersturmbannführer*; *SD-Untersturmbannführer*;
- Wilhelm von Ammon, ministerial counsellor of the Criminal Legislation and Administration Division (Abteilung IV) of the Reich Ministry of Justice and co-ordinator of proceedings against foreigners for offences against Reich occupations forces abroad;
- Wolfgang Mettgenberg, representative of the chief of the Criminal Legislation and Administration Division of the Reich Ministry of Justice, particularly supervising criminal offences against German occupational forces in occupied territories;
- Curt Rothenberger, state secretary of the Reich Ministry of Justice; deputy president of the Academy of German Law; *Gauführer* of the National Socialist Lawyers League;
- Josef Alstötter, chief of the Civil Law and Procedure Division (Abteilung VI) of the Reich Ministry of Justice; *SS-Oberführer*;
- Carl Westphal, ministerial counsellor of the Criminal Legislation and Administration Division of the Reich Ministry of Justice, officially responsible for questions of criminal procedure and penal execution within the Reich; Ministry co-ordinator for nullity pleas against adjudicated sentences;
- Hans Petersen, lay judge of the First Senate of the People's Court; lay judge of the Special Senate of the People's Court; *SA-Obergruppenführer*;
- Karl Engert, chief of the Penal Administration Division (Abteilung V) and of the secret Prison Inmate Transfer Division (Abteilung XV) of the Reich Ministry of Justice; *SS-Oberführer*; vice-president of the People's Court, *Ortsgruppenleiter* in the NSDAP Leadership Corps;
- Hermann Cuhorst, Chief Justice of the Special Court in Stuttgart; Chief Justice of

the First Criminal Senate of the Stuttgart District Court; member of the Leadership Corps of the Nazi Party at district executive level; sponsoring member of the SS;

- Paul Barnickel, senior public prosecutor of the People's Court; *SA-Sturmführer*;
- Günther Nebelung, Chief Justice of the Fourth Senate of the People's Court; *SA-Sturmführer*; *Ortsgruppenleiter in the NSDAP Leadership Corps.*

On 17 February 1947, the sixteen defendants pleaded not guilty to the individual indictments against them. Justice, however, would not be served on two of those indicted. Westphal committed suicide in Nuremberg Prison after the indictment hearing and prior to the commencement of the trial, and a mistrial was declared against the Engert, who failed to attend due to a reported physical condition that prevented his presence in court for most of the trial, which opened on 5 March 1947.

The accused had a plethora of defence advocates, indicative of the unusual imbalance between the highest level of legal practitioners about to plead and argue points of law and a prosecution case led by US army officer Brig.-Gen. Taylor, who had gained valuable experience in the previous Nuremberg Trials. His opening statement to the court included the following extracts:

This case is unusual in that the defendants are charged with crimes committed in the name of the law. These men, together with their deceased or fugitive colleagues, were the embodiment of what passed for justice in the Third Reich.

Most of the defendants have served, at various times, as judges, as state prosecutors, and as officials of the Reich Ministry of Justice. All but one are professional jurists; they are well accustomed to courts and courtrooms, though their present role may be new to them.

But a court is far more than a courtroom; it is a process and a spirit. It is a house of law, this the defendants know, or must have known in times past. I doubt that they ever forgot it. Indeed, the root of the accusation here is that those men, leaders of the German judicial system, consciously and deliberately suppressed the law, engaged in an unholy masquerade of brutish tyranny disguised as justice, and converted the German judicial system to an engine of despotism, conquest, pillage, and slaughter.

The defendants and their colleagues distorted, perverted, and finally accomplished the complete overthrow of justice and law in Germany. They made the system of courts an integral part of dictatorship. They established and operated special tribunals obedient only to the political dictates of the Hitler regime. They abolished all semblance of judicial independence. They brow-beat, bullied, and denied fundamental rights to those who came before the courts. The trials they conducted became horrible farces, with vestigial remnants of legal procedure which only served to mock the hapless victims.

The full content of the brigadier's opening statement amounted to a balanced and accurate case for the prosecution. His statement commenced what was to be a lengthy and finite case for the four judges who heard all the evidence and the defence arguments from a team of twenty-nine legal representatives. The prosecution case was presented by a team of five legal experts who undertook to prove to the court that crimes against humanity, primarily those committed against German nationals, were made possible by the revision of the laws relating to treason and high treason. These offences, normally rare, became commonplace during the Third Reich once the notorious People's Court had been empowered to define treason almost as it pleased and could therefore impose the death sentence for relatively minor offences.

After seven months of hearing evidence, during which 138 witnesses were called and some 2,093 pieces of documentary exhibits were introduced, the closing statements of the defendants were heard on 18 October. The trial hearing returned its judgment on 3 and 4 December 1947, the sentences imposed being announced on the latter date. Ten of the defendants were found guilty and four were acquitted:

> Oswald Rothaug—life imprisonment
> Franz Schlegelberger—life imprisonment
> Rudolf Oeschey—life imprisonment
> Herbert Klemm—life imprisonment
> Ernst Lautz—ten years' imprisonment
> Günther Joel—ten years' imprisonment
> Wilhelm von Ammon—ten years' imprisonment
> Wolfgang Mettgenberg—ten years' imprisonment
> Curt Rothenberger—seven years' imprisonment
> Josef Alstötter—five years' imprisonment
> Hans Petersen—acquitted
> Hermann Cuhorst—acquitted
> Paul Barnickel—acquitted
> Günther Nebelung—acquitted

The defendants who had been sentenced to life imprisonment ultimately had their sentences commuted to twenty years' imprisonment. However, all defendants had been released from custody by 1956, and those who had received lesser custodial sentences had been released by 1951.

Bibliography and Sources

Beck, E. R., *Under the Bombs: The German Home Front, 1942-1945* (University of Kentucky Press, 1986)

Bloxham, D., *Genocide on Trial* (Oxford University Press, 2001)

Brysac, S. B., *Resisting Hitler* (Oxford University Press, 2000)

Chorley, W. R., *Royal Air Force Bomber Command Losses* (Midland Counties, 1996)

Clark, F., *Agents by Moonlight* (Tempus Publishing, 1999)

Conway, J., *The Nazi Persecution of the Churches 1933-1945*, Toronto (1968)

Crankshaw, E., *Gestapo: Instrument of Tyranny* (Putnam, 1956)

'Das Geheimnis der Roten Kapelle' (The Secret of the Red Orchestra) in *Der Fortschritt* No. 45 (1950)

Davidson, E., *The Unmaking of Adolf Hitler* (University of Missouri, 1996)

Eschwege, H., 'Resistance of German Jews against the Nazi Regime' in *Leo Baeck Institute Year Book* vol. 15 (1970)

Ferencz, B. B., *An International Criminal Court*, 2 vols (Oceana Publications, 1980)

Fest, J., *Plotting Hitler's Death: The German Resistance to Hitler, 1933-1945* (Orion, 1997)

Fischer, R., *Stalin and German Communism* (Harvard University Press, 1948)

Foot, M. R. D., *SOE in the Low Countries* (St Ermin's Press, 2001)

Gerould, D., *Guillotine: Its legend and lore* (Blast Books, 1992)

Hoefer, F., 'The Nazi Penal System II', in *Journal of Criminal Law and Criminology* (1945)

Hoffmann, P., *The History of the German Resistance 1933-1945* (MIT Press, 1977)

Holmes, B. R. and A. F. Keele (eds), *When Truth was Treason* (University of Illinois Press, 1995)

Housden, M., *Resistance and Conformity in the Third Reich* (Routledge, 1997)

Judgment at Nuremberg (HMSO, 1946)

Koch, H., *In the name of the Volk: Political Justice in Hitler's Germany* (I. B. Tauris, 1997)

Koch, H., *The Hitler Youth: Origins and Development, 1922-1945* (Macdonald, 1975)

Lang, H.-J., *The Names of the Numbers* (Hoffmann and Campe, 2004)

Laska, V., *Women in the Resistance and in the Holocaust: The Voices of Eyewitnesses* (Greenwood Press, 1983)

Lifton, R. J., *The Nazi Doctors: Medical Killing and the Psychology of Genocide* (Basic Books, 1988)

Link, H., *The Church in East Prussia 1933-1945: History and Documents* (Munich, 1968)

Middlebrook, M. and C. Everitt, *The Bomber Command War Diaries* (Viking, 1985)

O'Neel, B., *39 New Saints You Should Know* (St Anthony Messenger Press, 2010)

Pringle, H., *The Master Plan: Himmler's Scholars and the Holocaust* (Hyperion, 2006)

Sadat, L. N., *The International Criminal Court and the Transformation of International Law* (Transnational Publishers, 2002)

Sagardoy, P. A., *Gelegen und ungelegen: Die Lebenshingabe von Sr. Restituta* (Christliche Innerlichkeit, 2001)

Schorn, H., *The Judge in the Third Reich: History and Documents* (Klostermann, 1959)

Stevenson, L., *Max Josef Metzger: Priest and Martyr* (SPCK, 1952)

Taylor, T., 'Nuremberg Trials: War Crimes Law and International Law' in *International Conciliation* No. 450 (Carnegie Endowment, 1949).

Taylor, T., *The Anatomy of the Nuremberg Trials* (Knopf, 1992)

Thacker, T., *Joseph Goebbels: Life and Death* (Palgrave Macmillan, 2009)

Turner, H. A., *Hitler's Thirty Days to Power: January 1933* (Bloomsbury, 1997)

Wachsmann, N., *Hitler's Prisons* (Yale University Press, 2004)

We Accuse: 800 Bloodstained Nazi Judges—Bastions of Adenauer's Militarist Regime (Committee for German Unity, 1959)

Welch, D., *The Third Reich: Politics and Propaganda* (Routledge, 1995)

British Library of Political and Economic Science, Kreisau Circle, GB 097 COLL MISC 0272

Bundesarchiv, Koblenz

Daily Mail report of the elimination of the SA, 2 July 1934

Imperial War Museum Archives, London

National Archives, Kew

New York Times: Hitler Beheaded American Woman, 1 December 1947

Observer, weekly newspaper of the Office of Military Government for Germany, Berlin, 1946

Plötzensee Memorial Centre, Hüttigpfad D-13627, Berlin-Charlottenburg-Wilmersdorf

The Times newspaper archives, London

US Government Printing Office (1946-1949): 'Trials of War Criminals Before the Nuremberg Military Tribunals Under Control Council Law No. 10'

United States of America *v.* Alstötter et al: 3 T.W.C. 1, 6 L.R.T.W.C. 1 and 14 A.D.I.L. 278, 1948

YIVO Institute for Jewish Research, 15 West 16th Street, New York, NY 10011

www.eyewitnesstohistory.com (Reichstag fire)

www.gdw-berlin.de (German Resistance Memorial)
www.jewishvirtuallibrary.org (August Hirt)
www.luebeckermaertyrer.de (Lübeck Martyrs)
www.resistance62.com/message_fillerin_oct1942.htm (Norbert Fillerin)
www.ushmm.org (US Holocaust Memorial Museum)
www.wiadomosci.gazeta.pl/kraj/1,34309,3593270.html (Walerjan Wróbel)